OFF-SCREEN CINEMA

OFF-SCREEN

CINEMA

Isidore Isou and the Lettrist Avant-Garde

KAIRA M. CABAÑAS

University of Chicago Press
Chicago and London

Kaira M. Cabañas is an art historian and visiting professor in the Departamento de Letras at Pontifical Catholic University of Rio de Janeiro.

The University of Chicago Press, Chicago 60637
The University of Chicago Press, Ltd., London

Printed in the United States of America

23 22 21 20 19 18 17 16 15 14   1 2 3 4 5

ISBN-13: 978-0-226-17445-7 (cloth)
ISBN-13: 978-0-226-17459-4 (paper)
ISBN-13: 978-0-226-17462-4 (e-book)
DOI: 10.7208/chicago/9780226174624.001.0001

Library of Congress Cataloging-in-Publication Data

Cabañas, Kaira Marie, 1974– author.
Off-screen cinema : Isidore Isou and the Lettrist avant-garde / Kaira M. Cabañas.
pages ; cm
Includes bibliographical references and index.
ISBN 978-0-226-17445-7 (cloth : alk. paper)
ISBN 978-0-226-17459-4 (pbk. : alk. paper)
ISBN 978-0-226-17462-4 (e-book)
1. Experimental films—France—History and criticism—20th century. 2. Cinematography—France—Special effects—History—20th century. 3. Lettrism in motion pictures. 4. Lettrism. 5. Isou, Isidore—Criticism and interpretation. I. Title.
PN1995.9.E96C33 2014
791.43'611—dc23

2014029550

∞ This paper meets the requirements of ANSI/NISO Z39.48-1992 (Permanence of Paper).

I love the cinema when it is insolent and does what it is not supposed to do.

Daniel, *Traité de bave et d'éternité*, 1951

No one in Europe knows how to scream anymore.

Antonin Artaud, 1935

CONTENTS

ACKNOWLEDGMENTS

THIS BOOK'S ORIGIN bespeaks a certain contretemps. I had begun the archival research that led to my first book, *The Myth of Nouveau Réalisme*, when, researching at the Archives de la Critique d'Art (then housed in Châteaugiron), I first read Frédérique Devaux's informative volume *Le cinéma lettriste: 1951–1991*. Before then, I had never heard of Lettrism, a movement still largely unaccounted for in the dominant histories of postwar art and experimental film. Subsequently, when I did see Lettrism mentioned in scholarly and critical works, it was largely referenced as a point of departure for individuals, in particular Guy Debord, who would go on to found the Situationist International. It is my hope that in the pages that follow a nuanced reading of postwar European artistic practices emerges, one that recognizes and clarifies the aesthetic contributions of Lettrist cinematic production, both on and off the screen, in the early 1950s and its afterlife in later generations.

The majority of this book was written in New York during my tenure as lecturer and director of Columbia University's MA program in modern art. While at Columbia, my colleagues in art history and film studies were especially supportive. I am thankful to Alexander Alberro, Jonathan Crary, Noam Elcott, Jane Gaines, Kellie Jones, Branden W. Joseph, and the late Philip Watts. Research assistant Rachel Silveri helped with various aspects of the manuscript's preparation, in addition to rights and image acquisition; her intelligence and utter reliability were a true gift. Staff member Emily Shaw also graciously gave of her time and expertise. The University Seminars at Columbia, through the Warner Fund, contributed toward the book's production and image fees. Additional assistance was provided by a research residency at the Museo Nacional Centro de Arte

Reina Sofia (MNCARS) in Madrid in the summer of 2012. More recently, during my time as a visiting professor in Rio de Janeiro, the Departamento de Letras at the Pontificia Universidade Católica (PUC-Rio) became a welcome home. I appreciate the department's support, especially that of its chair, Karl Erik Schøllhammer, and professor Ana Kiffer, with whom I share an enthusiasm for the work of Antonin Artaud.

The present study would not have been possible without the generosity of many individuals who have shared their expertise with me along the way. Above all, I am indebted to Frédéric Acquaviva for his discerning comments and spirit of collaboration, as well as his indefatigable sense of humor. Our work together on the exhibition *Specters of Artaud: Language and the Arts in the 1950s* was crucial in paving the way for this book's publication. P. Adams Sitney also warrants special recognition: I had my first conversations on Lettrist cinema with him while still a graduate student at Princeton. He also read the final manuscript, offering detailed observations and incisive critique with his characteristic generosity and wit. For their willingness to speak with me and to share their memories and their archives, I am particularly grateful to Michèle Bernstein, Catherine Goldstein, and the late Charlotte Wolman. Gérard Berréby, Jean-Michel Bouhours, Jean-Pierre Criqui, Laurence Bertrand Dorléac, Ginette Dufrêne, Bradley Eros, Fabrice Flahutez, Christine Guymer, Christian Lebrat, Marc'O, and Maurice Rajsfus each contributed to the project in various ways. Maurice Lemaître, though absolutely cantankerous when we met in person (in the true spirit of avant-garde provocation), has been a faithful correspondent, regularly sending me unsolicited material for my research.

This book has benefited from collections and archival resources housed in various institutions, including the Bibliothèque Kandinsky at the Centre Pompidou; the Département des Manuscrits, Bibliothèque Nationale de France; the Gaumont-Pathé Archives; the Beinecke Rare Book and Manuscript Library, Yale University; and the Museu d'Art Contemporani de Barcelona (MACBA) Study Center. It has also benefited from private collections, including the Archives Isou-Goldstein, Paris, and Archiv Acquaviva, Berlin. I am indebted to the staff, librarians, and archivists at each of these organizations. I also thank the many individuals, artists, museums, and estates that so kindly assisted with illustrations and permissions.

José Falconi must be specifically singled out for serving as a committed first reader, while Elizabeth Azen offered key guidance toward the finished project. Many other colleagues and friends have also graciously listened to, read, or responded to various aspects of this work. Among them, I will mention Lothar Baumgarten, Sonja Boos, Eric de Bruyn, Mela Dávila, Jesús Fuenmayor, Jennifer Josten, Birger Lipinski (who also

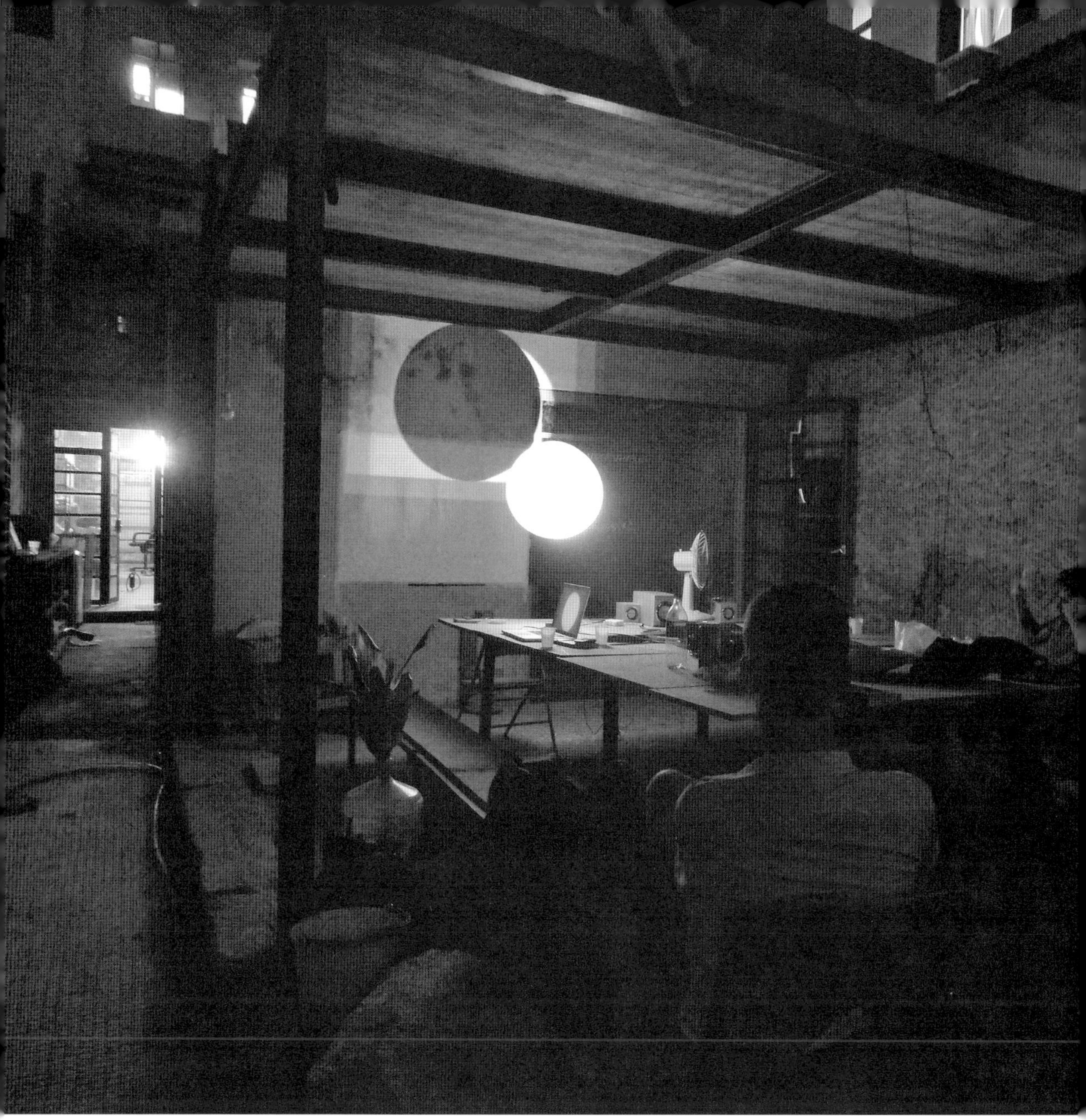

1. Gil J Wolman, *L'anticoncept*, 1951. Reconstruction with balloon, in the context of a seminar at the Universidade de Verão (Summer University), Rio de Janeiro. February 7, 2012. Photo: Rodrigo Garcia Dutra.

assisted with images), Ana Magalhães, Ivone Margulies, Sérgio Bruno Martins, Luiz Camillo Osorio, Amilcar Packer, Fernanda Pitta, Laercio Redondo, Jorge Ribalta, Matheus Rocha Pitta, Nadja Rottner, Daniel Steegmann, Ana Wambier, and Katja Zelljadt. Friends in Paris, including Jérôme Saint-Loubert Bié, Cécile Dazord, Christophe Giudicelli, Jian-Xing

Too, and Giovanna Zapperi, regularly sustained my enthusiasm for (and obsession with) this material. Former students also indulged my presentations and screenings of Lettrist film. The screening of *L'anticoncept* in Rio in 2011 (fig. 1) and the students' creative responses count among the most memorable. Fittingly then, *Off-Screen Cinema* is not only an account of Lettrist cinema but also a record of my conversations and dialogues with colleagues, students, and friends and of the ways that each contributed, perhaps unknowingly, to the study's final form.

The chapters in this volume draw upon material from my seminars and lectures presented in various contexts, including the MNCARS Study Center; MACBA; the Walker Art Center, Minneapolis; the Hirshhorn Museum and Sculpture Garden, Washington, DC; Capacete's Universidade de Verão (Summer University), Rio de Janeiro; the Cisneros Fontanals Art Foundation, Miami; the seminar "'If you can remember anything from the sixties, you weren't really there' 1955–1975: Sources and Methods II," organized by Sophie Cras and Emmanuel Guy at the École Normale Supérieure, Paris; the faculty seminar "Sites of Cinema," headed by Noam Elcott and Jane Gaines at Columbia University; the eighth edition of the Seminário Arte, Cultura e Fotografia, at the Museu de Arte Contemporânea da Universidade de São Paulo (MAC-USP); Tobi Maier's salon in Sao Pãulo; and, in conjunction with the exhibition *Interiors and Exteriors: Avant-Garde Itineraries in Postwar France*, curated by Jennifer Cohen and Marin Sarvé-Tarr at the University of Chicago's Smart Museum. So too, does the study develop aspects of my prior work published by *Grey Room*, MACBA, MNCARS, and the Walker Art Center and in the anthology *Consumato dal fuoco: Il cinema di Guy Debord* (2011). I would like to thank the students, audiences, organizers, curators, and editors at each of these venues for their support.

At the University of Chicago Press, executive editor Susan Bielstein deserves special acknowledgment for her backing of the project, as does Chicago's excellent editorial and production staff, including Anthony Burton and Joel Score. I am grateful to the two anonymous readers who critically commented on the manuscript and supported its publication. The elegance of the book's design is due to graphic designer Isaac Tobin. Finally, when researching and writing, day-to-day support counts just as much as the institutional sort. I continually benefit from the sustained love of family, my parents Humberto and Hermys, and dear friends. I owe you.

INTRODUCTION

The cinema has not evolved since the debut of the talkie.
René Clair, 1951

ON APRIL 20, 1951, Isidore Isou presented his film *Traité de bave et d'éternité* (On Venom and Eternity; fig. 2) in Cannes. Although the film was not officially entered in the city's film festival, it was widely publicized in the press and its screening constituted one of the festival's fringe events, including its very own jury. In this work, Isou employed *montage discrépant* (discrepant editing)—the purposeful nonsynchronization of sound and image—and also drew directly on the celluloid to exacerbate and produce what he called the *image ciselante* (chiseled image). On account of the film's screening in Cannes, Isou affirmed, "I am certain that *Traité de bave et d'éternité* will change cinema drastically and push it toward unexpected paths. It requires only that juries lend it an *attentive ear*."[1] Indeed, in the sound track to the film, Daniel, the protagonist, proclaims that photographic images will be destroyed *par la parole* (by speech).

In Isou's emphasis on aural perception and on speech as a way to counter the primacy of the filmed image, one hears echoes, as I have elsewhere argued, of dissident Surrealist Antonin Artaud. Anticipating the perceptual and psychological effects of sound's synchronization on cinema, in the interwar years Artaud declared, "There is no possible identification between sound and image. The image presents itself only in one dimension—it's the translation, the transposition of the real; sound, on the contrary, is unique and true—it bursts out into the room and acts,

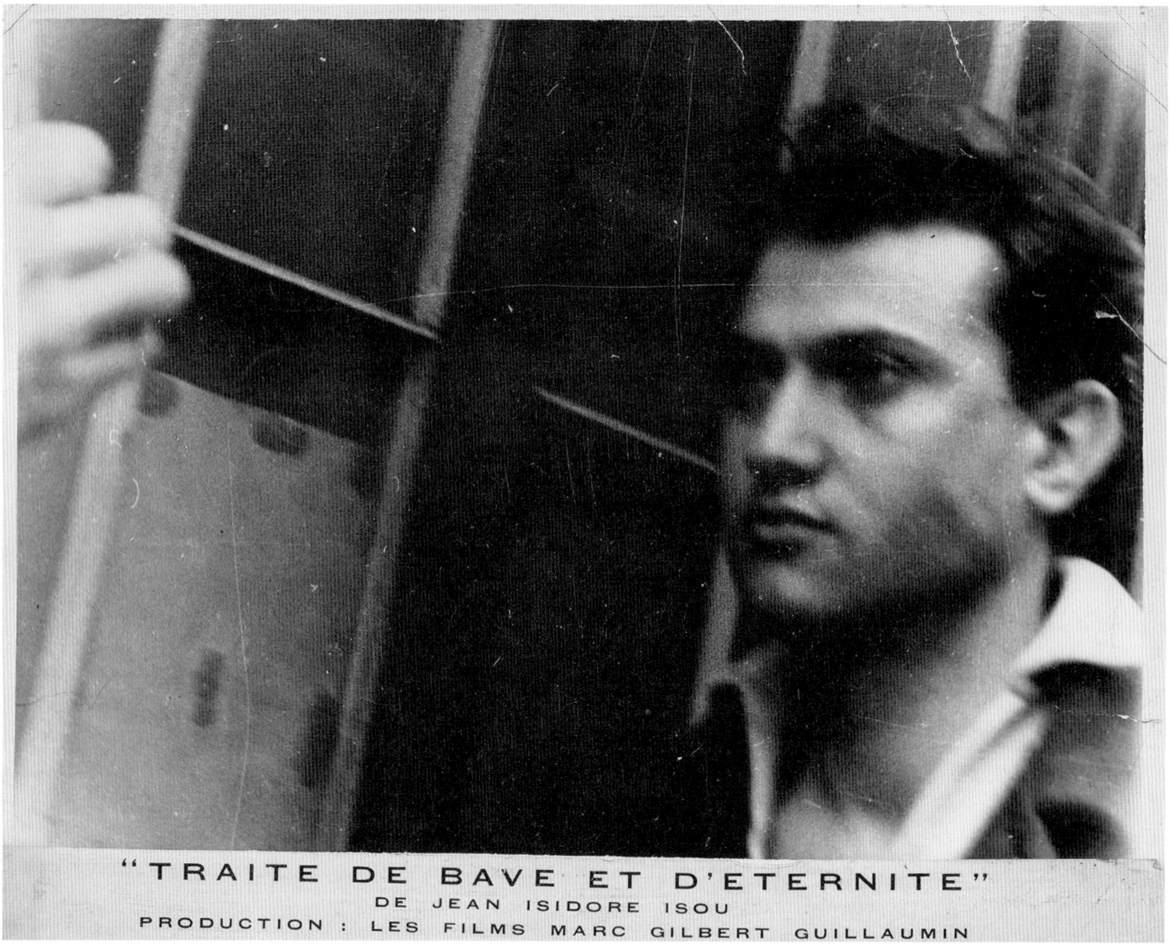

2. Press photograph for Isidore Isou's film *Traité de bave et d'éternité*, 1951.

by consequence, with much more intensity than the image."[2] At issue for Artaud was not the advent of the sound track per se, but rather the circumscription of sound to reproduce only speech. Artaud's resistance to words-on-film, words tethered to a face on the screen, is paralleled in Isou's lengthy treatise "Esthétique du cinéma" (Aesthetic of Cinema, 1952), while Artaud's emphasis on a purely visual cinema undergoes a historical reversal with Isou's and the Lettrists' systematic negation of photographic images in favor of sound.[3]

Off-Screen Cinema discusses the five core Lettrist films produced by Isou, Maurice Lemaître, Gil J Wolman, François Dufrêne, and Guy Debord in the years 1951–1952. From Isou's uncoupling of the unity of image and sound through *montage discrépant* to Wolman's use of a weather balloon instead of a flat image screen in *L'anticoncept* (1951) to Dufrêne's total abandonment of the filmstrip in favor of an exclusively live sound film,

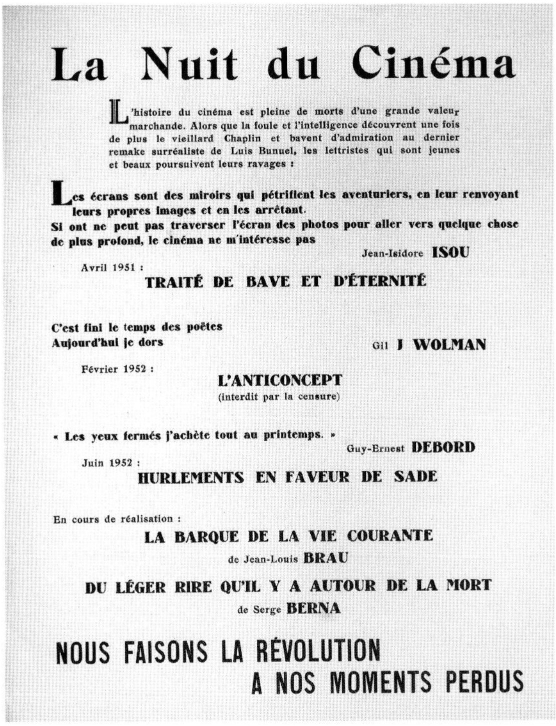

La Nuit du Cinéma

L'histoire du cinéma est pleine de morts d'une grande valeur marchande. Alors que la foule et l'intelligence découvrent une fois de plus le vieillard Chaplin et bavent d'admiration au dernier remake surréaliste de Luis Bunuel, les lettristes qui sont jeunes et beaux poursuivent leurs ravages :

Les écrans sont des miroirs qui pétrifient les aventuriers, en leur renvoyant leurs propres images et en les arrêtant.
Si ont ne peut pas traverser l'écran des photos pour aller vers quelque chose de plus profond, le cinéma ne m'intéresse pas

Jean-Isidore ISOU

Avril 1951 :

TRAITÉ DE BAVE ET D'ÉTERNITÉ

C'est fini le temps des poëtes
Aujourd'hui je dors

Gil J WOLMAN

Février 1952 :

L'ANTICONCEPT
(interdit par la censure)

« Les yeux fermés j'achète tout au printemps. »

Guy-Ernest DEBORD

Juin 1952 :

HURLEMENTS EN FAVEUR DE SADE

En cours de réalisation :

LA BARQUE DE LA VIE COURANTE
de Jean-Louis BRAU

DU LÉGER RIRE QU'IL Y A AUTOUR DE LA MORT
de Serge BERNA

NOUS FAISONS LA RÉVOLUTION
A NOS MOMENTS PERDUS

3. Tract listing the Lettrist film program for La Nuit du Cinéma, 1952.

each Lettrist film defied cinema's established conventions (e.g., continuity editing, synchronized sound, screen), and sometimes the necessity of its image support (i.e., film), in order to generate new conditions and communities of viewing (fig. 3). Crucial in this context is the Lettrists' aural conception of cinema, primarily through the embodied and volumetric predominance of sound and live performance. By foregrounding sound (though not always intelligible speech), as well as actual participation, the Lettrists worked to counter the dominance of vision and the reality effect produced with the advent of sound synchronization in 1927. The Lettrists consistently employed dissociative strategies in their films—disjunctures between speech and sound, sound and image, screen and space—in pursuit of an unmediated cinema consistent with their desire to move from the space of representation to the event itself.

That the Lettrists were committed to a cinema that implied spectators' active participation is no doubt informed by the context in which their work was produced. During World War II, under the restrictions of Nazi-occupied France, cinema had been conceived as a site for a particular form of governmentality. (Here *governmentality* should be understood, in the general sense offered by Michel Foucault, as "the conduct of conduct" and how specific forms of activity shape the behavior of individuals.[4])

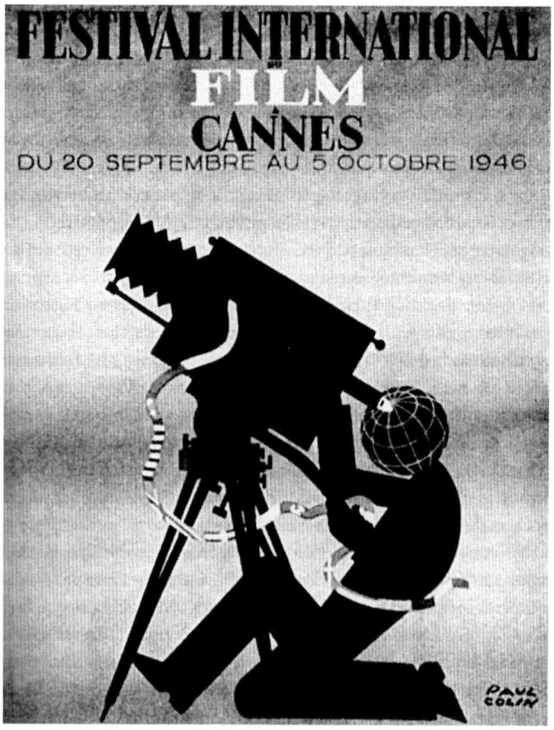

4. Paul Colin, poster for the first Festival International du Film à Cannes, September 20–October 5, 1946.

At the time, such governance extended from the types of films that could be shown, and the monitoring of the viewing public's behavior, to the Aryanization of the industry.[5] Subsequently, the first postwar decade was a time of intense reconstruction and political instability in France and also witnessed the expansion and eventual consolidation of the film industry. The Cannes Film Festival opened in 1946 (fig. 4); the Cinémathèque Française established its first screening room in 1947; and the appreciation of Hollywood cinema was on the rise: the Francophilic *An American in Paris* won best picture at the Oscars in 1952.[6] Lettrism, initially a poetry movement founded by Isou and Gabriel Pomerand in 1946, existed largely in the margins of this context.

> The Lettrists invented a great many of the working methods, the forms, and the structures widely used today throughout the international experimental cinema.
> *Dominique Noguez, 1978*

The twenty-first century has witnessed a growing interest in the moving image in contemporary art, which has helped prompt an investigation into the intertwined histories of art and film, from the origins of cinema to the present. This flurry of renewed attention to projected images is evinced in a series of international group exhibitions and their corresponding publications.[7] The artists presented in these exhibitions have often embraced projection as an alternative to or expansion of the conventions of painting and sculpture, incorporating aspects of photography, film, and performance in their work. That Lettrist cinema remains unaccounted for in these survey exhibitions is perhaps unsurprising given the notoriety and at times aggressive polemics of the group's members (I too weathered an afternoon of Lemaître's insults in researching this book), as well as the fact that archival documentation of the original screenings not only is scant but until very recently has been unavailable to a broader scholarly public.[8]

In English only a handful of texts on Lettrist cinema exist to date, and the movement does not appear in the existing general histories of experimental film.[9] Given that early Lettrist cinema forms the discursive context from which Guy Debord's films emerged, it remains surprising it is rarely addressed, even in the context of studies on Debord. In its final chapter, *Off-Screen Cinema* redresses this oversight by situating Lettrist film practice as central to an understanding of Debord's first film, *Hurlements en faveur de Sade* (Howls for Sade, 1952), as well as his subsequent theoretical elaboration and practice of *détournement*. While French publications offer chronological or brief accounts of individual Lettrist films, they often remain within the purview of Isou's and the other artists' discourse about their work.[10] This critical lacuna is exacerbated by the fact that first-, second-, and third-generation Lettrists often claim to be the exclusive arbiters of Lettrist works' interpretation. This book draws upon Lettrists' writing about their work, but also moves beyond what they say in order to align their film practices with broader cultural debates and issues that defined postwar French art and culture at the time.

While the critical literature on Lettrist cinema remains to be expanded, the films have been programmed in screening rooms in France thanks to committed curators and scholars, among them Frédéric Acquaviva, Bernard Blistène, Jean-Michel Bouhours, Nicole Brenez, and Dominique Noguez. And recently, the Lettrists have been garnering international attention and support. In 2005, the Museu d'Art Contemporani de Barcelona organized a Lettrist film program and publication titled *Próximamente en esta pantalla: El cine letrista, entre la discrepancia y la sublevación* (Coming Soon to This Screen: Lettrist Cinema between Discrepancy and Revolt). In 2012, the Moderna Museet in Stockholm organized a conference titled "All the King's Horses: Letterism Today?," which included a discussion of Lettrist film. That same year, Lettrist cinematic work and related archival material were featured at the Museo Nacional Centro de Arte Reina

Sofia in Madrid, in the exhibition *Specters of Artaud: Language and the Arts in the 1950s*, which I cocurated with Acquaviva and which included the first quadraphonic installation of Dufrêne's *Tambours du jugement premier* (Drums of the First Judgment, 1952), originally a live sound film with no visual images.[11]

Nevertheless, Lettrist films as a more or less coherent body of work remain largely unscreened and unexhibited in the United States. This absence is notable given Stan Brakhage's repeated affirmation that Isou's *Traité de bave et d'éternité* had a formidable influence on his mature aesthetic. Brakhage had been present at the film's screening at the San Francisco Museum of Modern Art (SFMoMA) on October 23, 1953, in the context of the "Art in Cinema" series, which was programmed by Frank Stauffacher. Subsequently, in the early 1960s, Brakhage exchanged two letters with Isou, confessing how the film continued to inspire him (see appendix).[12] After the SFMoMA screening, another screening of *Traité* likely took place at the Society of Cinema Arts in Los Angeles, thanks to archivist Raymond Rohauer (fig. 5).[13] Also in the LA area, an obscure literary magazine titled *Pendulum*, published by the California Institute of Technology, presented a short introduction to Lettrism, as well as some of the first English translations of Lettrist texts, including excerpts of theoretical writings on avant-garde cinema.[14] Among the few other publications and presentations: in 1955, Isou, Lemaître, and Jacques Spacagna performed Lettrist poetry in the film documentary *Around the World with Orson Welles* (fig. 6); in the 1950s and 1960s, copies of Rohauer's subtitled version of *Traité* circulated on the New York experimental film circuit; and in the early 1980s, Marjorie Keller invited Richard Foreman to give a lecture on *Traité* at the University of Rhode Island. In a recent

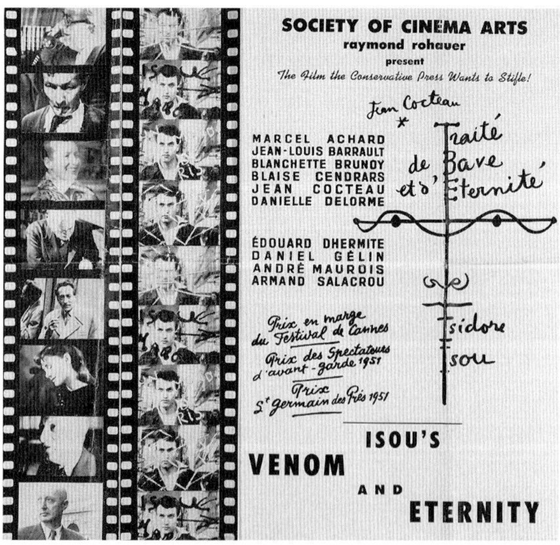

5. Raymond Rohauer, promotional brochure for Isidore Isou's film *Traité de bave et d'éternité* (1951), Society of Cinema Arts, Los Angeles, ca. 1953.

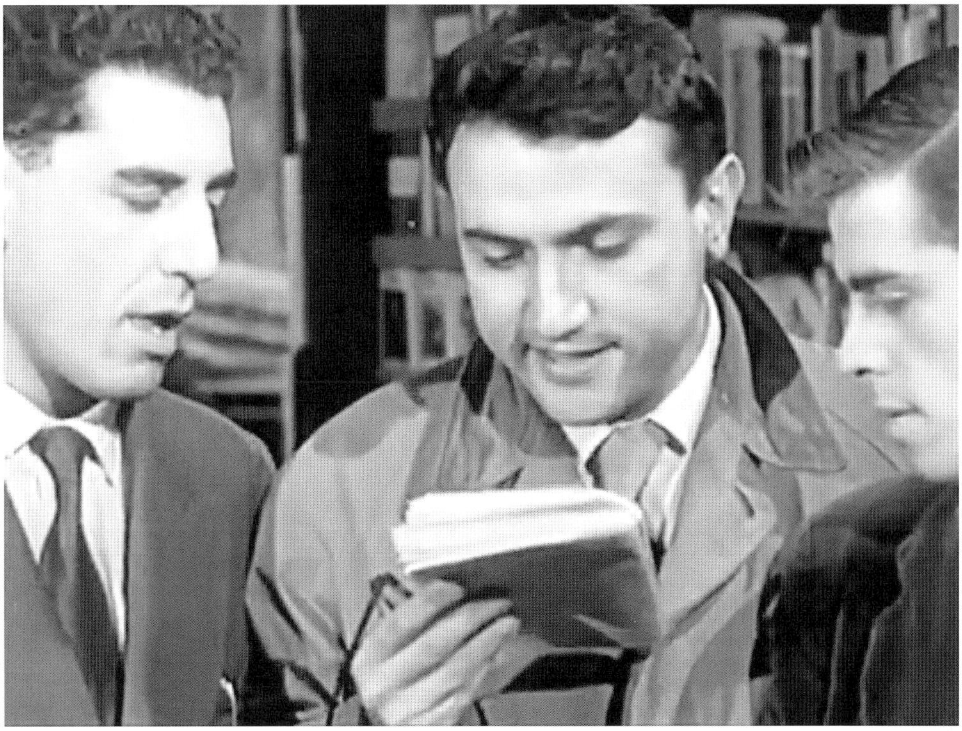

6. Maurice Lemaître, Isidore Isou, and Jacques Spacagna, in *Around the World with Orson Welles*, 1955. Frame enlargement.

conversation, Foreman recalled being deeply impressed by the film: "At the time, I would have listed it as one of my favorite ten films." He also noted that, curiously, "in Paris, the film was not very well known."[15] Apart from these scattered instances, the Lettrist films' American reception remains decidedly thin.[16]

TOWARD AN ISOUIENNE TRANSFORMATION OF CINEMA

Perhaps the single most important resource for studying early Lettrist film is *Ion*, a single-issue magazine dedicated exclusively to Lettrist work in cinema, which was published under the direction of Marc-Guilbert Guillaumin, otherwise known as Marc'O, in April 1952 (fig. 7). *Ion* includes Isou's "Esthétique du cinéma" and Marc'O's "Première manifestation d'un cinéma nucléaire" (First manifestation of a nuclear cinema), as well as the scripts for Wolman's *L'anticoncept*, Dufrêne's *Tambours du jugement premier*, Gabriel Pomerand's *La légende cruelle* (The Cruel Legend), and Debord's *Hurlements en faveur de Sade*.[17] Isou's contribution, with its preface, seven chapters, *envoi*, and appendix, takes up 114 of the magazine's 286 pages. In this extended essay, Isou demonstrates an intimate knowledge of the history of avant-garde cinema and meticulously develops his

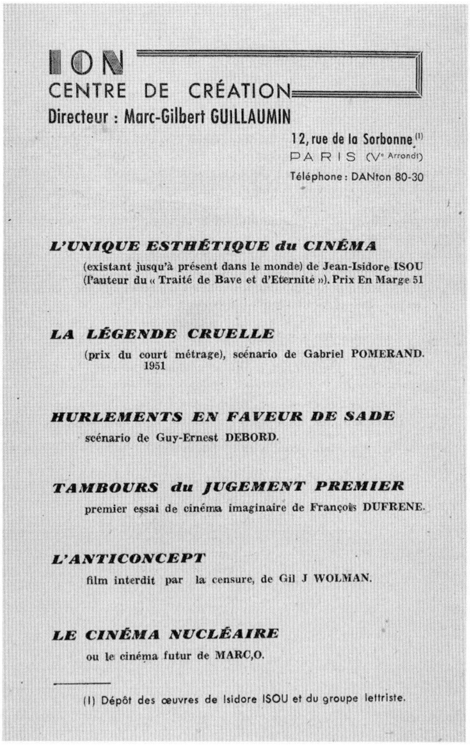
ION
CENTRE DE CRÉATION
Directeur : Marc-Gilbert GUILLAUMIN

12, rue de la Sorbonne (1)
PARIS (Ve Arrondt)
Téléphone : DANton 80-30

L'UNIQUE ESTHÉTIQUE du CINÉMA
(existant jusqu'à présent dans le monde) de Jean-Isidore ISOU (l'auteur du « Traité de Bave et d'Eternité »). Prix En Marge 51

LA LÉGENDE CRUELLE
(prix du court métrage), scénario de Gabriel POMERAND. 1951

HURLEMENTS EN FAVEUR DE SADE
scénario de Guy-Ernest DEBORD.

TAMBOURS du JUGEMENT PREMIER
premier essai de cinéma imaginaire de François DUFRENE.

L'ANTICONCEPT
film interdit par la censure, de Gil J WOLMAN.

LE CINÉMA NUCLÉAIRE
ou le cinéma futur de MARC,O.

(1) Dépôt des œuvres de Isidore ISOU et du groupe lettriste.

7. Flyer announcing the publication of *Ion*, April 1952.

argument for the transformation of the medium. What in large measure differentiates Lettrist film from that of the historical avant-garde is its engagement with the emergence and consolidation of the *film parlant* (talkie) as a specific form of sound film. For Isou, the development and perfection of sound technology for reproducing speech-on-film required a rethinking of "the problem of montage according to new foundations."[18] Accordingly, a central concern of Lettrist films was to experiment with the disjunction between *what* one sees and *how* one hears in a cinematic context.

Central to Isou's account of the history of cinema is the designation of two phases: the *amplique* (amplic) and the *ciselante* (chiseled). In its amplic phase, cinema explores the intrinsic elements of film in order to subject them to the development of the anecdote or subject matter; the secondary aspects of the art (its "flow" and "system of combinations," that is, editing) are similarly deployed to secure narrative coherence.[19] This history of editing with an eye to the successful communication of a story continued with the introduction of sound, which Isou claims to have constituted the final element in the "perfection of amplic montage."[20]

In this context, Isou critiques filmmakers and authors, among them René Clair and Georges Sadoul, who regard subject matter as essential to the art. Moreover, he refutes the pervasive misunderstanding of cinema

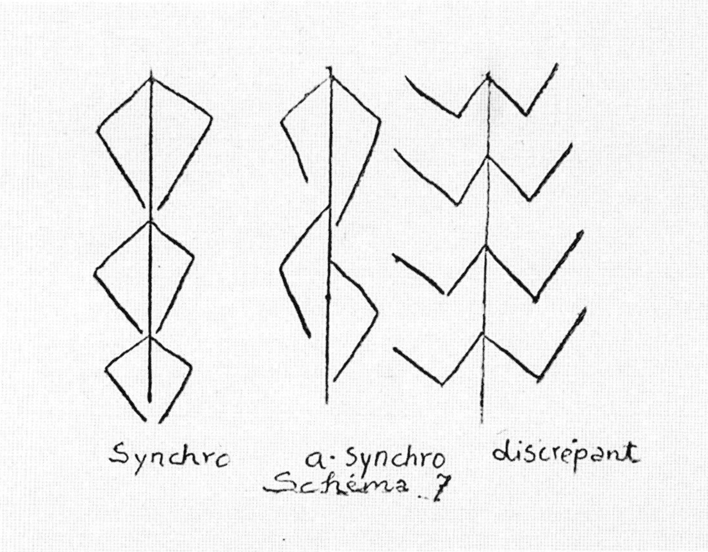

8. Isidore Isou's diagram explaining *montage discrépant* (discrepant editing), from his "Esthétique du cinéma," published in *Ion*, April 1952.

as primarily an art of movement. He recalls how when he asked students at the Institut des Hautes Etudes Cinématographiques "What is cinema?" they unsurprisingly responded "movement." As a result, he explains "the cinematograph became cinema."[21] To be sure, Isou disavows a definition of film that hews too closely to the medium's technological mechanisms and support, singling out those authors who confuse the development of technology with the critical elaboration of aesthetic strategies, as if the former drove the ruptures of the latter.

In "Esthétique," Isou outlines the procedures for achieving what he calls *cinéma discrépant* (discrepant cinema) and in so doing introduces his theory of *montage discrépant*—the uncoupling and radical individuation of the image and sound tracks. By means of such disjunctive editing, he proposes to inaugurate cinema's chiseled phase. Isou offers a sketch that visualizes different conceptualizations of montage practice (fig. 8). In this diagram the oblique lines to the left of each vertical line represent "sound," while those to the right represent "image." When synchronized, the two sets of lines work together to advance a central line or story, as in the illustration on the left, labeled "Synchro" for synchronization. In the middle illustration, depicting non- or asynchronic sound and image, the two sets of lines do not converge on the central vertical line, but they still remain oriented toward it and thus toward a central theme. In the final illustration, on the right, sound and image develop in opposing directions, away from the central axis and any governing story.

The primary purpose of *montage discrépant* was to ensure the semiotic rupture between the image track and sound track, giving sound total autonomy vis-à-vis the image. Isou thus criticized Soviet avant-garde cinema's indebtedness to overriding themes and the "*qualitatively new*" meanings that emerged through their juxtaposition of image and sound.[22] He understood meaningful relations, as visualized in the middle diagram for asynchronic montage, to obtain between image and sound in Soviet films even when the effect was nonnaturalist. Isou, by contrast, upholds not only the nonsychronization of sound and image but also their conceptual independence in the service of a discrepant and chiseled cinema. With regard to the image track, chiseling meant subjecting the filmstrip to a series of interventions, including scraping it with needles or painting on it with a brush to produce a chiseled image (see chapter 1). The chiseled image track was to signify as both referential and abstract, iconic and indexical.

Isou constantly refers to the "mechanics" of cinema's amplic and chiseled phases, ultimately claiming that the image track's chiseled phase could also open onto the development of a *métagraphique* language of color, whose application would "shift filmmakers' attention away from the problem of the essence of the photographic particle."[23] With his use of "mechanics" and repeated discussion of "particles," Isou idiosyncratically adopts the language of quantum physics as a way to further signal his work's departure from classical cinema. For Isou, the introduction of painted color on the filmstrip (e.g., abstract marks, frames of pure color, invented signs, all explored in Lemaître's films) interrupts the iconicity of the filmed image and insists on film's material status, but it also provides him with a foundation for a renewed narrative system. With his film-novel *Amos ou Introduction à la métagraphologie*, he inaugurated a new amplic phase in 1953.[24] This "film" presents a short story told in part through pictographic symbols originally painted in brightly colored gouache over black-and-white photographs, a few of which picture Isou (fig. 9). By placing the French text next to the image reproductions in a discrepant manner, *Amos* likewise explores the semiotic disjuncture between various modes of representation.

The presence of Lettrist poetic works on the films' sound tracks is also key. If Dada reduced poetry to phonemes (the smallest sound unit that forms meaningful contrasts between utterances), the Lettrist endeavor hinged on the question of bodily intonation, explored as a means by which to divide a phoneme's articulation internally. The Lettrists proposed a manner for the production of such sounds, by way of tongue clicks, hiccups, coughs, growls, and lisps. Isou, and subsequently Lemaître, invented complex notational systems to describe various means of intonation (fig. 10). At times their systems of notation incorporate international phonetic symbols; at other times, they relinquish letters in favor of other graphic signs. In each case, they enrich and systematize the possibilities for phonation and corresponding shifts in sound values.[25]

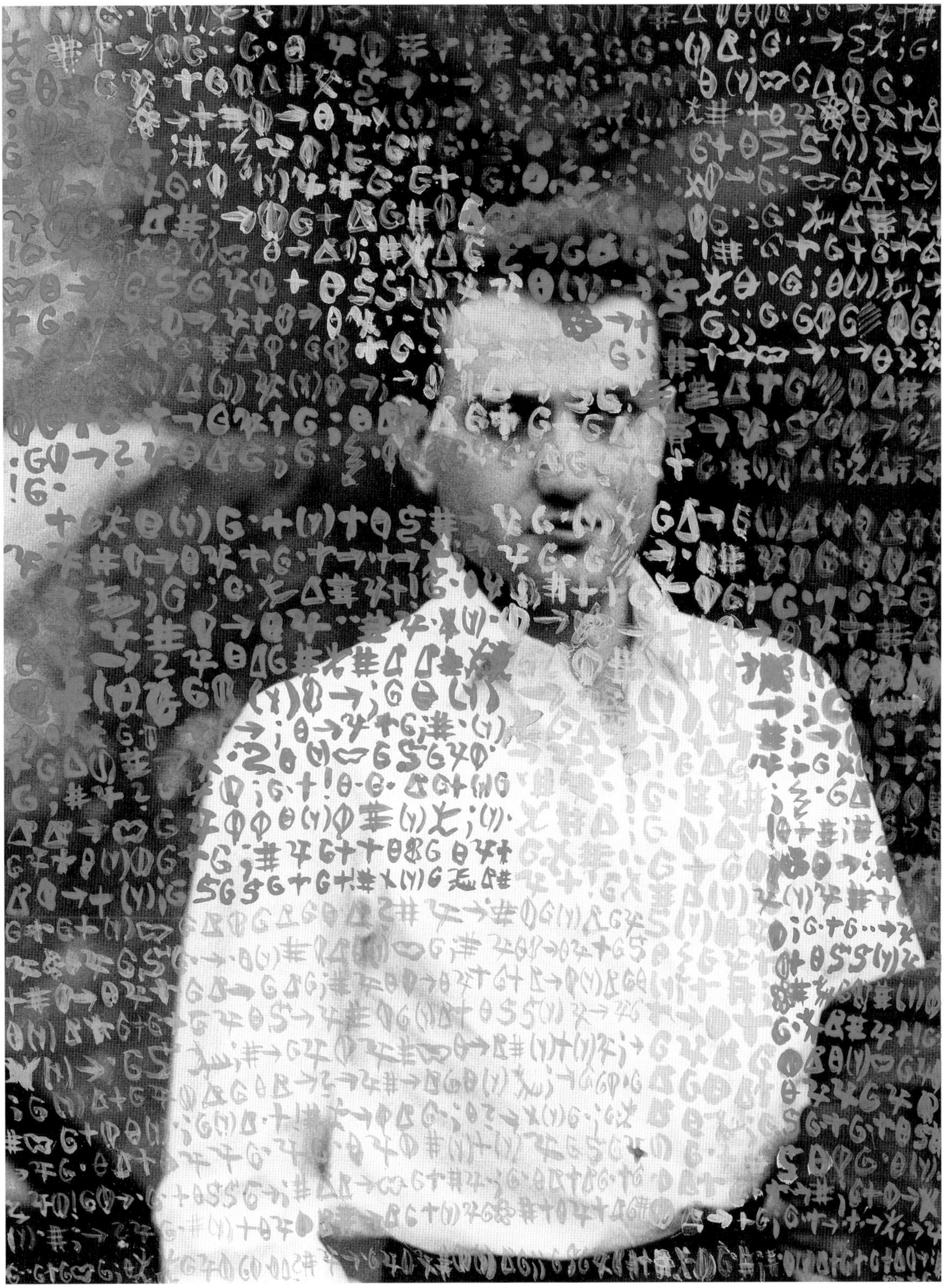

9. Isidore Isou, *Amos*, 1952. Original photograph with painted signs used as illustration in Isou's film novel *Amos ou Introduction à la métagraphologie*, 1953.

LE NOUVEL ALPHABET LETTRIQUE

1. Α (alpha)	=	*aspiration* (forte).
2. Β (beta)	=	*expiration* (forte).
3. Γ (gamma)	=	*zézaiement* (sifflement entre les dents comme un son de serpent).
4. Δ (delta)	=	*râle.*
5. Ε (epsilonn)	=	*grognement* (comme un chien prêt à aboyer).
6. Η (eta)	=	*ahanner (son rauque)* fait avec le gosier en gonflant le ventre.
7. Θ (theta)	=	*soupir* (fait simultanément avec le gosier, la bouche, le nez).
8. Κ (kappa)	=	*ronflement.*
9. Λ (lambda)	=	*gargariser* (avec l'air qui se débat entre la langue et le palais).
10. Μ (mu)	=	*gémissement.*
11. Ν (nu)	=	*hoquet.*
12. Ο (omicron)	=	*toux, toussotement.*
13. Π (pi)	=	*éternuement.*
14. Ρ (ro)	=	*claquement de langue.*
15. Σ (sigma)	=	*pètement* (avec les lèvres).
16. Τ (tau)	= =	*crépitement* (comme imiter le bruit d'une auto).
17. Υ (upsilonn)	=	*le son du crachat* (une sorte de peuh-pouah-ptiou ensemble).
18. Φ (phi)	=	*baiser* (bruyant)
19. Ψ (psi)	=	*sifflement* (simple, non mélodique).

10. Isidore Isou's notation system for a new alphabet, published in *Introduction à une nouvelle poésie et à une nouvelle musique* (Paris: Gallimard, 1947), 314.

With Lettrist poetry, the propositional content of language is displaced by the physicality of the utterance and the immediacy of aural sensation. Such a poetic practice did not imply, however, that a film's sound track could not include spoken (conceptual) language, but rather, as Artaud claimed in relation to theater, that the sound track should also make "language express what it does not ordinarily express."[26] The desire to develop language's expressive possibilities through the oral aspects of speech is further evinced in the Lettrists' shared fascination with the particularities of pronunciation, and later cries, as in the gurgles and screams found in the poetic work of Wolman and Dufrêne, whose individual elaborations of a physical poetry were known respectively as the *mégapneumie* and *crirythme* (figs. 11–12).[27] The Lettrists and Artaud each understood "language as [a] form of *Incantation*."[28] Language's rhythmic deployment and incantatory effect are perhaps nowhere more explicit than in the sustained presence of a Lettrist chorus on the sound tracks to Isou's and Lemaître's first films.

11. Gil J Wolman performing his *mégapneumie* in the recital *La poésie lettriste*, Théâtre Odéon, Paris, February 18, 1964. Frame enlargement.

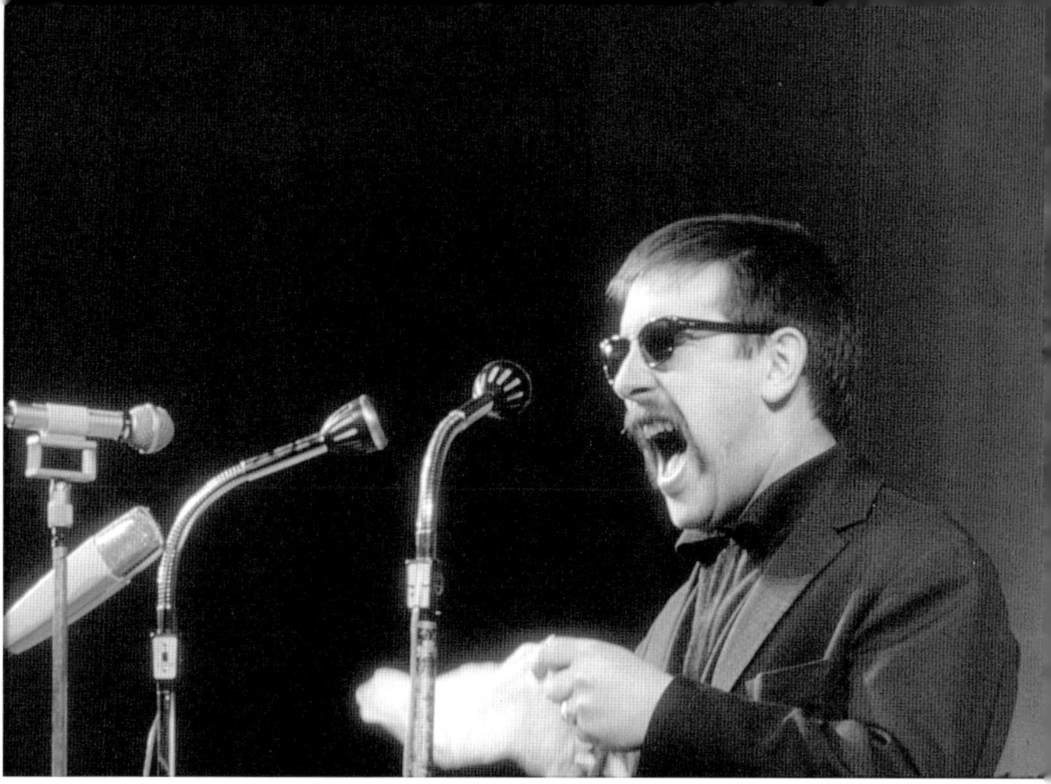

12. François Dufrêne performing his *crirythme* in the recital *La poésie lettriste*, Théâtre Odéon, Paris, February 18, 1964. Frame enlargement.

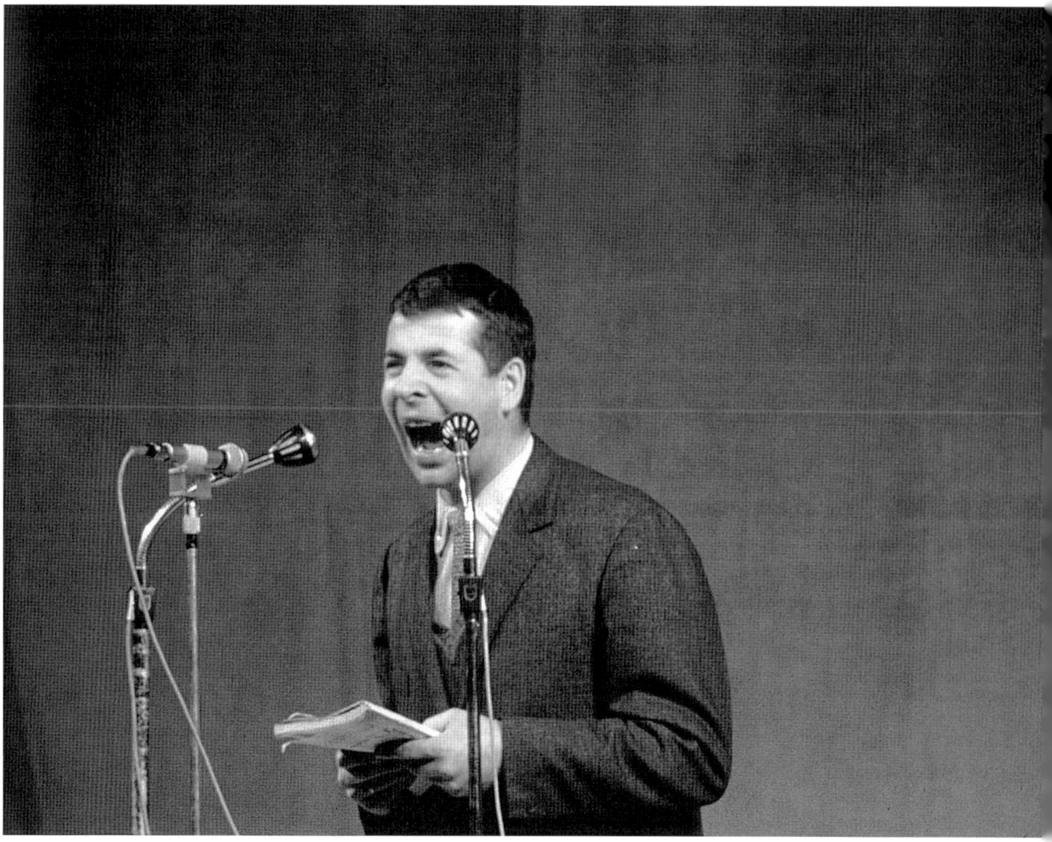

VOICE IN CINEMA

Beyond the chiseling on the image track, Isou claims to be pushing the elimination of the visual even further: "upcoming films will eliminate *the photo* from cinema."[29] This forecast for film produced without photography is astonishing, especially at the very moment when André Bazin was extolling the realist ontology of cinema, an ontology premised precisely on the icono-indexical properties of the filmed image (a subject I address in chapter 1). Yet Isou proposed the elimination of photography neither to promote the abstract animations of contemporary filmmakers like Robert Breer (then working in Paris, although there is no evidence he and Isou had knowledge of one another), nor to make the materiality of film the self-reflexive subject and object of film practice, as in the structural-materialist films of the following decade, when fixed camera position, flicker effect, loop printing, and re-photography off the screen became defining film techniques.[30] In the immediate postwar moment that concerns this study, Lettrist film challenged photographic reference in order to explore the possibilities of cinematic speech.[31] To this end, Isou writes of a potential collaboration with Debord in which the latter was to have declared, "The cinema is dead. There can be no more film. Let us proceed, if you like, to the debates."[32]

Isou's account of this exchange with Debord speaks to his and the Lettrists' investment in film as a social practice and, more specifically, in the legacy of the interwar ciné-club, whose programs regularly included debates. Many Lettrist films mine and refer to ciné-club conventions—that is, the tripartite structure of lecture, screening, and debate consolidated in the 1920s.[33] This legacy, which I explore in relation to Lemaître's film (chapter 2), is referenced in Isou's film when Daniel, the sound track protagonist, proclaims, "This is the first time that the ciné-club is introduced in the cinema [i.e., in his film]." Consequently, for the Lettrists film is not a thing (the filmstrip), nor is it exclusively the apparatus of projection (e.g., projector, light, screen) within which film's visual images unfold. Rather film is claimed as part of a social network in which spectators and their responses to the film are integral.

The Lettrist emphasis on debate and the liveness that is constitutive of the process of their films' screenings should be held apart from the set of practices that emerged subsequently and came to be known as expanded cinema.[34] Central to the development of expanded cinema was the interaction of performers and their images. As a kind of experimental cinema-theater, expanded cinema does share some characteristics with Lettrist film, but in expanded cinema the visual projection often remains a primary component: its central terms revolve around live action and filmed image, the screened body and the body screened.[35] By the mid-1960s, the moving image was more firmly ensconced among the materials of art, which at times approximated the display culture of modern mass media used for propaganda and advertising. I am thinking here, for example, of the creation of immersive environments like Stan VanDerBeek's *Movie-Drome* (1963) and what Liz Kotz wryly identifies as its "somatic, dreamlike address."[36] In the decade that followed, other artists turned to the "idea" of cinema, making use of ephemeral properties such as "light" and "time" as means by which to create films no longer tied to film as a material form. Yet such works of "paracinema" were often presented in the art gallery, and thus outside of cinema's institutional frame.[37]

By contrast, Lettrist cinema not only challenges cinematic conventions within the actual space of the cinema theater but also consistently interrogates speech. Lettrist films critically deploy speech toward the *détournement* of the visual image, both upholding the communicative function of language and casting doubt on it through the disintegration of language to the letter and the bodily production of sound. With the poetry audible on their sound tracks, Lettrist films operate toward a semiotic transfiguration of a public mode of address: the voice in cinema.[38] What Lettrist films in the years 1951–1952 undeniably share is their work on the voice in cinema as a discursive site that is neither neutral nor natural. Moreover, this voice is one produced both from within and without the parameters of what is seen on the screen.

HETERODOX MODERNISM

Aspects of Isou's appeal for a chiseled cinema—a whittling of the medium to its essential parts—seem to recall certain modernist affirmations, such as those of Clement Greenberg, whereby each art has its "unique and proper area of competence." Greenberg upheld the "purity" and "self-definition" of a medium with a vengeance: "The task of self-criticism became to eliminate from the specific effects of each art any and every effect that might conceivably be borrowed from or by the medium of any other art."[39] Hence, in the case of painting, his definition of modernism and medium specificity was defined by a teleological movement toward flatness.

Isou's discrepant cinema similarly takes an inward turn (what Isou calls *un mouvement d'introjection*) toward the constituent elements of film in order to research and chisel the *particules* (sound and image) of which it is made. "Discrepant montage," he explains, "diverts the tracks and makes them indifferent to one another."[40] Indeed, he negatively determines the specificity of the image and sound track in terms of their mutual indifference or nonrelation. Sound, rather than being subservient to the image, does not relate to, define, or otherwise inflect an image's meaning. Yet by insisting on *two* tracks, Isou betrays an understanding of modernism that would claim for a medium a single technical support or unique essence, a point I will return to below. There also obtain semiotic and material differences internal to each track, and thus additional differentiations.

If the Lettrists shared Artaud's resistance to the sound track, harnessing disjunctive and chiseling strategies to anti-illusionist and material ends, they supported a similarly aggressive approach to spectatorship. In 1999, in his thoughtful study on Artaud's film projects, Stephen Barber noted that "Artaud's cinema has only one direct successor: The Lettrist cinema of the early 1950s . . . with its emphasis on negation and its violent approach to spectatorship."[41] Artaud aimed to impact the spectator differently, insisting, especially with regard to theater, on the "spectacle acting not only as a reflection [of a prior text] but as a force."[42] He described his desire to "mesmerize the audience's sensibilities" and to "surround the spectator in the most physical ways, leaving him immersed in a constant pool of lights, images, movements, and sounds."[43] Similarly, Isou's sound track protagonist announces, "I want a film which will really hurt your eyes. . . . We should leave the cinema with a headache!"; Lemaître proposed a production company for professional spectators who were to actively interrupt commercial screenings in a decidedly more Brechtian fashion; and Wolman insisted on a physical and anticonceptual cinematic reception. In each instance, these artists oppose passive consumption, as well as spectacle's emergent ideological constraints in the service of the culture industry or film technology's alliance with the military and the state.

Beyond these individual experiments with an active and physical spectatorship, Lettrist cinema might also be considered through the lens of Artaud's heterodox modernism as put forth in his conceptualization of a Theater of Cruelty: "The theater, which is in *no thing* but makes use of everything—gestures, sounds, words, screams, light, darkness."[44] Theater, like film, does not possess a unique physical substrate to which the medium could claim to be reduced, whereby the medium's essence would be tied to a unique technical support. It follows that a study of Lettrist cinema also contributes to recent reconsiderations of the artistic medium within art history.[45] Equally, the work's recovery provides the conditions for thinking an alternative genealogy of avant-garde practices, one whose afterlife might be found less in the projected images we find in art galleries today than in the emphasis on speech we find in the tactics of contemporary art and media activists, from the Yes Men to Sharon Hayes, and in the aesthetico-political strategies of contemporary protests.[46]

The elusiveness of Lettrist cinema certainly raises methodological challenges when accounting for the specificity of the works and their varied and multiple effects. Their heterodox modernism is one that presents semiotic crossovers in both production and reception. But this does not mean that any material can be used willy-nilly toward any end. If Isou frames image and sound as indifferent to one another, he nevertheless also speaks to the potential crossovers and cross-contamination between media. Isou's commentator in *Traité* describes Daniel's ambition—"music within poetry, painting within the novel, and now the novel within the cinema"—thereby invoking how the conventions of one medium could expand the parameters of another. In the case of the sound track, Isou uses the bodily intonation of Lettrist poetry as a means to critique the supposed semiotic transparency of speech-on-film. With regard to the image track, scratches and paint streaks coexist with photographic reproductions. Each track reproduces sensory data (be it the profilmic visual or aural event), but works of Lettrist cinema further explore the materiality of the support, exploiting the tensions that ensue between the material and the referential, the literal and the symbolic, the abstract and the indexical. In so doing, they adopt elements from one medium (poetry, painting) to critique the illusionism and spectacular consolidation of another (sound-image relations in film).

Lettrist cinema offers a hybrid audiovisual experience for spectators: they are at once viewers of images, readers of text, and interpreters of textual marks and signs that interrupt filmed images, just as they are auditors of a debate and subject to the interruption of linguistic meaning by the eruption of seemingly senseless sounds. It is worth noting that such heterodox practices developed alongside the aestheticism and quasi-mystical silence imposed during film screenings that would increasingly define the cinephile culture of Paris and the critics and filmmakers associated with *Cahiers du cinéma*.[47] That a few filmmakers from that generation were actually present at Lettrist screenings (among them, Alain Resnais, Chris Marker, and Jean-Luc Godard) is also telling.[48] While largely unacknowledged, I wager that these filmmakers owe, at least in part, their development of certain aesthetic devices—from the use of imageless sequences with voice-over to heterogeneous montage aesthetics—to their early exposure to Lettrist film. Consequently, historians of their films might in the future also turn to Lettrism as one of the possible references for auteurist practices. Lemaître, for one, has maintained a sustained polemic across the decades accusing these filmmakers of plagiarism. A cursory review of the titles of some of his publications makes this aggressively clear: "Marguerite Duras: Pour en finir avec cet escroc et plagiaire généralisée" (Marguerite Duras: To Have Done with This Crook and Generalized Plagiarist, 1970), "Les nouvelles escroqueries

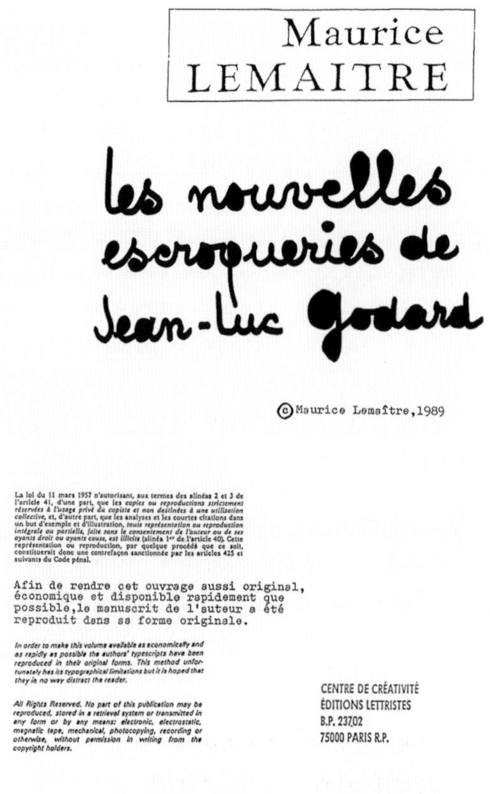

13. Maurice Lemaître, "Les nouvelles escroqueries de Jean-Luc Godard," 1989. Cover.

de Jean-Luc Godard" (The New Scams of Jean-Luc Godard, 1989; fig. 13).[49] Yet where the Lettrists engage a dialectic of the screen and the space of the audience to productive ends, these filmmakers contributed to and worked within film as it was materially defined and historicized as a medium.

Off-Screen Cinema pursues a line of inquiry that pushes beyond the formal boundaries of film to address aspects of cinema as an institution and a specific form of governmentality, as the "conduct of conduct" evoked above. Beyond the individual Lettrist film's turn to the voice in cinema, which largely unites these otherwise disparate works, each chapter charts a tension: between cinema as it is marked by operations of power and cinematic experimentation that proposed an alternative to dominant modes of film production and consumption in the 1950s. These individual filmmakers and their works instantiate their challenge to cinema through various means: the chiseling of official newsreel footage; the development of an alternative pedagogical model for educating the film public; the repurposing of the material support of a militarized vision (namely, a weather balloon); and, finally, the enabling of conditions for active spectatorship during what was, at the time, understood as an increasingly spectacular regime of passive consumption. Such tensions characterize the unique historicity of Lettrist cinema, aligning it with broader cultural and aesthetic debates, from the status of cinematic realism to the uses of film during war. It is also these tensions that inscribe these works within the discursive terrain called *cinema*. The Lettrists displayed a sustained commitment to the medium (film) in addition to the social and historically specific practices it entailed. They refused to be governed by film conceived as spectacle or propaganda and for that reason experimented, aggressively so, with other forms through which film as an art—but also as an art of government—might organize both its practice and its modes of reception.

This study is not a comprehensive account either of Lettrist film or of Lettrism as a movement.[50] Such a task would be gargantuan, given the proliferation of the Lettrists' production and their contributions across disciplines: from theater to dance, politics to antipsychiatry, mathematics to the economy. (Isou even wrote a volume addressing female sexuality.) Instead, I focus on the inaugural years of their experiments in cinema and the particular dialectic of what goes on and off the screen. Because I emphasize speech and the live elements that accompany the films, a few important Lettrist films do not receive sustained attention. These include Gabriel Pomerand's *La légende cruelle* (1951), which refilms the painting and drawing of Leonor Fini; Marc'O's *Closed Vision* (1954), which, while it exploits disjunctive editing, is indebted to a Surrealist aesthetic; and, finally, the aborted film project *La barque de la vie courante* (The Boat of Everyday Life, 1951–1952) by Jean-Louis Brau.[51] From the get-go, my ambition was to write a short history that would intervene within current historiographies of experimental film and modernist art history and at once serve as an invitation to future scholarship on the subject. It is my hope that other scholars will bring to bear new perspectives on this challenging, strange, and fascinating work. For now, let us turn to Isou's film, remembering that it will require an attentive ear.

ONE

TO SALIVATE IS NOT TO SPEAK, AS BORING AS WATCHING DUST

IN MID-APRIL 1951, rumors circulated as to whether Isidore Isou would attend the premiere of his first film, *Traité de bave et d'éternité* (On Venom and Eternity), which was programmed as a fringe event complementing the official Cannes Film Festival. Isou's short-term imprisonment on account of the publication of his book *Isou, ou La mécanique des femmes* (Isou, or The Mechanics of Women, 1949) had made him somewhat averse to publicity. Moreover, as a Romanian Jew, he feared that he could potentially be deported from France should another scandal ensue. It was thus Marc'O (Marc-Guilbert Guillaumin), the film's producer, and fellow Lettrists Jean-Louis Brau, François Dufrêne, Maurice Lemaître, and Gil J Wolman who transported the film reels to Cannes and there worked to promote Isou's film. A photograph from the time shows a group of young men, including Marc'O and Guy Debord, walking down a street in Cannes with Isou, who had finally arrived from Paris (fig. 14).[1]

Isou's presence in Cannes garnered considerable press attention. In the pages of *Combat*, one writer noted, "Isidore Isou is not happy, not at all happy that his real presence could be cast in doubt. Correction: Isidore Isou exists. He is there. . . . As for the film itself, *Traité de bave et d'éternité*, to whomever wants to see it, Isidore Isou will show a baggage claim ticket with which one may find, he says, the 5,200 meters of film."[2] If Isou's initial nonappearance raised doubts as to his actual attendance, he made sure to provide a preamble to his film, which was published in *Le film français (Cinémonde)*. Here, Isou declares his work's difference from the films of Orson Welles and the Neorealism of Roberto Rossellini and Vittorio De Sica, so popular at the time, and affirms, as noted in the introduction, "I am certain that the *Traité de bave et d'éternité* will change

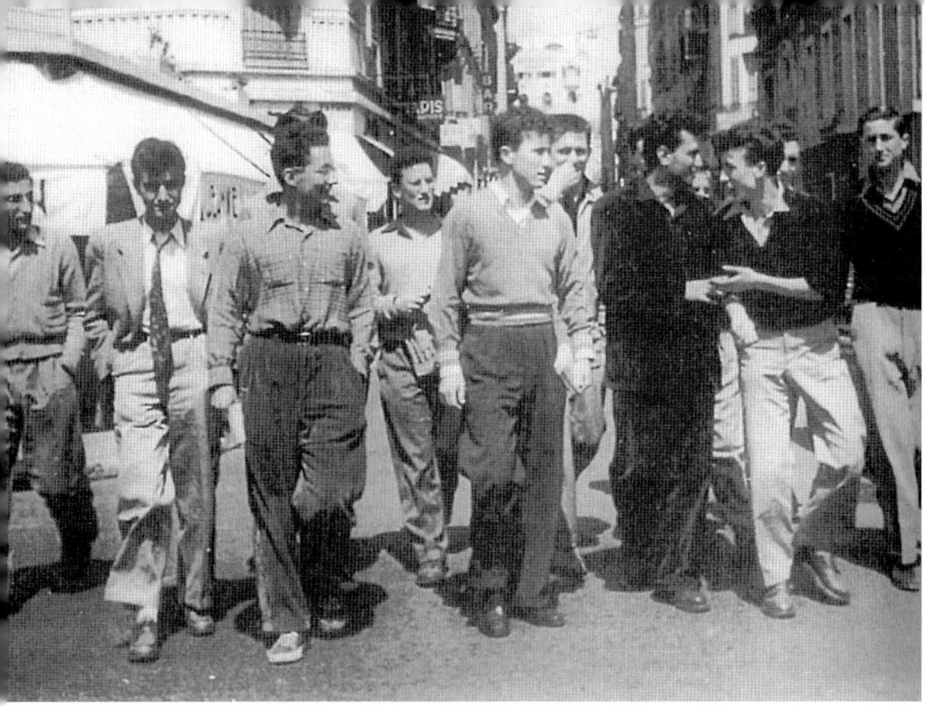

14. Marc'O and Guy Debord, among others, walk down a street in Cannes with Isidore Isou, who arrived from Paris. Cannes, 1951.

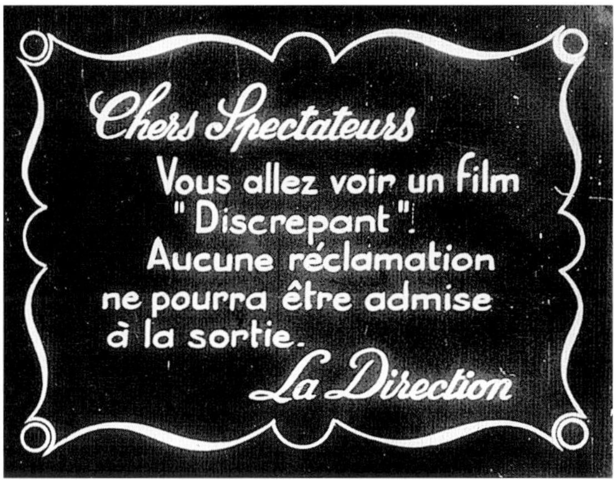

15. Isidore Isou, *Traité de bave et d'éternité*, 1951. Frame enlargement.

cinema drastically and push it toward unexpected paths. It requires only that juries lend it an *attentive ear*."[3]

Traité de bave et d'éternité premiered on Friday, April 20, at the Vox theater in Cannes. The film opens with an intertitle that announces, "Dear spectators / You will see a 'discrepant' film. No complaints will be accepted upon exit. The Management" (fig. 15). This shot is followed by a black sequence during which we hear a Lettrist chorus, before cutting to the opening credits and a rolling dedication to filmmakers "who brought something new or personal to the art of cinema" (D. W. Griffith, Abel Gance, Sergei Eisenstein, Luis Buñuel, Jean Cocteau, et al.). A short sequence introduces the covers of the various books penned by Isou, followed by the intertitle "Chapitre I: LE PRINCIPE" (Chapter 1: The

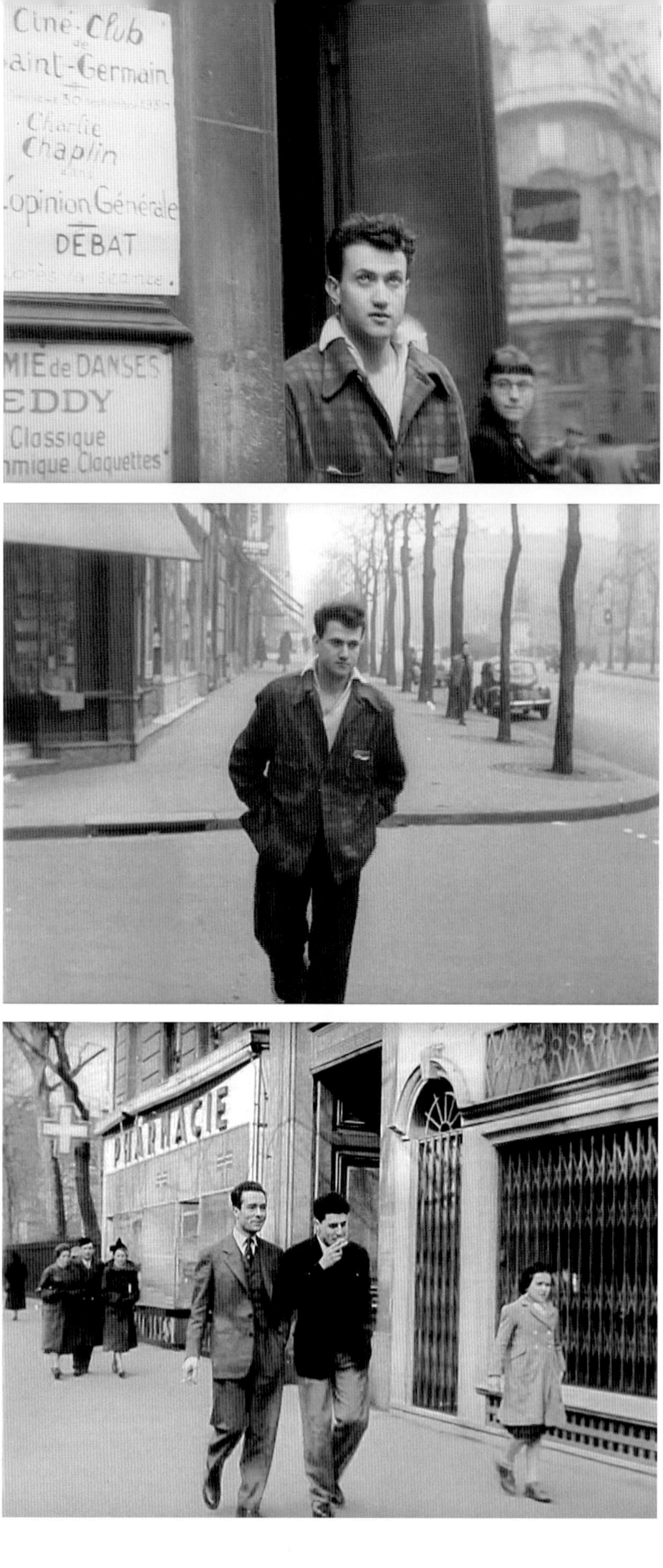

16. Isidore Isou, *Traité de bave et d'éternité*, 1951. Frame enlargements.

Principle). The shots that follow show Isou and his Lettrist cohort walking in the streets of Saint-Germain-des-Prés (fig. 16). But the sound track does not correspond to the images we see. In line with Isou's theory of *montage discrépant* (discrepant editing), the film uncouples the semantic unity of sound and image in order to insist on the two tracks' independent development. In this first of *Traité*'s three chapters, the sound track represents a film club debate; one listens to the protagonist, Daniel, defend his film theories amid the shouts of the public: "Decadent!" "You will piss off the spectators!" A commentator offers external reflection on Daniel. And all the while, the unrelenting rhythm of a Lettrist chorus occupies the acoustic background.

At approximately ten minutes, Daniel declares, "I want to separate the ear from its cinematic master: the eye." At twenty-three minutes, he asserts, "I want a film which will really hurt your eyes. . . . We should leave the cinema with a headache!" He shouts his proposal for a new cinema as best he can over the cantankerous public's hisses and boos.[4] The audience interruptions propel Daniel to advance his argument, in which he explains how photographic images will be destroyed *par la parole* (by speech). As if taking Daniel's words to their logical conclusion, for the screening at Cannes, Isou projected two-thirds of *Traité*'s without images, thereby failing to provide viewers with the purportedly most basic and constitutive element of a film: the image track. Only chapter 1 of the image track was completed at the time of the film's premiere; for chapters 2 and 3, the Vox was plunged into darkness, as the sound track voices were emitted from loudspeakers and acoustically filled the room. Isou's plea for an "attentive ear" thus proved to be a literal demand for the film's first audience.[5] The public and press were decidedly furious, while Jean Cocteau allegedly conveyed to Isou that the film was the "the most beautiful scandal of the entire festival."[6] To be sure, what the initial screening at Cannes put in relief was Isou's deprivileging of the image track in his pursuit of *montage discrépant*.

MOVEMENT OF SPEECH

Isou's theory of *montage discrépant* in part explains his lack of concern, or flagrant bravado, when choosing to present the final chapters of *Traité* without an image track. In doing so, he explicitly violated the consolidation of film's technical apparatus in the service of the continuity of movement, illusion, and narrative absorption.[7] But let us recall: "discrepant montage . . . diverts the tracks and makes them indifferent to one another."[8] In line with this assertion, the sound track was conceived as an independent entity and thereby complete even in the absence of the corresponding image track. During the film's second chapter, in the darkness of the Vox, one would hear the banal details of a love story involving Daniel, a woman named Eve, and another woman named Denise, and then in the final chapter be told that he and Eve attended a Lettrist recital. A voice-over defends Lettrist poetry, claiming that it is "more popular than Surrealist poetry." In the minutes that follow, Daniel concludes his theoretical defense of a new type of cinema. Daniel's inquiry in chapter 1—"Whoever said that the cinema, whose meaning is movement, must be absolutely the movement of the photograph and not the movement of the speech [*parole*]?"—underscores Isou's indifference to reproducing movement on the screen. To this end, I would like to suggest the extent to which the screening at Cannes foregrounded how Isou imagined the sound track as a site for recovering the phonetic substance of speech and the materiality of words.

Daniel's declarations were later echoed and formalized in Isou's "Esthétique du cinéma" (Aesthetic of Cinema, 1952) in a section dedicated to "la bande-paroles" (speech tracks). In this context, Isou describes how image-sound relations within montage practices had explored all possible subjects but how it remained for cinema to explore "*the secret chances* of speech and the nuances of sound combinations."[9] "Sound cinema," he declared, "was a *printing press for speech*."[10] Isou frames sound cinema as a recording technology but one that, like the printing press, results in language's codification and representation. With sound cinema or the talking film, speech is assimilated to the conceptual content of language, rather than harnessed toward phonation and revealing the process of enunciation. As a corrective, Isou argues for bringing the art of rhetoric to the sound track in cinema.[11] For Isou, rhetoric does not necessarily mean an art of persuasion tied exclusively to the communicative content of known words, but rather a means by which to "offer cinema speeches [*discours*] of a new kind [*genre inédit*]."[12]

This brings me to a consideration of *Traité*'s concluding sound track, which presents experiments in Lettrist poetry as an alternative to speech-on-film. The first recorded performance of Lettrist poetry presented in *Traité* 's third chapter is of "Marche" (March) by Dufrêne. The poem's rhythmic delivery is punctuated by shifts in volume. One can only imagine that with no visual image, in the darkness of the Vox, spectators were left with little semantic security to hold on to. While the poem's sounds conjure the orders and execution of military routine (a reading undoubtedly inflected by its "march" title), the audience would nevertheless have been confronted with a voice whose source they could not see or place in relation to the screen. Such a purely "acousmatic" situation goes against the grain of a cinema that attempts to fit sights to sounds in order to produce a visualized listening.[13] *Traité*'s first spectators were in a

17. François Dufrêne, “J’interroge et j’invective: Poème à hurler / À la mémoire d’Antonin Artaud,” 1949, published in *Ur*, no. 1, 1950.

Piètres pitres,
Totre botra botra titre ?
Totre batri ! batri !
Totre boutre (*bis*)
Totre ? butre
Vutre Katre voutre bôtre, bôtre...
Têtre, do : Tête-Kssêtre nat doussêtre,
Kssètre nat dongsètre nat têtre ?
Pouhkre (*bis*)
Empil surjoux empalex, empalex
Hogorax pempre yogogrex ollüngb ?
Somble règre, Kssamble Kssègre
Pohkre ! (*bis*)
Tègre empil jarssoux humpârux
Hugurix pïmpre yigüngrux ollüngb ?
(comme en *a parte*)
Kssulve nimvolve parèveulve
Krilva sèsrilve nimvolve parèveulve
(à nouveau hurlant)
Sèsrilve pulve ?
Pêhkre (*bis*)
Empil surjoux omparix pampre yungégrix ollüngb ?
Tètre, do : tètre-Kssètre nat dongssètre
Kssètre nat dongssètre nat tètre ?
(comme en *a parte*)
Peuyple pekpe, pekpe, pekpe ! virlokff
Irtounx velch hetchle topelfe
Yoktre lyogembounx
Bilche rlô ptyuvènrlô pulche !

doubly paradoxical situation: listening to a recorded voice that insisted on speech’s material source, the very body that was negated by the absence of a visual image.

While “Marche” may suggest militarized action, the subsequent poem, “J’interroge et j’invective” (I Question and I Accuse), reveals more bodily associations.[14] Dufrêne dedicates this poem “À la mémoire d’Antonin Artaud,” and throughout the poem one repeatedly hears /k/ as well as its phonetic equivalents: the hard /c/, /ck/, and /ch/ (fig. 17). The letter *K* appears infrequently in French, yet in the years 1946–1948 it has a continuous graphic presence in and is a regular phonetic element of Artaud’s post-Rodez writing and speech, a legacy that Dufrêne explicitly evokes.[15] With Dufrêne’s aggressive delivery of “*Peuyple pekpe, pekpe, pekpe*” and “*Glech ! Glamve ! pâhkre ! pahkre !*” we hear spit accumulate in his mouth and how he modifies phonation by forcefully filtering letters between his teeth. These instances of the body’s presence in speech suggest that *Traité de bave et d’éternité* would be better translated as “Treatise on Slobber and Eternity,” rather than its contemporary codification as “On Venom and Eternity.”[16] That the film’s speech track indulged in the recording of slobber, a bodily fluid that interferes with “proper” pronunciation and speech, was picked up by one reviewer whose subtitle contended, “to salivate is not to speak (French)” (fig. 18).[17] What the sound track of

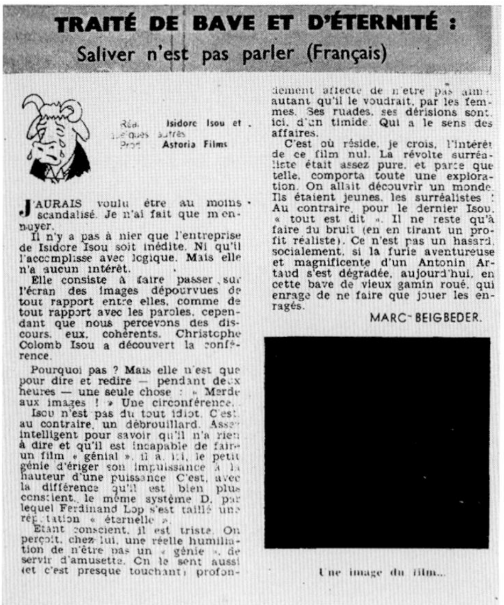

TRAITÉ DE BAVE ET D'ÉTERNITÉ :

Saliver n'est pas parler (Français)

Réal. Isidore Isou et quelques autres
Prod. Astoria Films

J'AURAIS voulu être au moins scandalisé. Je n'ai fait que m'ennuyer.

Il n'y a pas à nier que l'entreprise de Isidore Isou soit inédite. Ni qu'il l'accomplisse avec logique. Mais elle n'a aucun intérêt.

Elle consiste à faire passer sur l'écran des images dépourvues de tout rapport entre elles, comme de tout rapport avec les paroles, cependant que nous percevons des discours, eux, cohérents. Christophe Colomb Isou a découvert la conférence.

Pourquoi pas ? Mais elle n'est que pour dire et redire — pendant deux heures — une seule chose : « Merde aux images ! » Une circonférence.

Isou n'est pas du tout idiot. C'est au contraire, un débrouillard. Assez intelligent pour savoir qu'il n'a rien à dire et qu'il est incapable de faire un film « génial », il a, lui, le petit génie d'ériger son impuissance à la hauteur d'une puissance. C'est, avec la différence qu'il est bien plus conscient, le même système D. par lequel Ferdinand Lop s'est taillé une réputation « éternelle ».

Etant conscient, il est triste. On perçoit, chez lui, une réelle humiliation de n'être pas un « génie », de servir d'amusette. On le sent aussi (et c'est presque touchant) profondément affecté de n'être pas aimé autant qu'il le voudrait, par les femmes. Ses ruades, ses dérisions sont, ici, d'un timide. Qui a le sens des affaires.

C'est où réside, je crois, l'intérêt de ce film nul. La révolte surréaliste était assez pure, et parce que telle, comporta toute une exploration. On allait découvrir un monde. Ils étaient jeunes, les surréalistes ! Au contraire, pour le dernier Isou, « tout est dit ». Il ne reste qu'à faire du bruit (en en tirant un profit réaliste). Ce n'est pas un hasard, socialement, si la furie aventureuse et magnificente d'un Antonin Artaud s'est dégradée, aujourd'hui, en cette bave de vieux gamin roué, qui enrage de ne faire que jouer les enragés.

MARC-BEIGBEDER.

Une image du film...

18. Marc Beigbeder, *"Traité de bave et d'éternité:* Saliver n'est pas parler (Français)," n.d.

Lettrist poetry discloses, in no uncertain terms, is the bodily, organic basis of speech. Wolman will extend these investigations in the final minutes of *L'anticoncept*, when we hear him pant, gag, and scream.

By using Lettrist poetry as part of the sound track's experimental conceit, Isou lays claim to bodily intonation and its signifying possibilities for sound in cinema. Such a stance runs counter to how sound recording in relation to speech has, until recently, been framed. If the image track *represents* the space-time accessible to the camera through, for example, framing and point of view, the sound track has been claimed to *reproduce* sonic material.[18] Within these terms, and with regard to speech-on-film, Jean-Louis Baudry affirms "that in cinema—as in the case of all talking machines—one does not hear an image of the sounds but the *sounds themselves*."[19] Such a stance upholds the semiotic incommensurabilty between the iconicity of photography and the indexical trace of sound as means of specifying two recording technologies. Baudry's argument finds further support for the semiotic neutrality of speech recording by turning to the voice's discursive status in other disciplines: "Hence, no doubt, one of the basic reasons for the privileged status of voice in idealist philosophy and in religion: voice does not lend itself to games of illusion . . . between the real and its figurativity (because voice cannot be represented figuratively)."[20] Baudry aligns voice with the ideality of meaning and thereby assimilates an understanding of voice to the conceptual content of speech, to what words, independent of their phonation, literally say.

Isou rejects the idealist alignment of speech with pure thought and stresses how the body effects verbal signification and how intonation insists on the materiality of speech through tone, modulation, cadence, and

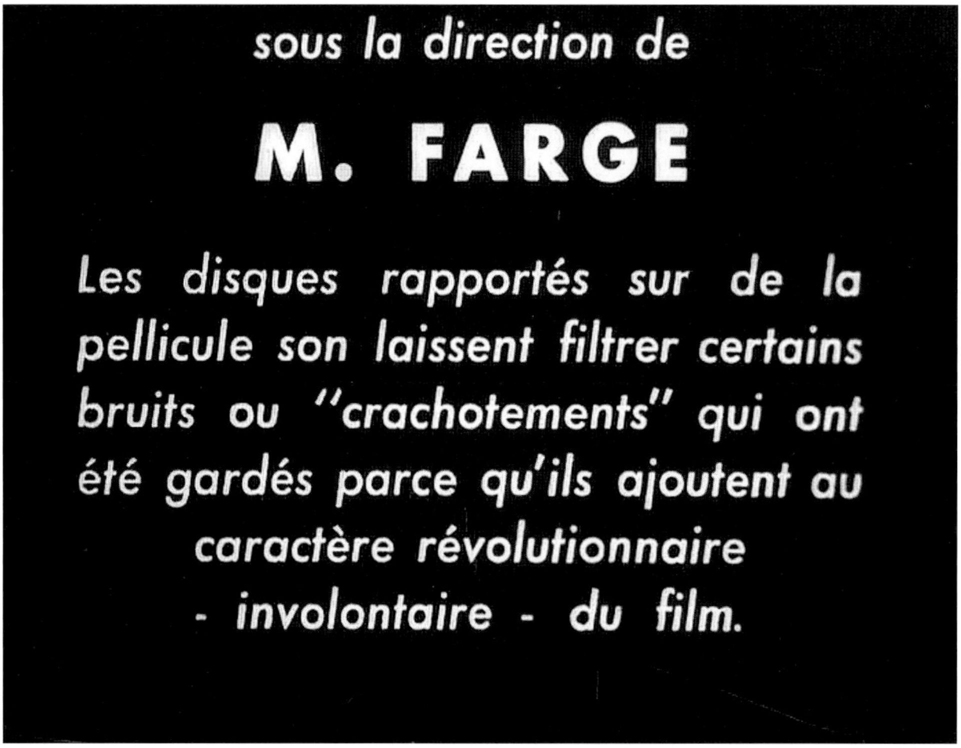

19. Isidore Isou, *Traité de bave et d'éternité*, 1951. Frame enlargement.

inflection. What is more, *Traité* foregrounds the materiality (as opposed to transparency) of recording by transferring an unusual, outdated technology of sound recording onto film's more advanced optical sound track. At approximately three and a half minutes, an intertitle explains (fig. 19):

> The sound was first recorded on vinyl with the kind help of Robert Beauvais, Gisèle Parry, and Caron, under the direction of M. Farge. The disks when transferred to the film retain certain noises or "crackling," which have been kept because they contribute to the—involuntary—revolutionary character of the film.

With *Traité*'s faulty transfer of sound, Isou uses one type of sound technology to remediate another. *Remediation* usually describes the condition whereby a medium "appropriates the techniques, forms and social significance of other media and attempts to rival or refashion them *in the name of the real*."[21] Consequently, it most frequently refers to media that replace older technologies in the service of more accurately reproducing reality. Hence, for example, the conception of television as an advanced form of radio. In contrast to this drive toward technological supersession coupled with realist ambition, Isou engages with a process that Pavle Levi has termed "retrograde remediation."[22] That is, he uses a

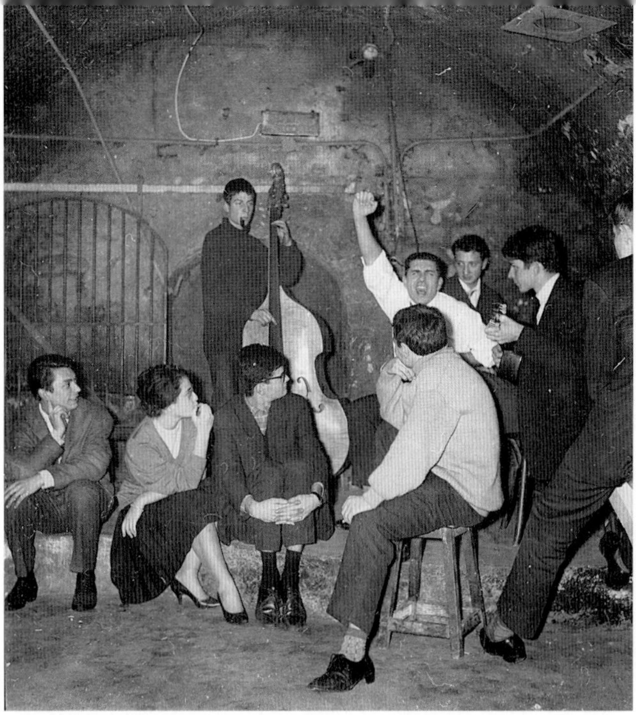

20. Maurice Lemaître (with arm raised) at Le Tabou, ca. 1959. Photographer unknown.

newer technological medium (optical track) *inadequately* by transferring an older medium (vinyl) onto it, drawing attention to the material and signifying properties of the original recording: the noise and crackle to which the intertitle refers.[23] His sound track implicates sound recording as a signifying practice and complicates a realist semiotics of listening in which the recording (sign) is taken to be equivalent to its referent (acoustic event). In this way, Isou's purposely flawed sound track counters the dominant practice of self-effacing sound work in commercial cinema, whereby good sound recording "rewards the suspension of disbelief with perceptual fantasy."[24] Here Isou's emphasis on the materiality of recording finds a parallel in his investigation into the material basis of speech. Each contributes to the specificity of his heterodox modernism: he uses Lettrist poetry together with the sound's second-rate transfer to critique the notion of the semiotic transparency of speech-on-film.

Isou and his fellow Lettrists brought their poetic experimentation to the public arena of performed speech at mythic venues such as Le Tabou, where live Lettrist poetry performances displaced the propositional content of language in favor of the physical, organic basis of speech and the immediacy of aural sensation (fig. 20). *Traité*'s impure and less than technically precise sound recording instead responds to Isou's perhaps surprising interest in the productive (not just reproductive) possibilities of sound and speech technology.[25] My claims with regard to the film's sound track point to an alternative genealogy for postwar European poetry's increasing attention to the body and use of recording technologies. One might then consider *Traité*'s sound track as a possible origin for the insistence on bodily sounds progressively explored by Dufrêne, Wolman, and Brau. With their *poésie physique* (physical poetry), each abandoned the written poetic score (which was still preserved in the poetic work of Isou and Lemaître) in order to experiment with the aural perspectives offered by the microphone's mediation in the amplification of bodily sounds (I take up this issue in relation to Wolman in chapter 3). Henri Chopin's *poésie sonore* (sound poetry) would go further, exploring the productive possibilities of the magnetophone.[26]

MOST REVOLTING FILM IN THE HISTORY OF CINEMA

From Cannes, Isou returned to Paris, where he completed *Traité* on May 23, 1951. As in the previously completed first chapter, he refrained from producing the visualized listening situation typical of image-sound relations in cinema. Instead he provoked a dismantling of realist expectations with regard to the images one sees. The final film with image track includes three chapters, "Le principe," "Le développement," and "La preuve." The first, as described above, includes shots of Isou and other Lettrists walking around Saint-Germain-des-Pr és, while the sound track represents a film club debate. In the remainder of the film, Isou experiments with the *ciselure* (chiseling) of the visual image through the manipulation of the celluloid by writing on the film, presenting sequences in negative, and inverting shots to suggest 180-degree camera rotation. Chapter 2 includes a rendezvous with a woman and found footage culled from the trash bins of specialized film labs, among them the Services Cinématographiques du Ministère des Armées, while the previously mentioned love story unfolds on the sound track (fig. 21). Chapter 3 features Lettrists such as Dufrêne and Marc'O; cameos by avant-garde figures such as Jean Cocteau, Marcel Achard, and Armand Salacrou; and the use of clear and countdown leader—all in conjunction with a sound track that concludes the film club debate and features the aforementioned Lettrist poetry recordings, which are paired with black-and-white abstract sequences to suggest a structural parallel between the whittling of semantic reference in speech (Lettrist poetry) and the abstract (chiseled) images projected on the screen (fig. 22).

The very day of its completion *Traité de bave et d'éternité* was screened at the Ciné-Club Avant-Garde 52, which was directed by Armand Cauliez at the Musée de l'Homme, a key location for early screenings of Lettrist films. Due to its last-minute programming, the showing went unannounced in the ciné-club's listing, published earlier that month in the pages of *Cinéma 51*.[27] At this time, the film's reception was lukewarm at best. Eight months later, however, the debates surrounding Isou's film

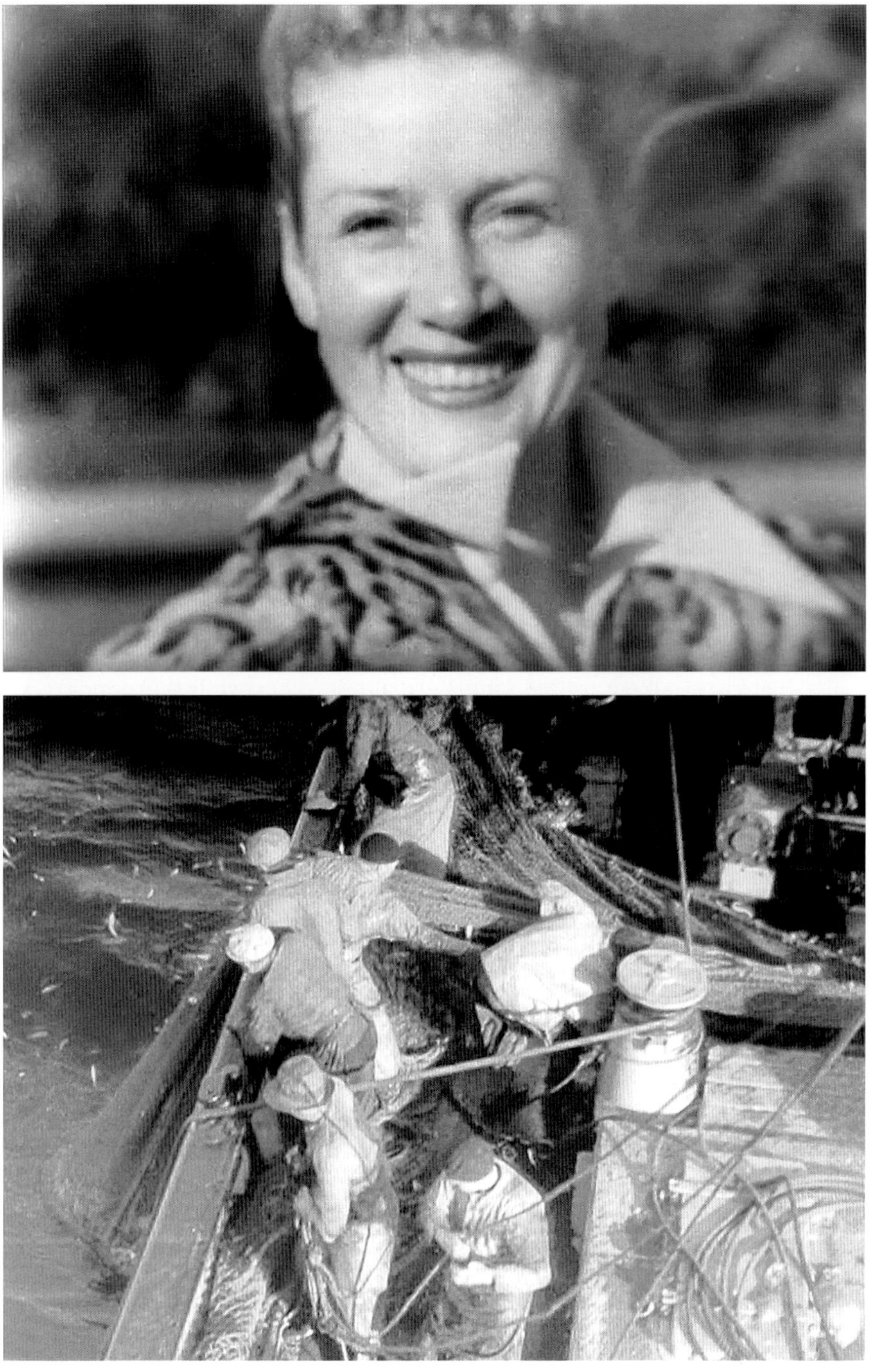

21. Isidore Isou, *Traité de bave et d'éternité*, 1951.
Frame enlargements.

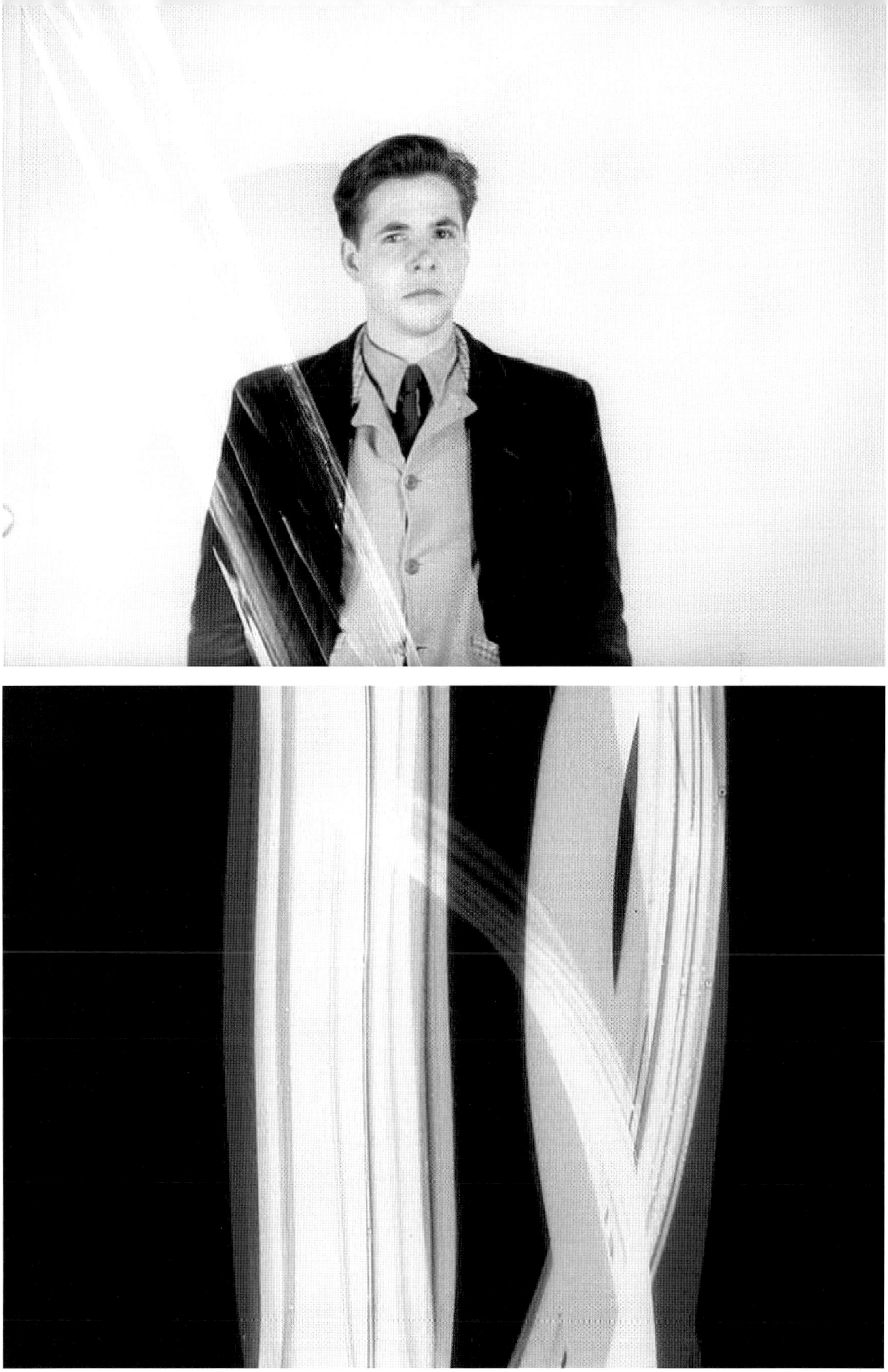

22. Isidore Isou, *Traité de bave et d'éternité*, 1951.
Frame enlargements.

again escalated. From January 25 to February 7, 1952, *Traité de bave et d'éternité* was officially released at the Studio de l'Etoile, the onetime home of Henri Langlois's Cercle du Cinéma, the precursor to the Cinémathèque Française. Various emerging filmmakers and artists attended *Traité*'s screenings, among them Jean-Luc Godard and Yves Klein, who each informally participated in the Lettrist milieu.[28] Klein's exposure to Lettrist film in part explains his abandonment of painting's conventional support, a subject I return to in the epilogue.

Traité's progamming was accompanied by the usual publicity, including a poster designed by Jean Cocteau (fig. 23). On the poster one could read the actors' names as well as a list of prizes the film had received: the "Prix en marge du Festival de Cannes," "Prix des Spectateurs d'avant-garde 1951," and "Prix St. Germain des Prés 1951." At the bottom of the poster are two additional taglines: "The film that the conformist press want to suppress" and "The film that the youth and avant-garde exalt." Isou and his friends also posted fliers and handed out leaflets to people waiting in line at nearby cinemas, declaring that *Traité* was "the most revolting film in the history of cinema." On account of their aggressive campaign, Isou and one of his cohort were taken to the police station, more than likely for disturbing the public order. The strategy is one Isou would advocate again four months later when he wrote, "We must have an effect on the theater managers and their public, either by leaflets or by direct communication."[29]

The response to the film's official release in Paris recalled the film's initial reception in Cannes. One press notice in the "La scène et l'écran" (Stage and Screen) section of *Le Figaro* was titled "Applause, Insults, and Booing Welcome the Film of Isidore Isou."[30] A day later a critic reviewing the film maintained that its "obsessive verbal delirium . . . quickly exhausts the attention."[31] Another writer described Isou's filmic enterprise as having "no interest" and seemingly reproduced a frame from the film: a black photogram that uncannily prefigures the primary material of Debord's film *Hurlements en faveur de Sade* (Howls for Sade), which would premiere five months later (see fig. 18).[32] These authors not only criticized the film but also Isou's person, calling him a "presumptuous young man."[33] The fascist press described him as "a little Jew called Isidore Jewel" (un petit juif, nommé Isidore Bijou) and renamed the film *Traité de cave et de publicité* (Treatise on the Cellar and on Advertising).[34] A distressed critic described how "the majority of shots are—voluntarily—scratched or blurred. At five minutes you laugh; at ten minutes you are bored; at twenty minutes you leave."[35]

Amid this contentious reception, Maurice Schérer (the pseudonym of Eric Rohmer) provided a more measured, if ambivalent, critique in the pages of *Cahiers du cinéma*'s March 1952 issue (fig. 24): "Isou here

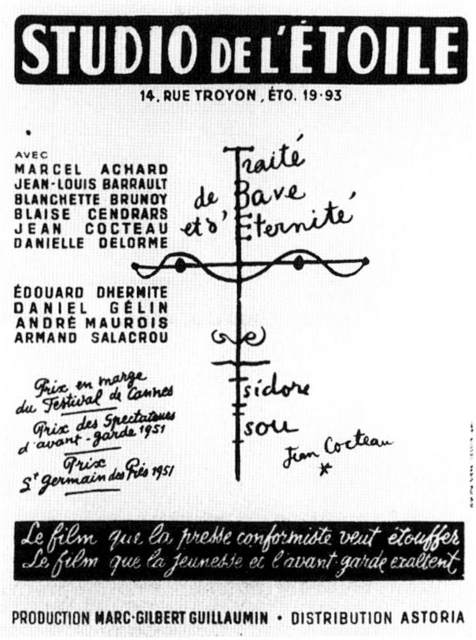

23. Jean Cocteau, poster for *Traité de bave et d'éternité* (1951), release at the Studio de l'Étoile, 1952.

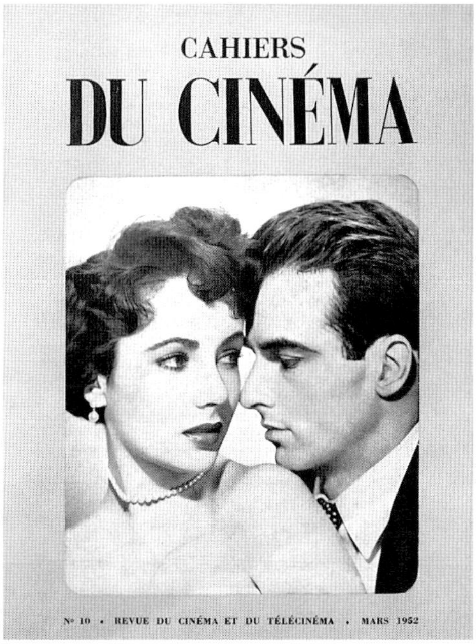

24. *Cahiers du cinéma*, no. 10, March 1952. Cover.

demonstrates a certain cinematographic sensibility and—contrary to the avant-gardists of 1930, who tried to make film the playground for all their pictorial, musical, and literary theories—the problems he intends to solve are *of a specifically cinematographic order*."[36] In this statement one hears the kernel of film aestheticism that would struggle for a foothold in film culture in Paris in these years. While Schérer mildly mocks Lettrist experiments and suggests that it would be easy not to take Isou's film seriously, he nevertheless aligns with him, at least in part: "As Isou rightly said, some innovation could be brought into the art of photography."[37] Such attention to the specificity of the filmed image would increasingly characterize the Parisian cinephile culture and the critics and filmmakers associated with *Cahiers du cinéma*.[38] It comes as little surprise, then, that Schérer's attention was drawn not so much to the question of sound and speech in *Traité* (what he refers to as "the provocative variety of tone") as to the status of Isou's shots and how they echo the "desire to seek things as they are" (désir de solliciter les choses telles qu'elles sont).[39]

Schérer ultimately restricts his comments to the original shots filmed by Isou in chapter 1 of *Traité*—shots untouched by the handmade, chiseled marks that pervade chapters 2 and 3. He notes the lack of expression on the actor's face and affirms, "Finally, I believe it is my duty to say that the first chapter, in which we are shown Isou walking on the Boulevard Saint-Germain, 'hooked' me a thousand times more than the best non-commercial films I have ever seen."[40] For this young critic and aspiring filmmaker, photographic innovation derived from stylistic rigor and a dogged insistence on what he calls the "brute power of the image" (pouvoir brut de l'image), rather than from interventions on the filmstrip. Yet it is precisely this power of the image, one based on film's indexical relation to the real, that Isou undermined through his use of found footage together with his chiseling on the negative and positive emulsion by means of scissors, needles, and ink.

ARCHIVAL LOOKING

The practice of making new films from the footage of earlier films is virtually as old as cinema itself. Examples of how "films beget films" extend from the 1898 representation of the Dreyfus affair to Frank Capra's *Why We Fight* series (1943–1944) made for the US War Department.[41] Indeed, just four years prior to the release of Isou's *Traité de bave et d'éternité*, Nicole Védrès completed *Paris 1900* (1947; fig. 25), made entirely from preexisting newsreel footage drawn from more than seven hundred films housed in public and private collections.[42] Following the film's screening at Cannes in 1947, André Bazin issued the following statement:

> We do not, however, believe that the authors' merit is diminished by their exclusive use of all the archival documents [*documents cinématographiques d'époque*]. On the contrary, their success is due to a subtle working of the medium, to the intelligence of their selection from vast material; to the delicate and intelligent editing, to all the tools of exquisite taste and of culture.[43]

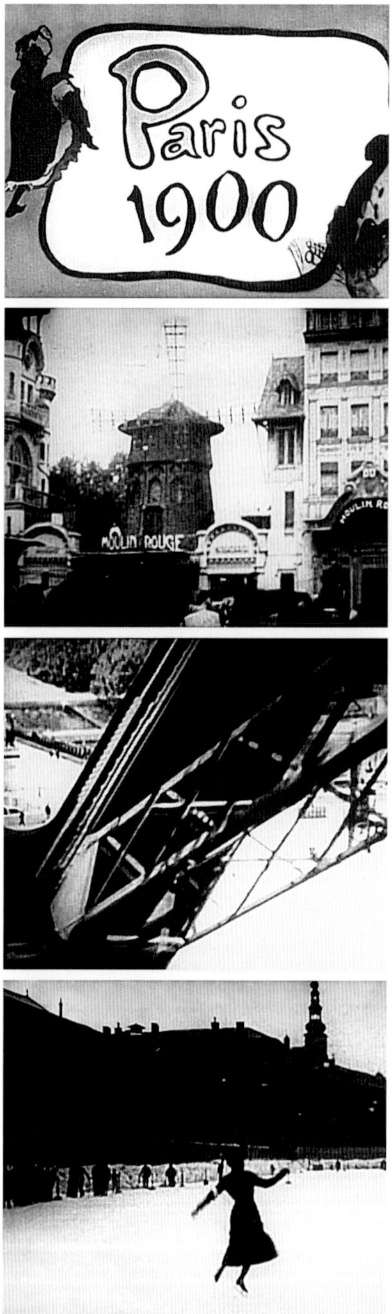

25. Nicole Védrès, *Paris 1900*, 1947. Frame enlargements.

Bazin might praise Védrès's and her team's careful editing of newsreel footage in *Paris 1900*, but he does not address how the historical footage actively framed reality. Through its montage of shots—from the Moulin Rouge to street vendors, historical monuments to trends in women's fashion—the film participates in the conceit of documentary realism, whereby the archival shots (or "statements," in the Foucaultian sense) are understood to emanate from concrete historical referents (in this case, Paris in the years 1900–1914). Thus they ground the film's discourse on a historical reality presumed to be both true and unmediated by the camera's framing. The film's voice-over narration then redoubles the visual scenes through its verbal account of historical subjects, including technological progress (e.g., the Eiffel Tower, the subterranean metro) and the emergence of women in sports. Isou was indebted to Védrès's film as a precedent (unacknowledged, as far as I know, in Isou's writing). Yet his use of found footage in *Traité* inscribes itself within a genealogy of experimental film practices, wherein media images and found footage are treated as part of the very materials of history rather than as images of history itself.[44] Significantly, Isou's experimental use of found footage arrives early on the international scene, in 1951, anticipating its use in American avant-garde cinema in the years 1955–1965.[45]

Rather than maintaining the representational integrity of found footage shots and recombining them into montage sequences, Isou changes the shots' appearance by directly drawing on the celluloid. For example, at approximately thirty-nine minutes into *Traité*, a shot frames a French and a Vietnamese diplomat (or other official public figures) against the sky, as they stand at attention side by side. The Frenchman wears a white suit with a dark belt and a tie that waves in the wind; the Vietmanese man is dressed in more traditional ceremonial attire with visible symbols on his shirt. In this shot, Isou initially only chiseled the eyes of the two figures. Like a blindfold that blocks their vision and at once their identities, the marks eventually become larger, shimmering and waving across their faces for the duration of the shot. In the subsequent shot, the marks become even more expansive in response to the increased number of figures in the image. From behind the fluctuating and undulating line, four men await on the tarmac while a fifth descends an airplane (fig. 26). Their identities, too, are obfuscated by Isou's marks.

This shot cuts to a close-up of two men; their faces are covered by white globular disks that morph into a horizontal band as they shift their bodies and exit frame left; the band eventually extends beyond the foreground figures' faces so as to engulf background figures as well. Between the flickering movement of the chiseled frames and the movement of the figures, one catches glimpses of diplomatic gestures (the requisite handshake) as well as the officials' sartorial signifiers, including the pin in the lapel of the Frenchman and the symbols on the shirt of the Vietnamese man. The edited shots thus document the same historical event, whose specific setting is revealed in the next shot, in which Isou's lines, executed frame by frame, follow the figures' descent of the steps of a temple. The final two shots of the sequence show three and four naval figures on a ship's deck; Isou occults their faces in both the medium and the long shot. In the medium shot, the word *honneur* is legible on a plaque on the ship's exterior wall (fig. 27). Next, the film returns to the streets of Paris.

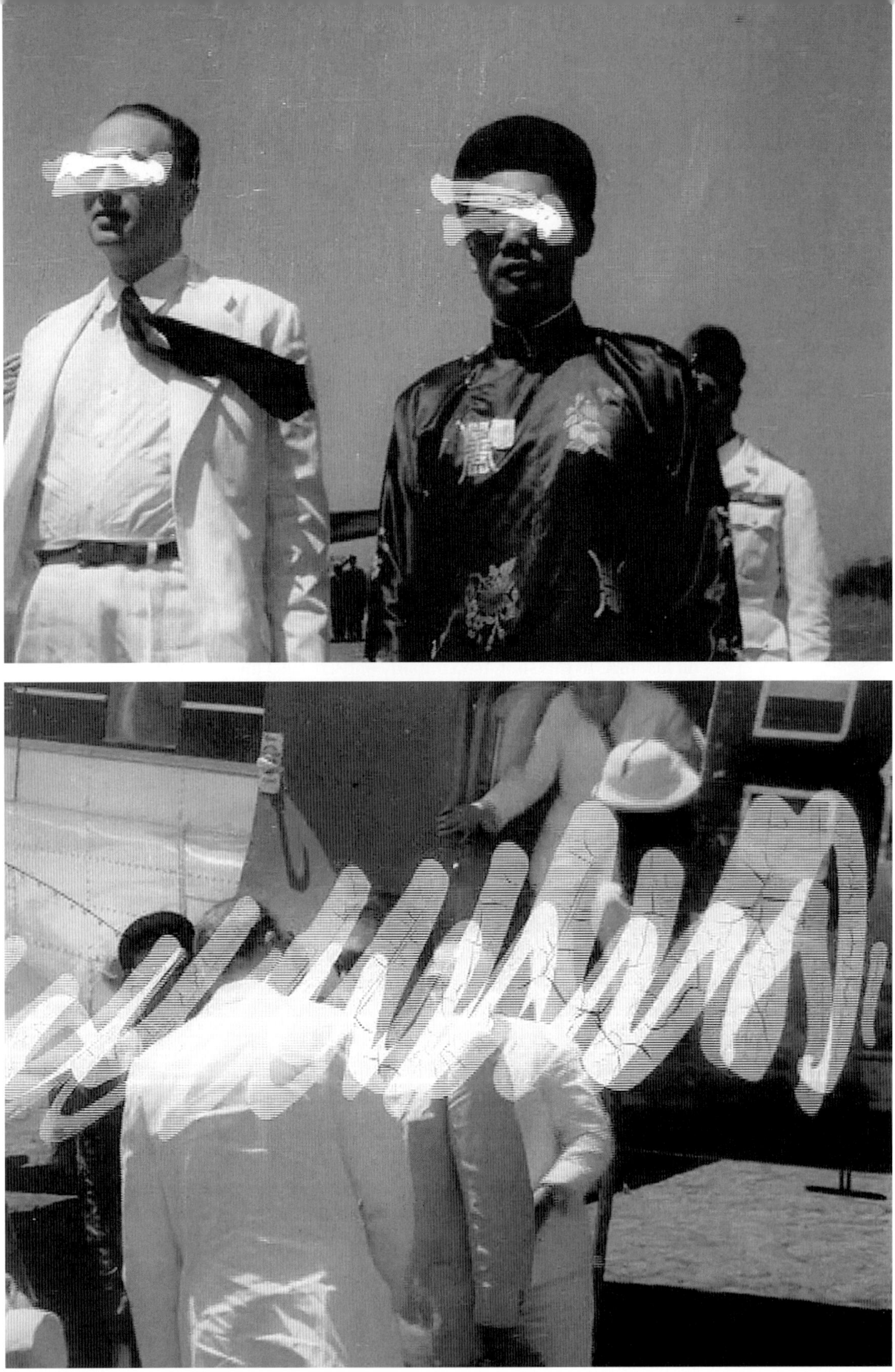

26. Isidore Isou, *Traité de bave et d'éternité*, 1951.
Frame enlargements.

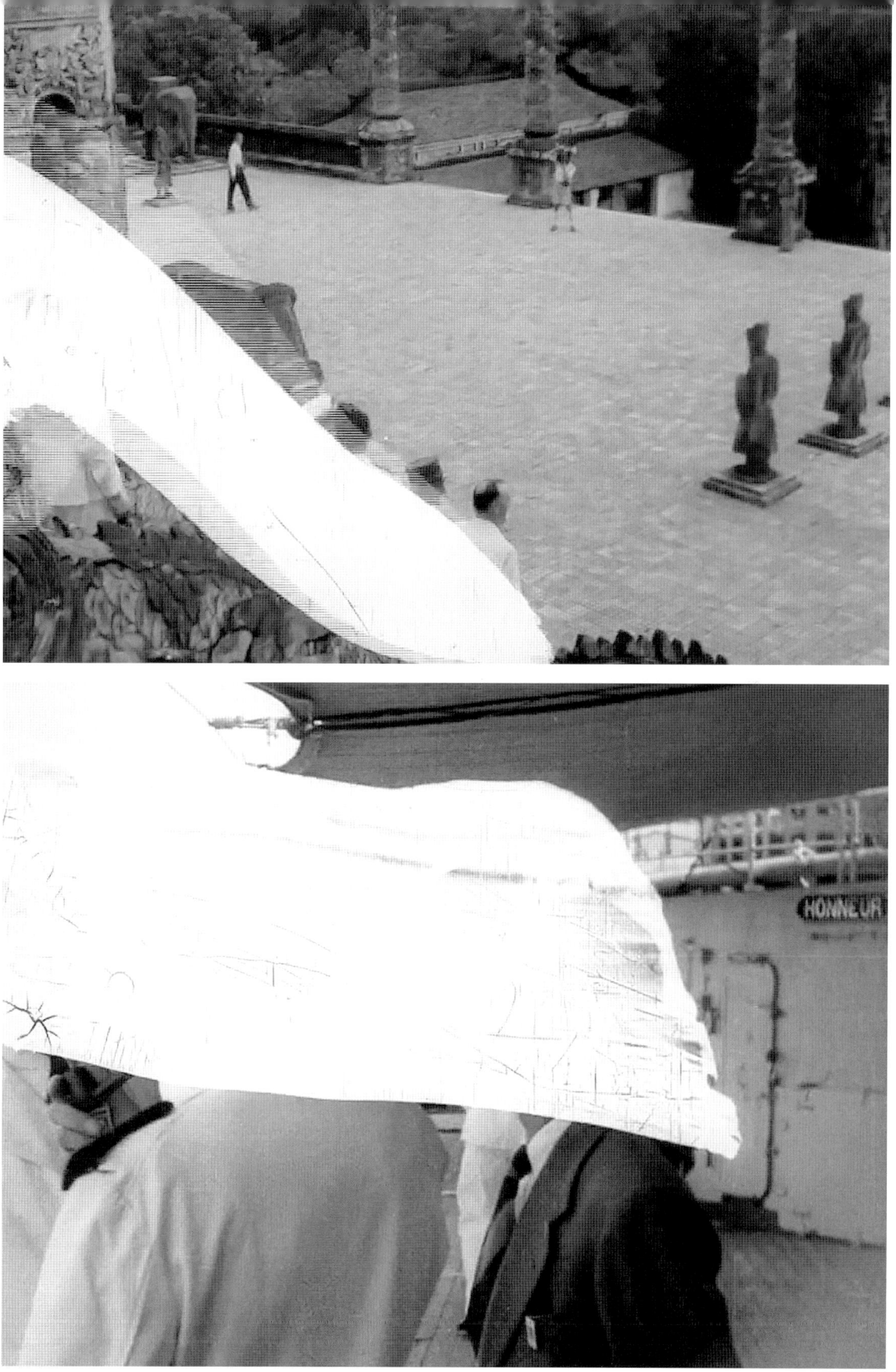

27. Isidore Isou, *Traité de bave et d'éternité*, 1951. Frame enlargements.

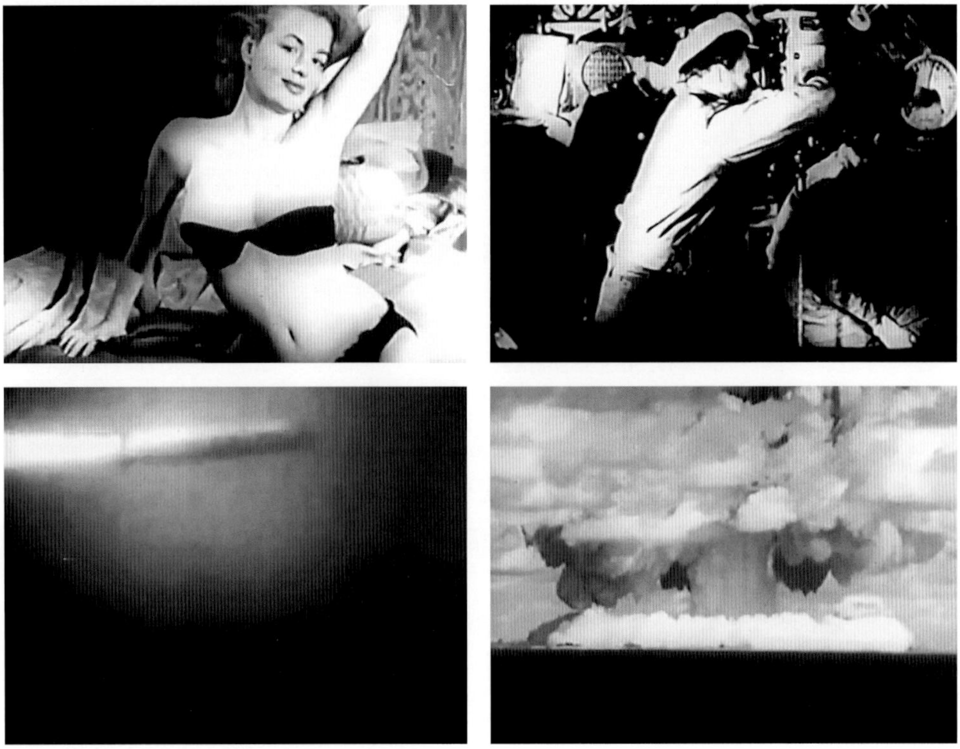

28. Bruce Conner, *A MOVIE*, 1958. Frame enlargements.

Insofar as the found footage's meaning is not propelled by its editing, *Traité* deviates from other experimental found footage films, which often mine the legacy of the historical avant-garde and the principles of Eisensteinian montage. It is worth noting that in *Traité* the found footage rarely shows weapons in action—that is, the movement of planes, ships, or torpedos. The relative stasis of the figures in its shots, and the ceremonial pageantry so often on display, differ notably from the use of found footage in subsequent experimental collage films, such as Bruce Conner's *A MOVIE* (1958), a key example in studies on the use of found footage in experimental film.[46]

Conner's twelve-minute film includes some 180 found shots from a variety of international sources—a chase scene from a western, military tanks on the move, a car crash, and so on—with black leader of different lengths spliced between them. The heterogeneous image track unfolds alongside the musical accompaniment of Ottorino Respighi's *Pines of Rome* (1924). In the first section, as Kevin Hatch maintains, "the shots blend smoothly, owing to their similar short lengths and matched directionality (cars, horses, and tanks all move from left to right)."[47] The second section involves aerial vehicles (e.g., blimps, airplanes) and a well-known sequence of submarine, periscope, scantily clad woman, torpedo, and mushroom cloud (fig. 28). The movement of the mushroom cloud as it spreads across the sky is continued in the next shot, which shows surfers perilously riding waves. The overriding organizational principle of *A MOVIE* matches movement across the shots, just as the montage sequence torpedo/woman/explosion conjures metaphoric links between military aggression and sexual desire.[48]

If in Conner's film movement *within the shot* impels the movement *from shot to shot* (what Eisenstein termed "rhythmic montage"), within *Traité*'s found footage sequences Isou's marks draw attention to the discursive organization of profilmic reality, rather than relying on the formal requirements or metaphorical associations engendered by montage.[49] In Isou's other found footage sequences, however, few marks obscure the figures' faces or the context. In shots depicting no identifiable state officials, Isou presents the figures and their settings with minimal visible intervention on his part. By primarily restricting his thicker, obfuscating marks to the faces of public figures, Isou establishes discursive differences within his use of found footage shots, and consequently a differentiated economy of visual representations. This consistent relation between a shot's visual marking and its content—marked officials versus unmarked civilians; generals whose identities are obscured versus soldiers whose faces are seen—is striking and is sustained throughout most of *Traité*'s second chapter (fig. 29; see also fig. 31). The distinction evinces how Isou's mark-making on the celluloid is wholly motivated by what the found footage represents. It is not indifferent, despite what he and some of his commentators claim.[50]

In the 1950s, at the time Isou was developing his work in film, André Bazin was elaborating a conception of modernist realism based on the ontology of the filmic image. Bazin's famous formula "forbidden montage" is premised on film's indexicality, and thus its potential to make available the random and contingent, the accidental and antisystematic, within the domain of the visual image. Bazin's understanding of realism should not, however, be framed within the terms of verisimilitude or of perceptual equivalence between film and so-called profilmic reality. Bazin's attentiveness to the "density of profilmic reality" was matched, as Ivone Margulies maintains, by his understanding of the "complex layering of referential modes."[51] Within these terms, Bazinian realism emerges from the tension between the singularity of the profilmic event and its filmic registration, the indexical recording of the former always exceeding the representational dictates of the latter.

With *Traité*, the 1950s subjective investment in realism as the contingent and antisystematic finds its experimental alternative. By working at the intersection of filmic representation and its erasure, Isou puts into practice an alternative politics of looking at the precise moment when

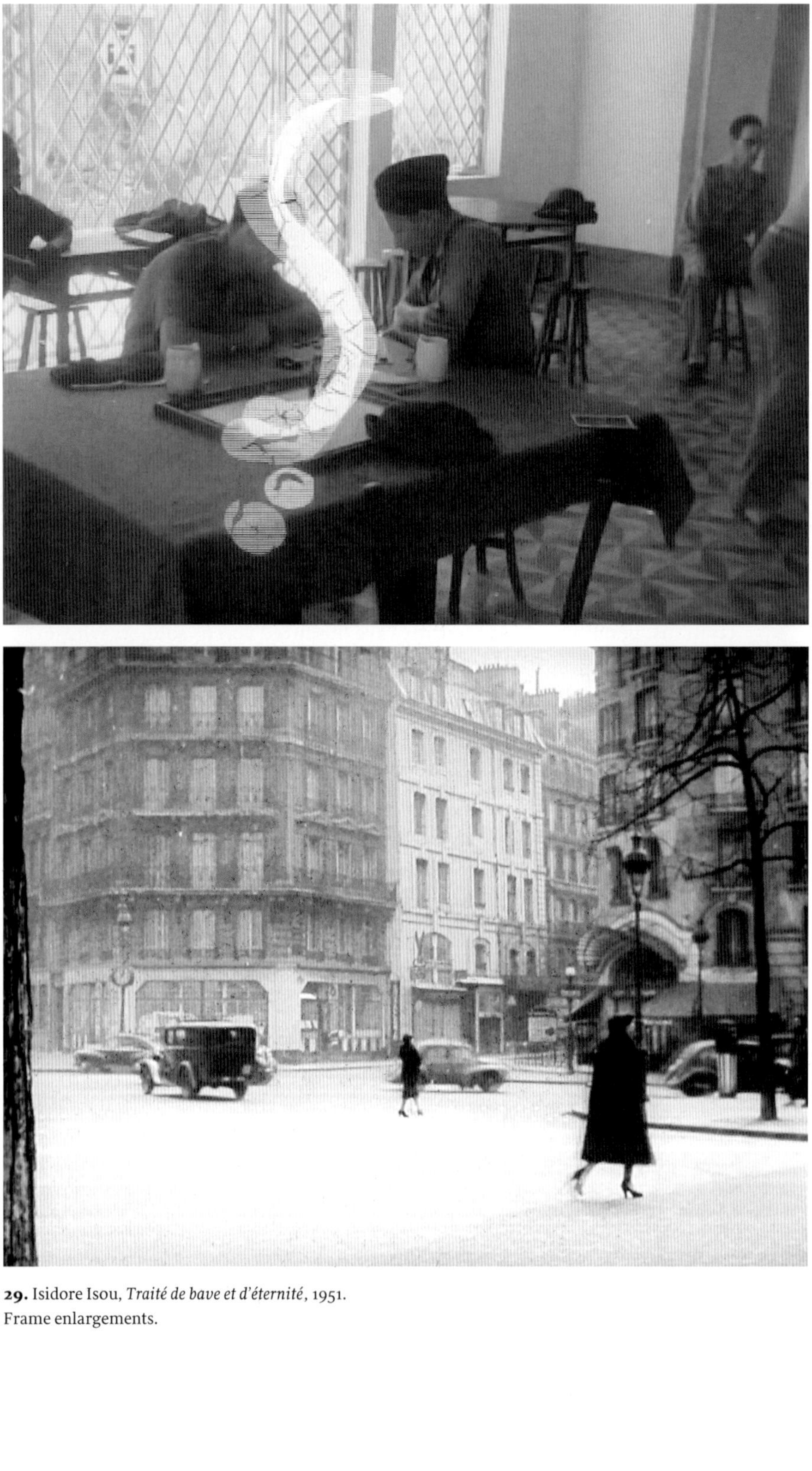

29. Isidore Isou, *Traité de bave et d'éternité*, 1951.
Frame enlargements.

understandings of what constitutes realism in film were decidedly at stake, from the ontological realism of Bazin to the representations of the working class by Italian Neorealist filmmakers. Moreover, Isou's use of found footage connects his work to the status of archival documents and to the recording and representation of history. At the historical moment when Isou produced *Traité*, the use of footage from the Service Cinématographique des Armées was a far from innocent choice, given the fraught context of the First Indochina War. Vietnam was precariously teetering between French control, Chinese and Communist influence, and national independence. In France in the early 1950s, the Cold War as well as anticolonialist movements precipitated a moment of intellectual radicalization. What was known as France's "Dirty War" increasingly gave the lie to the country's *mission civilisatrice*: the pillaging of villages, abuse of prisoners, and horrors of the French occupation of Vietnam were increasingly being exposed through soldiers' firsthand accounts in the contemporary press.[52] In this context, Isou's more assertive chiseling may have emerged from the thorny issue of how to deal with official images. Isou makes it impossible to identify the state representatives who are defaced, thereby potentially avoiding prosecution.[53]

In the early 1950s, shots similar to those used in *Traité* were a regular part of the accounts of the war in Indochina presented at cinemas in the form of *actualités*. An analysis of the newsreels archived at Gaumont-Pathé discloses how the coverage of current events extended from the "problem" of Indochina to the success of the Palm Tree military operation. Some reports show the movement of war (e.g., beach landings, parachutists), while others feature officials such as General de Lattre de Tassigny and their formal duties. "Indochine: L'arrivée du Général de Lattre," for example, distributed in theaters as world news, proceeds from images of a plane landing to the general and other officers descending from the plane to a sequence composed of shots showing the requisite handshakes and salute of the troops (fig. 30). The editing of the sequence parallels that in the found footage employed by Isou. But given the film's newsreel status, a voice-over doubles the visual scene by describing the general's arrival, his investiture as *haut-commissaire* of the region, and his declared intent to "return safety and prosperity in Indochina."[54]

The extent to which Isou's interventions on archival found footage may be a response to the use of photography and film in news and state propaganda is hard to know. In any case, it is on the individual frames of shots from the Services Cinématographiques du Ministère des Armées that Isou began his experiments with chiseling the photographic image, thereby placing his mark-making and its particular effect squarely within images of war. At approximately forty-six minutes, after shots of the streets of Paris and a refilmed photograph of Isou reclining in an armchair, *Traité*

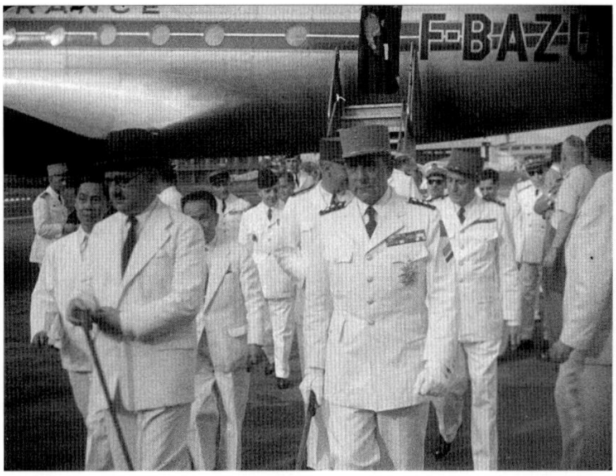

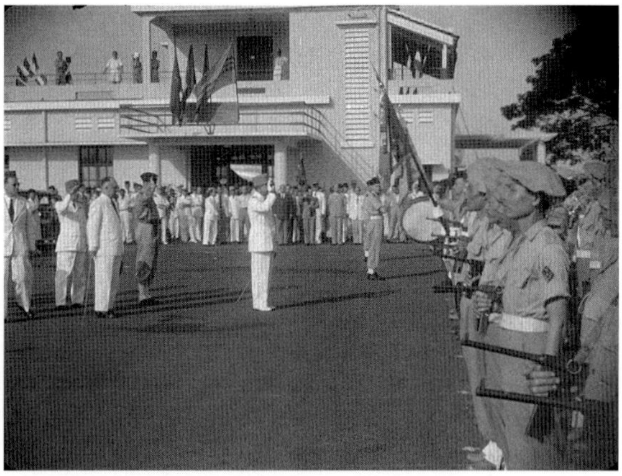

30. "Indochine: L'arrivée du Général de Lattre," *Journal Actualité (Journal Gaumont)*, sound film, black-and-white, 13 seconds. Gaumont-Pathé Archives, Paris. Frame enlargements.

returns to the scene of the found footage. One shot shows various officials on a boat. In the foreground, the two figures' faces are barely visible given the large black **V** that has been chiseled on the filmstrip; each arm of the **V** extends across one of the figure's faces. As another figure enters the shot on the lower right, he too is immediately covered with black marks. The next shot shows an official mission: ten men walk through the landscape, as Isou's black horizontal lines follow their forward march. Tellingly, given the subtle logic behind his mark-making, the next shot presents unchiseled Vietnamese as they cut tree logs (fig. 31). The sequence's final shot takes us to a balcony lined with officials, including a Catholic priest. Isou's marks mask the identity of the building and officials, but a French flag confirms the setting as occupied Vietnam (fig. 32). In the course of *Traité*'s second chapter Isou's found footage increasingly transitions toward a broader ceremonial context of colonization and war, thereby calling attention to the performative dimensions of profilmic reality.

It was in fact Maurice Lemaître who applied most of the streaks (*rayures*) and undertook the scraping (*grattage*) of images. Based on his own involvement in the *Traité*'s production, and contrary to most critics' claims, which ventriloquize Isou, Lemaître affirms, "It is mistaken to see [the chiseling] as independent of the images, except perhaps later [toward the end], when the editor that I was was tired of punctually scratching, *hiding the faces* of people appearing in the shots taken from the Service Cinématographique des Armées."[55] Lemaître confesses that the marks are not distinct from what the images represent, and that any departure from "hiding the faces" was due to his physical fatigue as chiseler on behalf of Isou. In the same context, he warns against attributing "to those long bands . . . any logic, a so-called logos, as if the bands were aimed to carry in themselves their reason of being and wanted to offer another image of the image, *beyond the image*."[56] If we heed Lemaître's warning that the bands offer no "image beyond the image," what the chiseling accom-

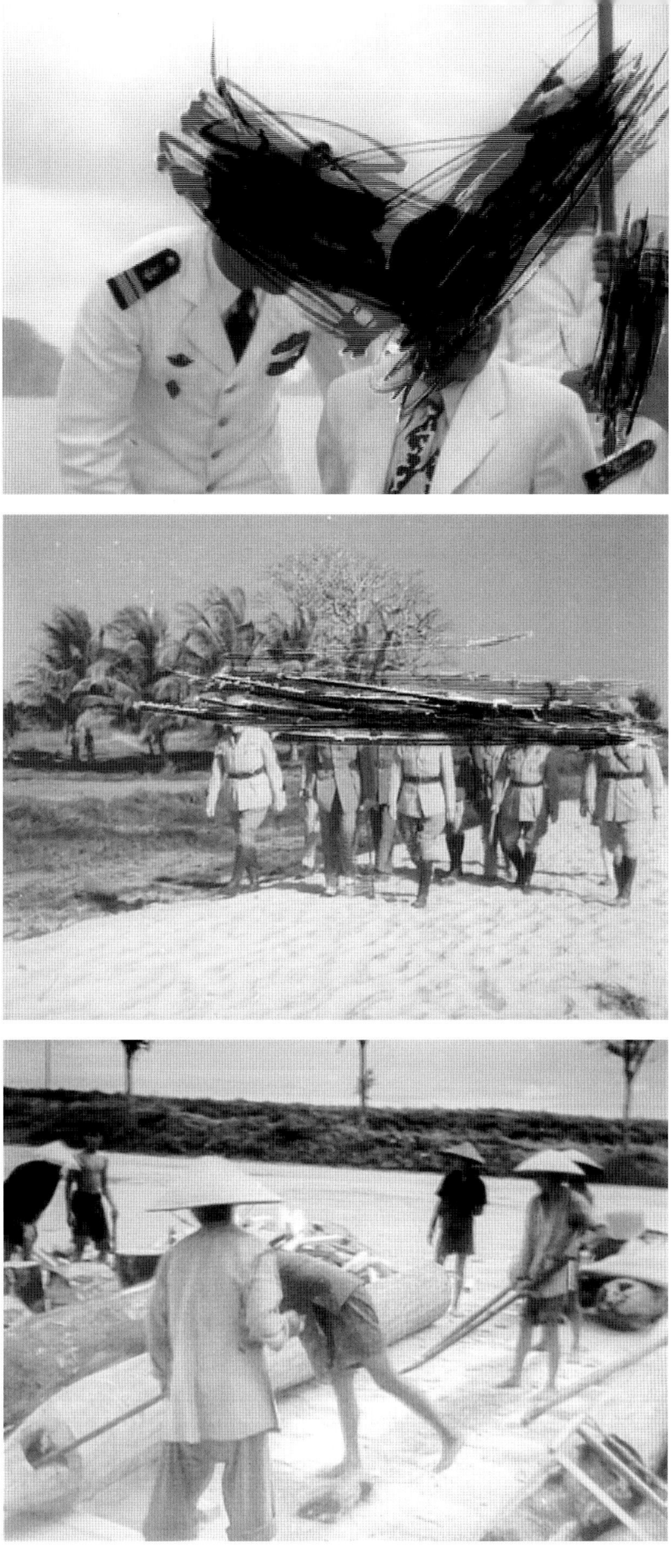

31. Isidore Isou, *Traité de bave et d'éternité*, 1951. Frame enlargements.

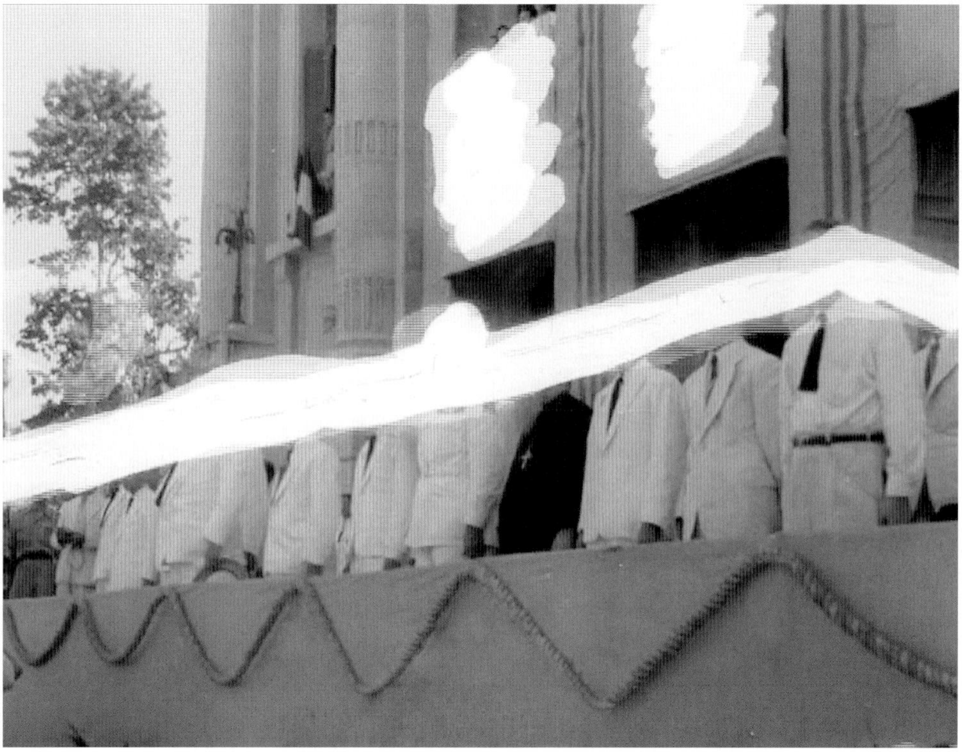

32. Isidore Isou, *Traité de bave et d'éternité*, 1951. Frame enlargement.

plishes is—in each instance where a figure might be identified as a specific diplomat, general, or other military or state representative—a redirection of attention away from individual identity to the *subject of discourse*, from individual acts to the *discursive context* in which the customs, gestures, and movements of an event unfold.

While it is impossible to verify the end for which the found footage used in *Traité* was intended, such shots, edited together, could have been integrated into the chain of an argument or news report whose ideological meaning would have been consolidated through the requisite voice-over narration, as in the newsreel "Indochine: L'arrivée du Général de Lattre." By contrast, in chapter 2 of *Traité* we primarily listen to the vicissitudes of Daniel's love affairs on the sound track. Bereft of the newsreel's urgent tone, the found footage sequences do not achieve any heightened dramatic effect, nor does the mismatched sound expose or satirize the visual images.[57] For some critics, the result was a film that was "as boring as [watching] dust."[58] The lack of rhythmic editing provoked another critic to claim, after the May 23 screening, "the montage inspires nothing but boredom."[59]

Isou and Bazin share a historical moment. Moreover, they both share a rejection of discursive montage. Bazin's dictum of "forbidden montage" finds its dialectical counterpart in Isou's theory of *montage discrépant*, which was premised on disavowing the conceptual unity montage affords among images but especially between image and sound. Bazin's realism privileges the shot, the image's visuality, and the contingency and antisystematicity that may arise within it. Isou's chiseling of the image disrupts photographic images' icono-indexical relation to the real, undoing any naive belief in images' referentiality through a materialist attention to the filmstrip as support. *Traité de bave et d'éternité* challenges the transparency of archival documents' reproduction of reality but does so without abandoning historical or, more precisely, certain cinematic "truths." In short, Isou's work on found footage interrogates the type of visibility cinema as an institution upholds.

Such a reading takes into account the fact that Isou's found footage sequences would have been wholly legible as contemporary and familiar to viewers in 1951–1952. Given the contemporaneity of the images used to justify the war, his use of found footage is doubly archival. He uses archival footage in the literal sense as a document (namely, as the material facts of history), but he manipulates it in such a way that it is also understood as part of a system that governs history's appearance. In this latter sense, Isou's work anticipates the archive as articulated by Foucault: "that which defines the mode of occurrence of the statement-thing: it is *the system of its functioning*."[60] By incorporating representations of recent history in his film, Isou puts in relief how the French state regulates the perception of war, how it frames reality in a determinate way. *Traité* diverts the shots' exhibition and propagandistic value as filmed news by eliminating the customary voice-over narration. The chiseled shots direct attention away from the *what* of the image to the *how* of the footage's framing but also—and this is crucial—the events' staging. Isou's film shifts our focus to the conventions of war and nationalism on display, while in other shots drawing attention to the divergent everyday contexts of war at home and abroad.[61] As a result, the cumulative effect of the second chapter's diverse shots is not to show the unity of the French empire but the streets of Paris seemingly untouched by the images of destruction from a colonized land to which French "universalism" and "Union française" had laid claim.[62]

In Isou's found footage sequences, the chiseled marks shudder and vibrate, insisting on the materiality of the filmstrip, as they conceal, distort, and redirect attention in the preexisting images. Understood in this way, Isou's claim to "detach us from the photo and its reality, *making us indifferent to it*" is true only insofar as reality is taken to be pure facts and archival images are taken to be images of history itself.[63] Perhaps this is what Isou meant when he wrote, "Discrepant montage crushes the certainties of the 'positive' and turns them into lies."[64] By taking the found footage shots out of their normal circuit of distribution and reception, Isou's chiseling reveals how reality is discursively organized by techniques of power—from the explicit use of military force to the way cinema frames certain historical facts. What emerges in *Traité* is not indifference to the reality presented in the photographic image but an alternative politics of what looking at archival images as images of history might mean.

When watching *Traité de bave et d'éternité*, contemporary spectators were viewers of images as well as interpreters of marks and signs that interrupted the filmed images. So too were they auditors of a debate about a new kind of cinema, a love story, and the materiality of speech as emphasized through recordings of Lettrist poetry. *Traité* thus provided an object lesson—Isou called it a manifesto—on how to listen in the cinema but also how to see in ways that highlight the medium's signifying properties. In the case of found footage, his chiseled marks put in relief the performativity of profilmic reality. Lematîre would extend such an object lesson by using the cinema as a platform for pedagogy through his various proposals and attempts to instruct the filmgoing public. It is to Lematîre's particular form of public education that I now turn.

TWO

FRENCH CINEMA DIES OF SUFFOCATION

IMAGINE A FILM CLUB in Paris. You are watching the world premiere of a film whose action exceeds the boundaries of the screen. Various live interventions, from people scripted to stand in front of the projection beam to unplanned yells and screams, compete with the projected film's images and sounds. Approximately forty-seven minutes into the screening, a man gets up on stage and cuts the screen with a knife, then climbs through to its other side. Despite the destruction of the projection surface (and with it the spatial illusionism it usually supports), the film's abstract images continue to unfold on its remains, in the space around and between its tattered edges. As we witness these events, they are simultaneously described on the film's sound track, causing a semantic overlap between verbal description and live action. At fifty-two minutes, after various cacophonous sounds and a chorus of Lettrist poetry, a voice-over enumerates the "mass of cinematographic inventions" introduced by the film, including the screen's destruction in preparation for a new screen; the transformation of filmic representation into a theatrical combination; and, vis-à-vis the image, an expansion of Isidore Isou's *ciselure* (chiseling) and *montage discrépant* (discrepant editing). The film is none other than Maurice Lemaître's *Le film est déjà commencé?* (Has the Film Already Started?, 1951; fig. 33).[1]

As the film nears its end, we see black-and-white shots covered by abstract designs and accompanied by another voice-over that details various press responses to the film. We hear how, in the pages of *Echo des travailleurs de la pellicule*, Roger Diamil inveighs against the film and its author:

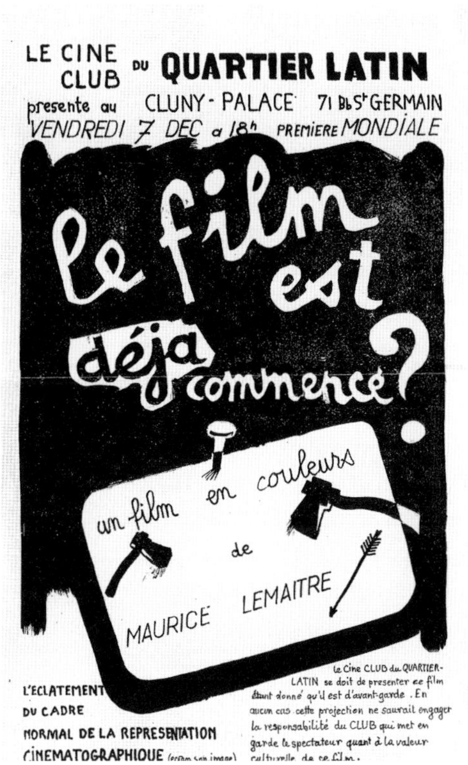

33. Poster for the screening of Maurice Lemaître's film *Le film est déjà commencé?*, 1951.

> While increased wages are refused to our workers, tired from the daily hard labor in capitalist factories . . . daddy's boys like Maurice Lemaître find a way to throw money out of the window . . . to make a film without any value, neither ideological nor even artistic. All unite against the threat.

On the opposite end of the political spectrum, François Derais, writing for *France-toujours*, maintains, "French cinema dies of suffocation under the appalling caresses of these strangers [*métèques*] who want to destroy that which is the most beautiful and noble among us: the French people's tradition of taste for work well done, taste that has made us world renowned." If the former criticism frames the film as an outrage to leftist politics and the plight of the proletariat, the latter contends that it constitutes an insult to French aesthetic discretion. Religion, too, is apparently susceptible to the film's threat. The writer for *Le Catholique libéré* asserts, "In the face of [the film], the believer, who is an intelligent censor, and anxious to guard our children from bad examples, should prohibit, and really feel like a soldier of Christ, supported in his effort by the mystery of the incarnation."[2]

While the reviews suggest the variegated contours of the political context in which Lemaître screened his film, what is notable here is how the press response is mysteriously coterminous with and included as part of the screening, ostensibly the film's premiere. Moreover, the voice-over indicates that "Last night, in a cinema on the Left Bank, was the world premiere of Maurice Lemaître's film with the strange and promising title *Le film est déjà commencé?*"[3] Thus, depending on the vantage from which one thinks through the temporal relation between "last night" and the present moment of the premiere, we are either watching a film whose premiere has already taken place, or we are at a premiere in which the film's sound track anticipates and reproduces a press reception that does not yet exist. Given the impossibility of premieres both yesterday and today, the fictive nature of the press reports reproduced on the film's sound track become increasingly aporetic.

Whether these fictional accounts are true or commensurate with the film's actual reception is less at issue than how Lemaître's sound track appropriates an institutional context (that is, the press review) in which film is understood and recognized as film. The particular stakes of this gesture become clear when one considers that, with the exception of a few announcements in the pages of *Cinéma 51* and *France-soir* (fig. 34), there are no known reviews of his film's premiere.[4] By inventing the film's press reception, Lemaître ironically legitimizes his work as a film (albeit one rejected by a fake press) and transforms the screening into an event whose effects are registered both within and beyond the cinema's institutional frame.[5] What emerges as central to Lemaître's film practice is not only the physical space in which the film is projected and the live interventions that transpire therein, but also the multiple forums—from the press review to the ciné-club—for discussing, debating, and legitimating what constitutes cinema.

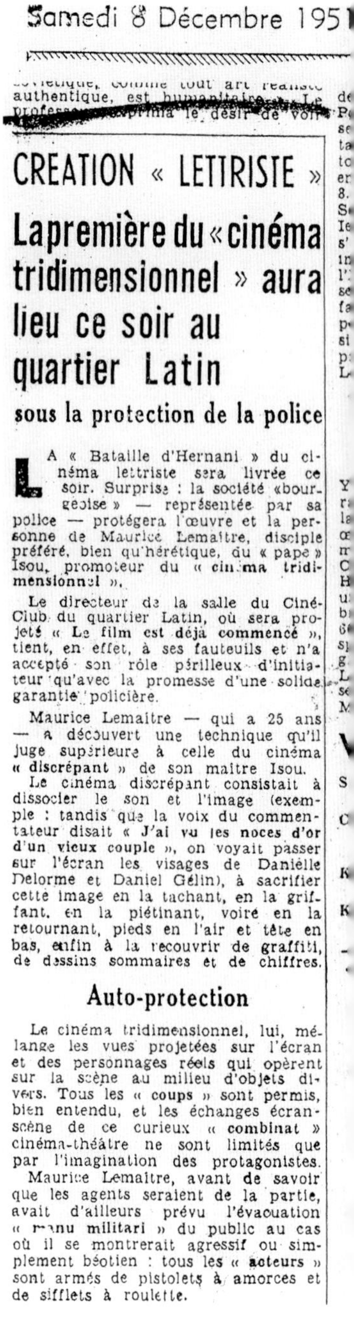

Samedi 8 Décembre 1951

CREATION « LETTRISTE »

La première du « cinéma tridimensionnel » aura lieu ce soir au quartier Latin

sous la protection de la police

LA « Bataille d'Hernani » du cinéma lettriste sera livrée ce soir. Surprise : la société « bourgeoise » — représentée par sa police — protégera l'œuvre et la personne de Maurice Lemaitre, disciple préféré, bien qu'hérétique, du « pape » Isou, promoteur du « cinéma tridimensionnel ».

Le directeur de la salle du Ciné-Club du quartier Latin, où sera projeté « Le film est déjà commencé », tient, en effet, à ses fauteuils et n'a accepté son rôle périlleux d'initiateur qu'avec la promesse d'une solide garantie policière.

Maurice Lemaitre — qui a 25 ans — a découvert une technique qu'il juge supérieure à celle du cinéma « discrépant » de son maître Isou.

Le cinéma discrépant consistait à dissocier le son et l'image (exemple : tandis que la voix du commentateur disait « J'ai vu les noces d'or d'un vieux couple », on voyait passer sur l'écran les visages de Danièlle Delorme et Daniel Gélin), à sacrifier cette image en la tachant, en la griffant, en la piétinant, voire en la retournant, pieds en l'air et tête en bas, enfin à la recouvrir de graffiti, de dessins sommaires et de chiffres.

Auto-protection

Le cinéma tridimensionnel, lui, mélange les vues projetées sur l'écran et des personnages réels qui opèrent sur la scène au milieu d'objets divers. Tous les « coups » sont permis, bien entendu, et les échanges écran-scène de ce curieux « combinat » cinéma-théâtre ne sont limités que par l'imagination des protagonistes.

Maurice Lemaitre, avant de savoir que les agents seraient de la partie, avait d'ailleurs prévu l'évacuation « manu militari » du public au cas où il se montrerait agressif ou simplement béotien : tous les « acteurs » sont armés de pistolets à amorces et de sifflets à roulette.

34. "La première du 'cinéma tridimensionnel' aura lieu sous la protection de la police," *France-soir*, December 8, 1951.

CINÉ-CLUBS TO SYNCINEMA

Having worked as an assistant on Isou's film, Lemaître turned to his own film work with the production of *Le film est déjà commencé?* It was first presented in part on November 12, 1951, at the Ciné-Club Avant-Garde 52 at the Musée de l'Homme.[6] This was soon followed by its so-called world premiere, on December 7

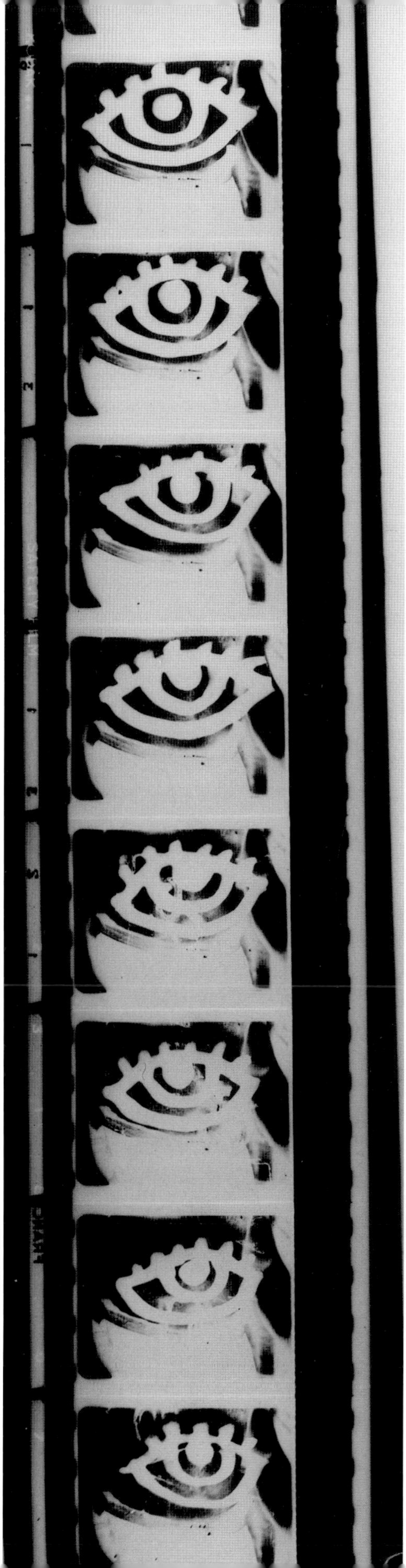

35. Maurice Lemaître, *Le film est déjà commencé?*, 1951. Filmstrip detail.

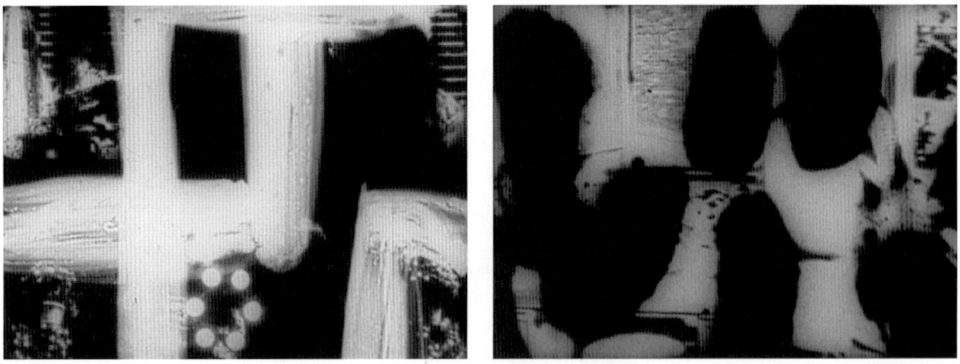

36. Maurice Lemaître, *Le film est déjà commencé?*, 1951. Frame enlargements.

at the Ciné-Club du Quartier Latin at Cluny Palace on the Boulevard St. Germain. Dedicated to Isou, Lemaître's film explored the further possibilities of *montage discrépant* and the chiseling of the filmed image. Some marks are abstract and others visibly iconic: letters, words, numbers and other kinds of symbols appear both over the photographic images and on abstract backgrounds (fig. 35). Unlike Isou in *Traité de bave et d'éternité* (On Venom and Eternity), Lemaître hand-colored his film to the extent that only a handful of shots remain untouched by the almost kaleidoscopic array of colors and their varied applications. Entire sequences appear overexposed and underexposed or are projected in negative; others show Hollywood logos and commercial advertising. The film includes abstract flicker sequences of alternating black and white that produce mild stroboscopic effects and sequences of pure color that interrupt the film's movement (figs. 36–38). The film repeatedly calls attention to its unique status and departure from classical cinema through intertitles such as "un film pas comme les autres" (a film unlike any other; fig. 39).

With regard to the film's sound track, Lemaître claims, "While Isou composed for the first time in film his sound in the manner of Proust, I introduced mine in the style of Joyce."[7] Lemaître implies that *Traité*'s sound track could be read in part as the interior monologue of the figure seen walking in the streets of Paris (played by Isou and voiced by Albert J. Legros), and thereby as an instance of rationally communicating subjective experience. Lemaître's repeated reference to Joycean prose in relation to his own work aims instead to capture the sonic complexity of *Le film est déjà commencé?*, which beyond those instances in which it details its own mise-en-scène, experiments with flashbacks, paradoxes, wordplay, word invention, and seeming stream-of-consciousness technique. At approximately forty-four minutes, one hears:

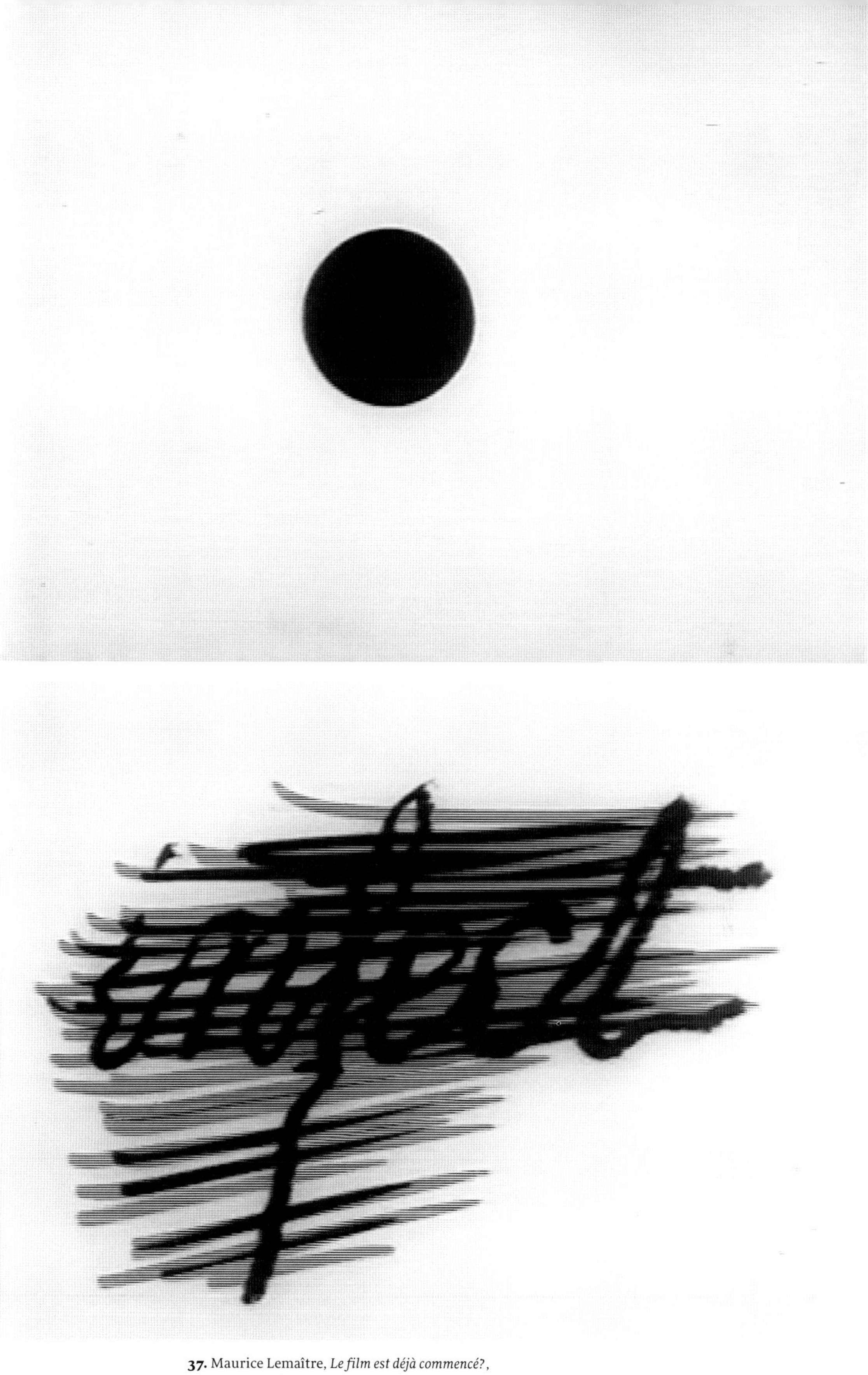

37. Maurice Lemaître, *Le film est déjà commencé?*, 1951. Frame enlargements.

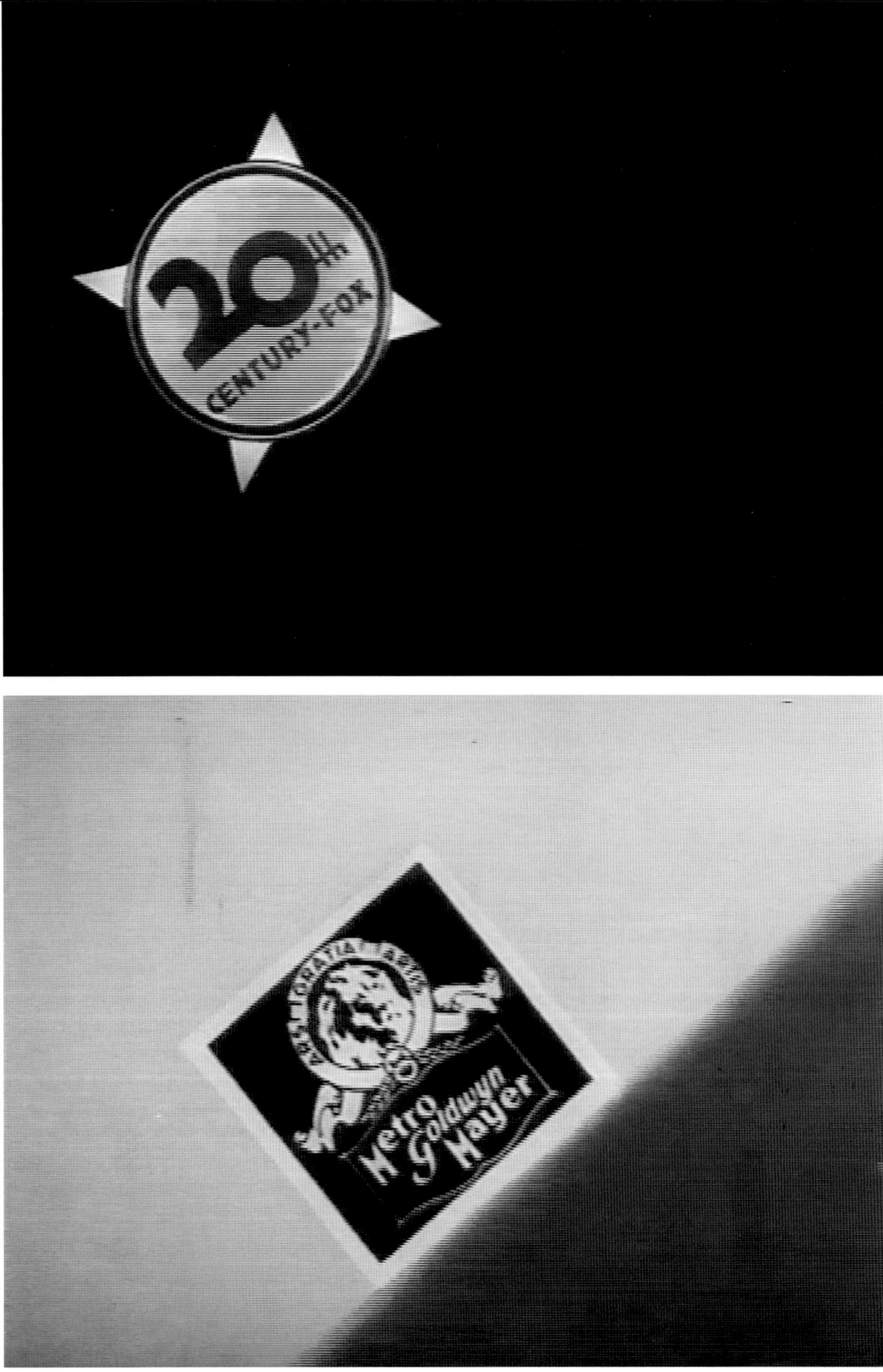

38. Maurice Lemaître, *Le film est déjà commencé?*, 1951. Frame enlargements.

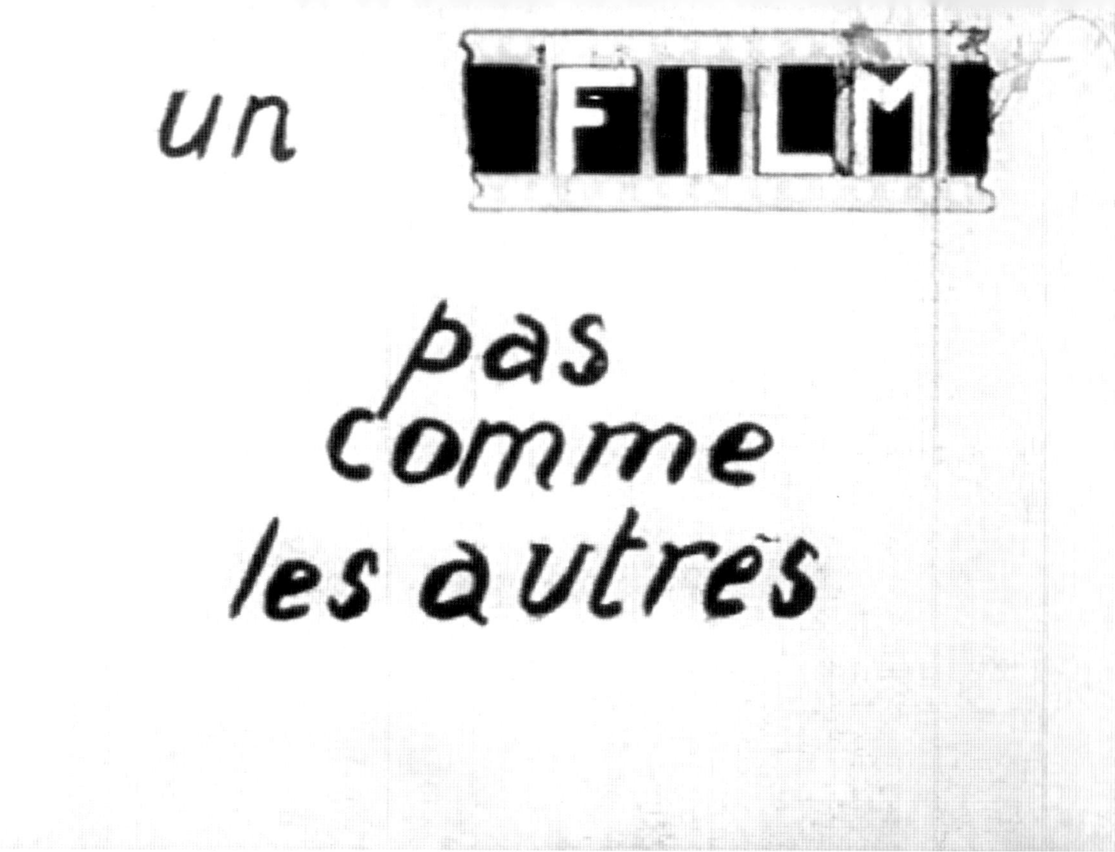

39. Maurice Lemaître, *Le film est déjà commencé?*, 1951. Frame enlargement.

> tavaritchbrokchnovieff qu'est-ce qu'on joue sur les boulevards tu manges maintenant out u t'en vas I had a gal once at the end of town it was like l'Angleterrde 1697 24 avril pleure le plus grand ses musiciens: Henry Purcell mort à like dipping in a barrel of honé donnez-moi un paquet de gauloises si tu crois petite je ne sais pas ce qui lui a pris tu n'est pas ca-pa-ble-de il ne sais rien faire de ses dix doigts heureusement qu'il a ses parents qui lui donnent a manger sans cela qu'est-ce que tu ferais on vous appelle au téléphone. . . . il est mort en Espagne où quelque part en voulant rejoindre les forces françaises libres I am sorry gonna fuck you balls votre père est un sous-Apollinaire.

Such syntactical disjunctures and shifts in language provoke a range of semantic associations and dissociations. The passage is immediately followed by a voice explaining that the phrases will become increasingly incomprehensible and exacerbated by technical deformations, which include playing the sound track in reverse.[8]

With *Le film est déjà commencé?* as with *Traité*, there is much more that could be said about the formal experimentation within the film itself: from the disjuncture between image and sound to the formal panoply of

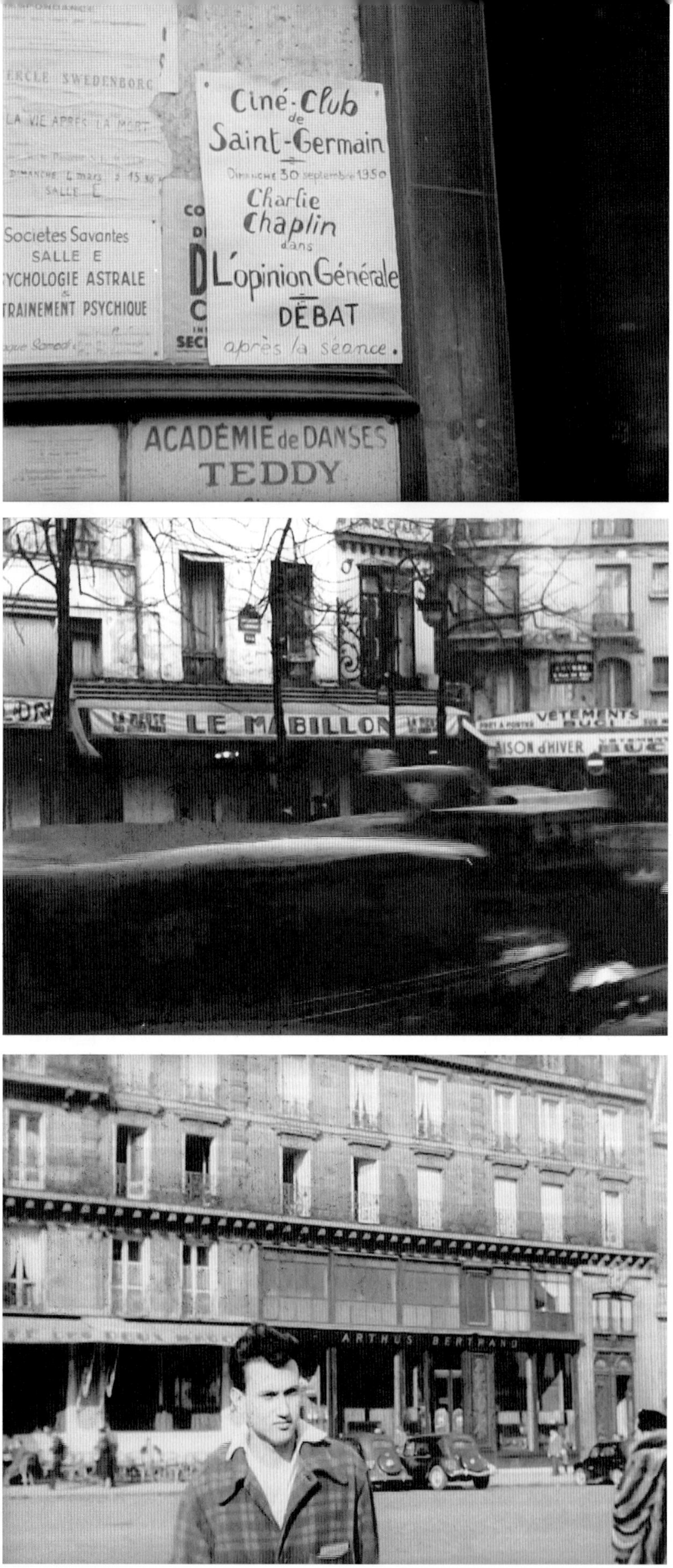

40. Isidore Isou, *Traité de bave et d'éternité*, 1951. Frame enlargements.

images and speech's attendant manipulations. In this context, it is significant that Isou chose to reproduce a ciné-club debate on the sound track to *Traité*, while his *dérive*-like meanderings on the image track begin with his departure from the Ciné-Club de Saint-Germain and a visible flyer that announces "DEBAT après la séance" (Debate after the screening). Cameos of avant-garde haunts such as the cafés Le Mabillon and Les Deux Magots follow this shot, as the voice-over continues with its justification for a new aesthetic in cinema (fig. 40). When complete, *Traité*'s sound track allowed Isou to explain his work in the time that it took to screen the film. He inscribed a debate about the very film one attended within the materials of his film, while also provoking live debate at each of its screenings.

Isou's recourse to film club debate foregrounds film's constitutive outside—that is, the alternate cinema network, whose origin in the 1920s provided a context for avant-garde film and first strove to define and uphold film as an art.[9] Indeed, what Lettrist film mobilizes in no uncertain terms are the live elements that form part of ciné-clubs' social organization—namely, the tripartite format of short introductory lecture, screening, and postscreening debate, first codified by Charles Léger in the 1920s.[10] For the Lettrists the ciné-clubs did more than provide an actual venue. The social form of verbal communication they engendered came to define both the content and the structure of Isou's and Lemaitre's first films.

By focusing on the ciné-club—as a communicative practice inscribed both within and outside the actual materials of Lettrist film—I propose an alternative film history, one in which the heterodox modernism of the Lettrists is key.[11] While Isou's sound track largely seeks to define what he calls discrepant cinema, Lemaître designated his film as a "séance de cinéma," taking his cue from the French term for film screening and elaborating it through what he called "syncinema," a kind of film performance that moved Lettrist film beyond the image and sound tracks and toward experimentation with the spaces of the screen and of projection, with what goes on both on and off the screen. Here, filmic specificity derives from the heterogeneity of the cinematic medium, which includes the activity of at once the body and speech that Lemaître would exploit in order to create what Isou calls "le premier film en relief vivant" (the first film with live relief).[12]

COMING SOON TO A THEATER NEAR YOU

In the published script to *Le film est déjà commencé?* Lemaître included a third column of text with the heading "*salle*" in addition to those columns designating the sound and image track (fig. 41). Here *salle* refers not only to the space of the theater but also to the audience, drawing attention

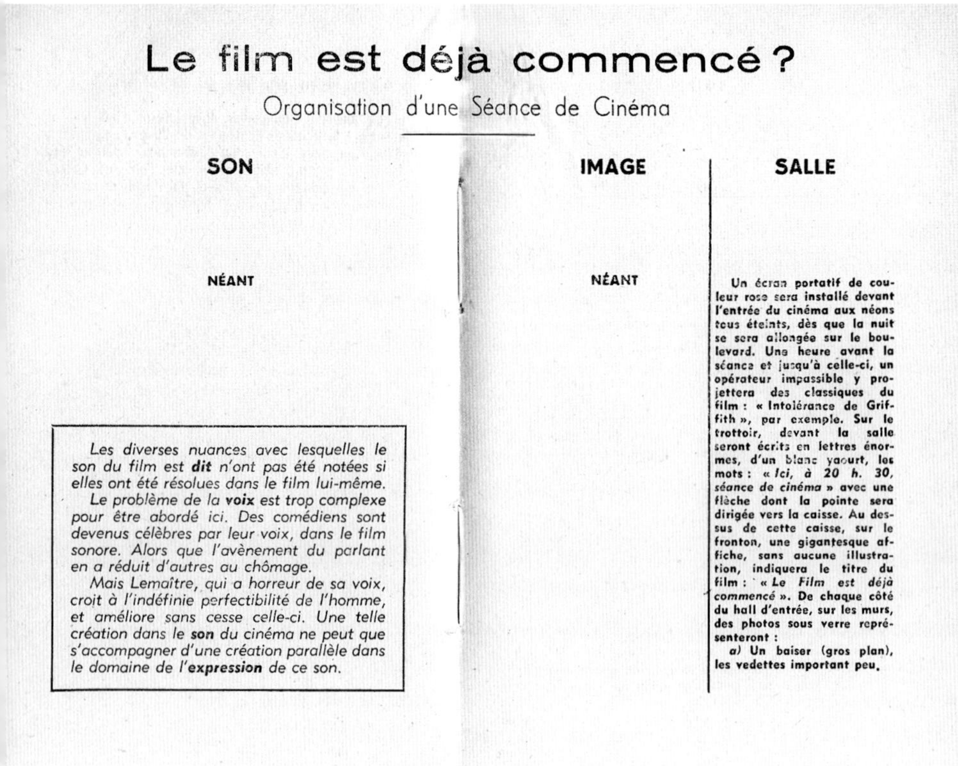

Le film est déjà commencé ?

Organisation d'une Séance de Cinéma

SON	IMAGE	SALLE
NÉANT	NÉANT	Un écran portatif de couleur rose sera installé devant l'entrée du cinéma aux néons tous éteints, dès que la nuit se sera allongée sur le boulevard. Une heure avant la séance et jusqu'à celle-ci, un opérateur impassible y projettera des classiques du film : « Intolérance de Griffith », par exemple. Sur le trottoir, devant la salle seront écrits en lettres énormes, d'un blanc yaourt, les mots : « *Ici, à 20 h. 30, séance de cinéma* » avec une flèche dont la pointe sera dirigée vers la caisse. Au dessus de cette caisse, sur le fronton, une gigantesque affiche, sans aucune illustration, indiquera le titre du film : « *Le Film est déjà commencé* ». De chaque côté du hall d'entrée, sur les murs, des photos sous verre représenteront : *a)* Un baiser (gros plan), les vedettes important peu.

*Les diverses nuances avec lesquelles le son du film est **dit** n'ont pas été notées si elles ont été résolues dans le film lui-même.*

*Le problème de la **voix** est trop complexe pour être abordé ici. Des comédiens sont devenus célèbres par leur voix, dans le film sonore. Alors que l'avènement du parlant en a réduit d'autres au chômage.*

*Mais Lemaître, qui a horreur de sa voix, croit à l'indéfinie perfectibilité de l'homme, et améliore sans cesse celle-ci. Une telle création dans le **son** du cinéma ne peut que s'accompagner d'une création parallèle dans le domaine de l'**expression** de ce son.*

41. Maurice Lemaître, *Le film est déjà commencé?* (Paris: Éditions André Bonne, 1952). Interior spread.

to the environmental and, more specifically, spectatorial situation that occurs exterior to film's technological support. In this column, Lemaître outlines how *Le film est déjà commencé?* begins:

> A pink-colored portable screen will be installed at the entrance to the cinema. . . . An hour before the screening . . . an impassive operator will project on it cinema classics: for example, *Intolerance* by Griffith. On the sidewalk, in front of the theater, will be written in enormous yogurt-white letters, the words: "Here, at 8:30 p.m., cinema séance," with an arrow pointing to the register.[13]

Lemaître continues by specifying that, even though the film is announced for 8:30, the audience should wait for an hour, while accomplices on the building's second floor beat dusty rugs and throw buckets of ice over those waiting in line below in the hope of provoking an exchange of insults. Once inside the theater, the audience would see that the screen is not the customary flat rectangle but is transformed by colored pieces of drapery placed on it and moving objects suspended in front of it. While spectators find their seats, the concluding minutes of a western would be shown.

When it ends, the spectators would then be asked to evacuate the theater and it would be cleaned. Eventually, back in the theater, the film director would begin a defense of his film, which should be interrupted by booing from the crowd. Next the operator of the cinema should accuse the filmmaker of having made a work in contradiction of his ideas on cinema and begin to tear the film off the reel, while another person, introducing him- or herself as the film producer, tries to save the celluloid.

Insofar as these events are surely staged as a form of avant-garde provocation, thereby recalling the anarchic performances of the historical avant-garde, Lemaître here (as with his fake press accounts) stages the scandal of the film before any scandal actually occurs. What is more, these actions described in the *salle* column are subsequently reproduced in the film's sound track. So, approximately nineteen minutes into the film, we see an abstract sequence of undulating pink; the title of Griffith's film *Intolerance*, which appears in letter groups across four shots (the first shot showing "IN," followed by "to," "LÉ," and "Ran"); and, finally, a pulsing intertitle that reads "CINÉ." As the images of letters and words proceed, we hear the following:

> Voice 6:
>
> Behold how the representation of Maurice LEMAITRE's film will proceed: A pink-colored portable screen will be installed at the entrance to the cinema. . . . An hour before the screening . . . an impassive operator will project on it cinema classics: for example, *Intolerance* by Griffith. On the sidewalk, in front of the theater, will be written in enormous yogurt-white letters, the words: "Here, at 8:30 p.m., cinema séance," with an arrow pointing to the register.[14]

Unlike the instructions for the prescreening events noted at the outset in the *salle* column, this sequence is eventually followed by voices that utter specific insults like "ce film est infect!" (that film is vile) while, according to the script, the actual theater space remains in silence.[15] As the sound track and image track unfold, the cinema remains silent until page 127, where Lemaître calls for the curtains to close in order to install a new screen. At this moment, approximately twenty-five minutes into the film, the film literally begins again as the curtain opens and the sound track describes the irregularity of the screen. "Voice 6" continues:

> That screen will not be rectangular, but a form made strange by a number of vibrant colored cloths placed on certain parts of it, as well as by different objects hanging in front of it. The cloth and objects could be put in motion by scene changers [*machinistes*] during the film. In

> the course of the projection, heads, hands, and hats will be placed in front of the projection beam in order to cover the images. . . . During these proceedings, the spectators will continue to sit down. Once that is finished—or almost—the word "End" will appear on that extraordinary screen, accompanied by triumphant music.[16]

As we listen to this description, we see sequences of pure color as well as abstract marks on the film's shots. Next the film's title appears, followed by the name of its author, just as we see the word "FIN" come into view, letter by letter, to the sound of triumphant music, as noted in the voice-over (and script). The film refuses the absorption and directional force of narrative film through repeated references, both visual and verbal, to its own beginning and end, as well as to future installments, through intertitles such as "PROCHAINEMENT SUR CET ECRAN" (Next on this screen; fig. 42). As suggested in this chapter's opening passages, the staggered repetition between live event and its sound track representation eventually begins to temporally coincide.

With no reviews, eyewitness testimony, or other documentation, my account of the overlap between verbal representation and live performance relies on the published script. On pages 138–39, the sound track column describes that a spotlight be directed toward a couple just as the *salle* column notes that a couple appear on stage and begin to kiss; on pages 164–65 the sound track indicates how an extra (*figurant*) "will stand up in the theater and shoot at the screen with a revolver. Another will tear the screen with knife-blows and will pass through to the other side of the screen into the wings, or will attack the wall."[17] With the exception of gunshots fired at the screen, the *salle* column details the screen's destruction and how the film will continue to be projected on its tattered surface. *Le film est déjà commencé?* alternates the coincidence between sound track and action on the stage, with sound track and no scripted performance (as indicated by "Silence" in the *salle* column). All the while the formal experimentation with chiseled images unfurls before the spectator. The penultimate line of the sound track describes how the final reel of the film cannot be found, while film extras dressed as police enter the theater and blow their whistles.

42. Maurice Lemaître, *Le film est déjà commencé?*, 1951. Frame enlargements.

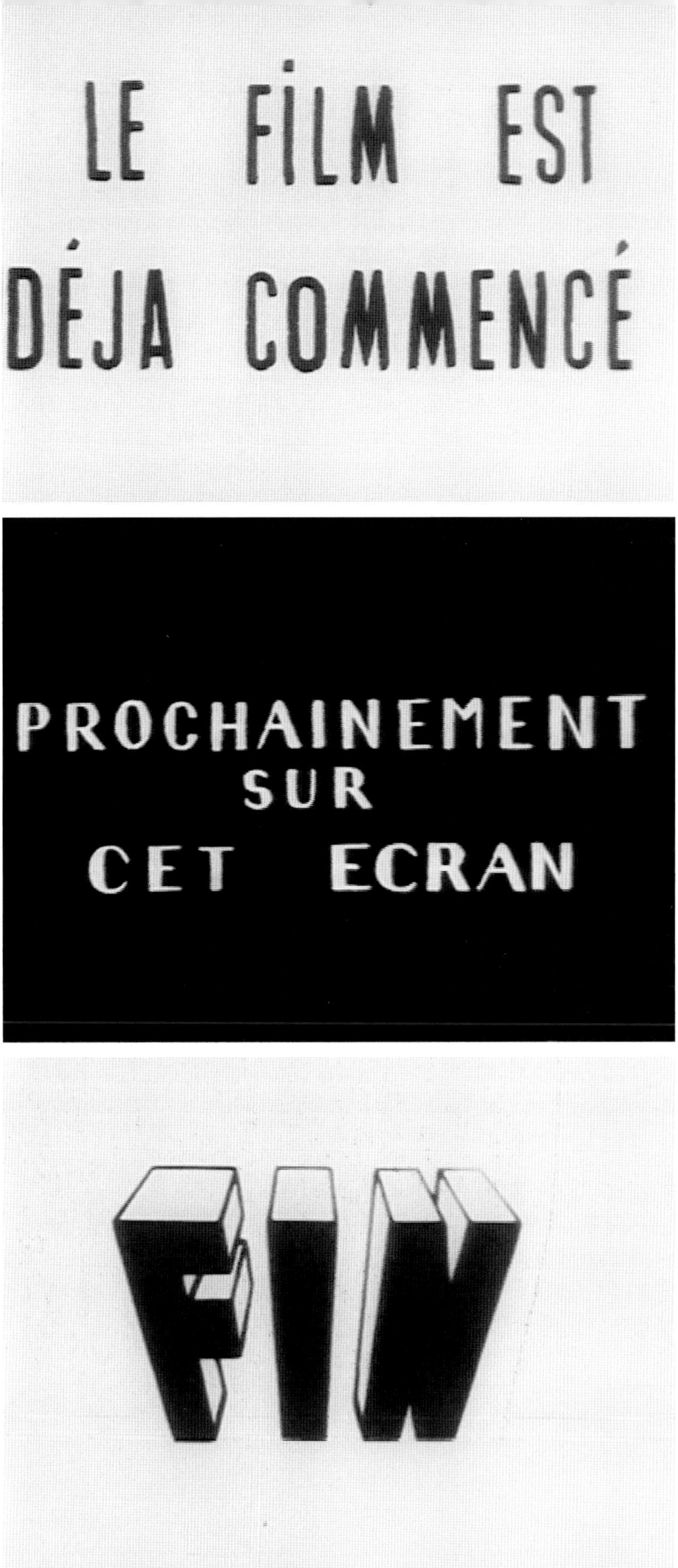

DISCOVER THE CULPRIT!

Before addressing other aspects of *Le film est déjà commencé?*, I would like to turn my attention to Lemaître's largely unremarked proposal "Base d'une éducation cinématographique du public par la critique permanente" (Basis for the public's cinematographic education through permanent critique; fig. 43), published first in the second issue of *Ur: La dictature lettriste* in 1952 and subsequently in the book *Le film est déjà commencé?* In this proposal, purportedly submitted to the Association de la Critique Cinématographique, Lemaître calls for a production company for chiseled films that will "redirect the spectators' demand for narrative films" (détourner la demande des spectateurs des bandes ampliques).[18] The production company's employees would be required to go to a minimum of three screenings a day and to "interrupt and comment on . . . the theater's normal representation." Inspectors would be charged with "overseeing the latter, the [proper] exercise of the profession, and finding replacements in the event of failure to sufficiently critique."[19]

Although the company was never founded and its activities, to the best of my knowledge, were never implemented, Lemaître's "Base d'une éducation cinématographique" offers specific instructions for the use of professional spectators who could carry out his challenge to commercial cinema. Lemaître describes the language and frequency of interruptions as well as the film genres to be disrupted, which include everything from crime-thrillers (*films policiers*) to romances. But what is particular about Lemaître's proposed disturbances is the agency given to the voice of the professional spectator in the modulation of a film's meaning. For example, he writes, regarding the crime-thriller:

> In the case in which the identification of the criminal is obvious, do not miss any opportunity to clarify this as such through assessments of his person ("he has a nasty face [*sale gueule*], so it must be him"), even if the character is likable. This attitude will increase ordinary spectators' sickening impression of "déjà vu," given that they are already disappointed by the perception of the character's guilt.
>
> On the other hand, if the criminal is difficult to identify, choose, while waiting, any character from the film (likable, if possible) and accuse him systematically. Crime-thrillers are almost always moral (or have a moral) and since spectators normally do not pay attention to this aspect of the work, it is necessary to demonstrate revolting cynicism and perfect amorality during the interruptions. This will highlight the real pleasure of the people in the theater by not letting them enjoy in good conscience.[20]

43. Maurice Lemaître, “Base d’une éducation cinématographique du public par la critique permanente,” *Ur: La dictature lettriste*, no. 2 (1952), 19–20.

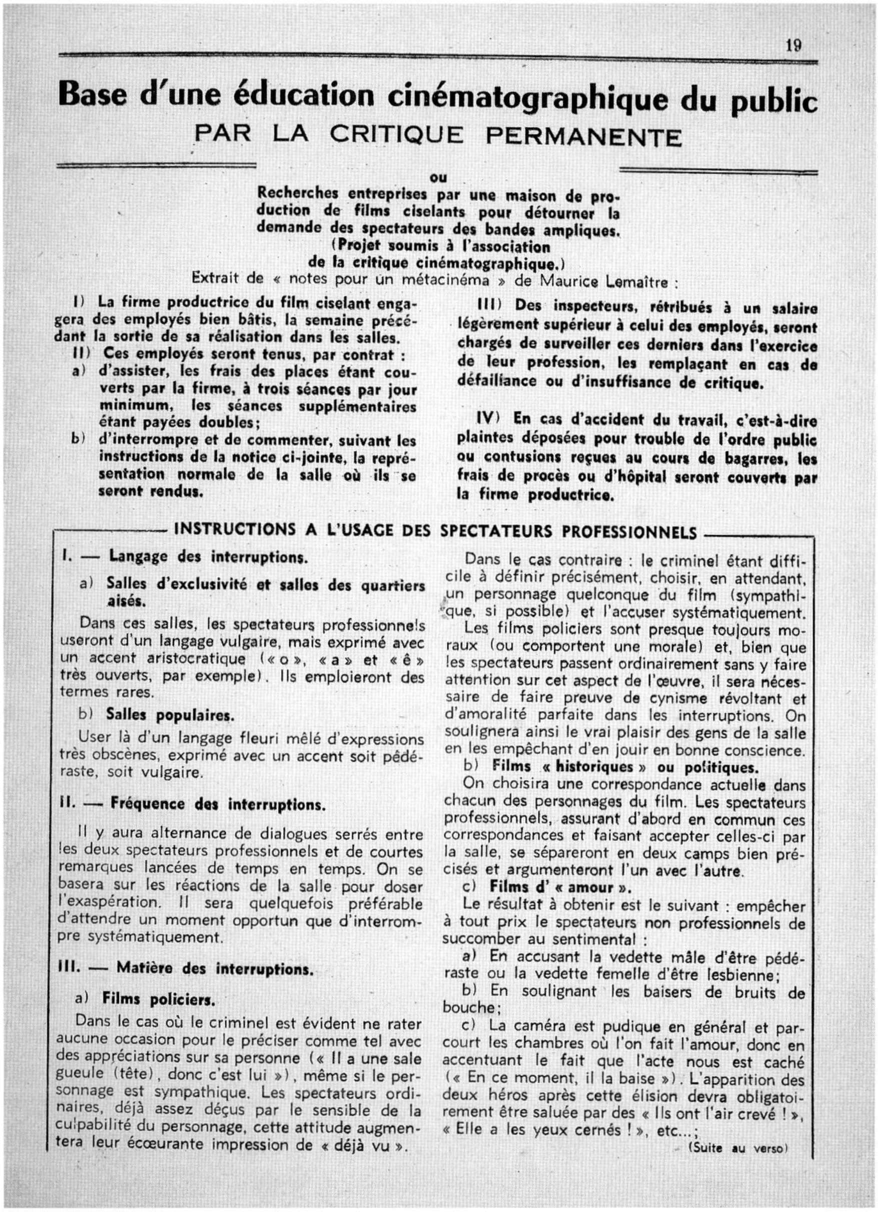

19

Base d'une éducation cinématographique du public
PAR LA CRITIQUE PERMANENTE

ou
Recherches entreprises par une maison de production de films ciselants pour détourner la demande des spectateurs des bandes ampliques.
(Projet soumis à l'association de la critique cinématographique.)
Extrait de « notes pour un métacinéma » de Maurice Lemaître :

I) La firme productrice du film ciselant engagera des employés bien bâtis, la semaine précédant la sortie de sa réalisation dans les salles.
II) Ces employés seront tenus, par contrat :
a) d'assister, les frais des places étant couverts par la firme, à trois séances par jour minimum, les séances supplémentaires étant payées doubles;
b) d'interrompre et de commenter, suivant les instructions de la notice ci-jointe, la représentation normale de la salle où ils se seront rendus.

III) Des inspecteurs, rétribués à un salaire légèrement supérieur à celui des employés, seront chargés de surveiller ces derniers dans l'exercice de leur profession, les remplaçant en cas de défaillance ou d'insuffisance de critique.

IV) En cas d'accident du travail, c'est-à-dire plaintes déposées pour trouble de l'ordre public ou contusions reçues au cours de bagarres, les frais de procès ou d'hôpital seront couverts par la firme productrice.

INSTRUCTIONS A L'USAGE DES SPECTATEURS PROFESSIONNELS

I. — Langage des interruptions.

a) **Salles d'exclusivité et salles des quartiers aisés.**

Dans ces salles, les spectateurs professionnels useront d'un langage vulgaire, mais exprimé avec un accent aristocratique (« o », « a » et « ê » très ouverts, par exemple). Ils emploieront des termes rares.

b) **Salles populaires.**

User là d'un langage fleuri mêlé d'expressions très obscènes, exprimé avec un accent soit pédéraste, soit vulgaire.

II. — Fréquence des interruptions.

Il y aura alternance de dialogues serrés entre les deux spectateurs professionnels et de courtes remarques lancées de temps en temps. On se basera sur les réactions de la salle pour doser l'exaspération. Il sera quelquefois préférable d'attendre un moment opportun que d'interrompre systématiquement.

III. — Matière des interruptions.

a) **Films policiers.**

Dans le cas où le criminel est évident ne rater aucune occasion pour le préciser comme tel avec des appréciations sur sa personne (« Il a une sale gueule (tête), donc c'est lui »), même si le personnage est sympathique. Les spectateurs ordinaires, déjà assez déçus par le sensible de la culpabilité du personnage, cette attitude augmentera leur écœurante impression de « déjà vu ».

Dans le cas contraire : le criminel étant difficile à définir précisément, choisir, en attendant, un personnage quelconque du film (sympathique, si possible) et l'accuser systématiquement.

Les films policiers sont presque toujours moraux (ou comportent une morale) et, bien que les spectateurs passent ordinairement sans y faire attention sur cet aspect de l'œuvre, il sera nécessaire de faire preuve de cynisme révoltant et d'amoralité parfaite dans les interruptions. On soulignera ainsi le vrai plaisir des gens de la salle en les empêchant d'en jouir en bonne conscience.

b) **Films « historiques » ou politiques.**

On choisira une correspondance actuelle dans chacun des personnages du film. Les spectateurs professionnels, assurant d'abord en commun ces correspondances et faisant accepter celles-ci par la salle, se sépareront en deux camps bien précisés et argumenteront l'un avec l'autre.

c) **Films d' « amour ».**

Le résultat à obtenir est le suivant : empêcher à tout prix le spectateurs non professionnels de succomber au sentimental :

a) En accusant la vedette mâle d'être pédéraste ou la vedette femelle d'être lesbienne;

b) En soulignant les baisers de bruits de bouche;

c) La caméra est pudique en général et parcourt les chambres où l'on fait l'amour, donc en accentuant le fait que l'acte nous est caché (« En ce moment, il la baise »). L'apparition des deux héros après cette élision devra obligatoirement être saluée par des « Ils ont l'air crevé ! », « Elle a les yeux cernés ! », etc...;

(Suite au verso)

Here the professional spectator’s speech denaturalizes the image’s narrative meaning—on the one hand, through an exaggerated attention to physiognomic characteristics, and on the other hand, through an arbitrary accusation possibly at odds with a film’s narrative conceit.

Lemaître prefigures the interruptive strategies of professional spectators in various intertitles presented in the course of *Le film est déjà commencé?* For example, approximately halfway into the film, spectators are prompted: “Vous découvrirez le coupable!” (You will discover

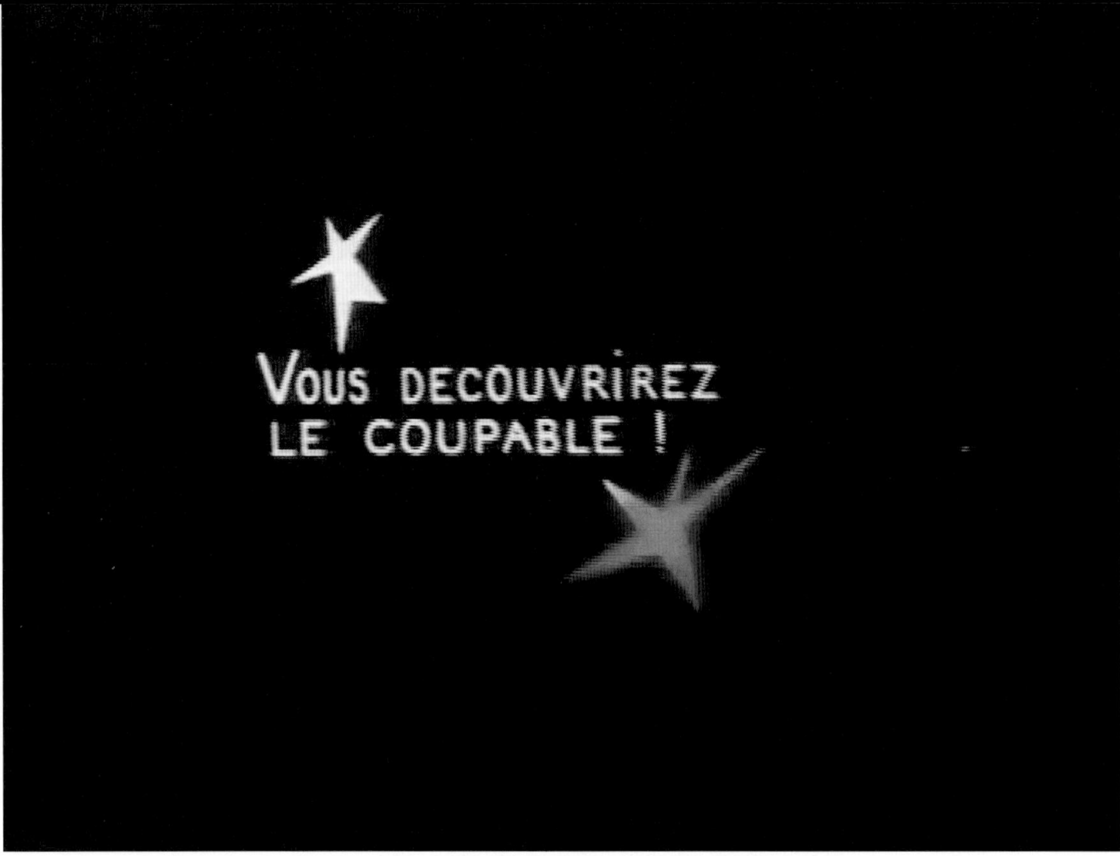

44. Maurice Lemaître, *Le film est déjà commencé?*, 1951. Frame enlargement.

the culprit!; fig. 44). Subsequently, his prospective "production" company did receive a small, albeit noteworthy, write-up in the contemporary press. On March 27, 1952, in the pages of *Ciné-coulisses*, a brief column describes the potential use of these salaried "voyeurs" and their proposed deployment of "a flowery language in neighborhood cinemas." In addition to the counter–crime-thriller strategy outlined above, the column's author mentions how Lemaître's professional spectators would draw attention to bodily functions normally kept from view by revealing what remains unseen in films, and cites "pipi" as an example. Yet what is most telling is the critic's designation of these cinema workers as "*active* contemplation professionals," thereby isolating how the production company's primary task was to target normative viewing practices understood as passive.[21]

The professional spectator's exercise of active contemplation depends on how their speech is mobilized as a means by which to modify a film's meaning. By deploying live speech to counter the specific sound-image relations upheld in a film, Lemaître's proposal constitutes a historical reformulation and dialectical reversal of the Kuleshov effect, of which he was aware.[22] In the late 1910s and early 1920s, Lev Kuleshov edited together a short film in which the expressionless face of Ivan Mozhukhin was juxtaposed to other shots. He recalls, "I created a montage experiment. . . . I alternated the same shot of Mozhukhin with various other shots (a plate of soup, a girl, a child's coffin), and these shots acquired a different meaning."[23] By using Mozhukhin's face as the constant image against which to juxtapose other shots, Kuleshov demonstrated that the same footage of an actor can accrue different meanings (e.g., an expression of hunger, tenderness, or grief) through editing and the contiguous relations between shots. Lemaître's professional spectators would have extended this visual lesson of montage by redirecting its effects from the relation between shots to the relation between a shot and live speech.

Situating Lemaître's proposal in relation to Kulsehov's experiment allows us to consider what it might mean to our understanding of a shot of an individual's face (Mozhukhin's, for instance) to have one of Lemaître's professional spectators assert, "He looks evil. He has an evil gaze. It must be him." Such a thought experiment points to how semantic meaning could be altered through the addition of speech potentially at odds with a film's diegetic universe and use of continuity editing. For when faced with an actor in a crime-thriller, a typical spectator invests the character with the properties attributed to him or her through the casting and voice-over speech that are characteristic of the genre. Lemaître's professional spectator would be a sort of heckler, challenging such pat identifications and thereby disrupting the narrative fantasy. In the wake of sound synchronization and the speech track's triumph, Lemaître's proposal for the public's cinematographic education, his recourse to live speech in relation to the moving image, points to language's performative force in cinema: saying something equals doing something to the image's meaning.

In the case of romance films, Lemaître maintains that the nonprofessional spectators should not be allowed to "succumb to the sentimental." To avoid such affective reception, he recommends that professional spectators accuse the on-screen stars of homosexuality and lesbianism as a means to thwart normative heterosexual-romantic identifications, and use onomatopoeia such as "miam-miam" (yum-yum) to stress the actors' bodily functions—that is, the eating or even the urinating mentioned above.[24] On the one hand, he taps into homophobic fears and entrenched prejudices to counter identification with the heteronormativity of Hollywood film. On the other hand, he encourages the eruption of abject, bodily sounds that are ordinarily both absent from the space of the screen and prohibited within the space of the theater.

With this proposal, as with *Le film est déjà commencé?*, Lemaître extends the audience participation and debate reproduced on the sound track of Isou's *Traité de bave et d'éternité* to an investigation of the film's projection as an event, one that also constitutes an elaboration of the role of the film lecturer in early cinema or the era of animated pictures. In early cinema the lecturer's speech was often used to compensate for the perceived insufficiency of the image and thereby served as a "narrative helper."[25] Alternatively, as Tom Gunning explains, the lecturer "builds an atmosphere of expectation" about the "astonishing properties which the [film] attraction about to be revealed will possess."[26] In either case, early lecturers emphasized the act of display and focused the spectator's attention on the attraction. Through their performances, both the film lecturer and Lemaître's professional spectators discourage contemplative absorption in the moving image. This type of direct address, which responds to the composite mode of early cinema, would be taken up by other artists in Lemaître's wake (I am thinking here, for example, of Marcel Broodthaers, to whom I refer in the epilogue). But rather than mediate the shock of the film attraction, Lemaître's professional spectators comprise a live element specifically orchestrated to undermine the narrative meanings films produce and thus provoke the public's active reception. Lemaître's critique, however, extended beyond Hollywood genres and commercial cinema to include the culture of the Parisian ciné-clubs and their particular methods and objectives when teaching film.

SUPERFLUOUS DIGRESSIONS

Ciné-clubs existed outside of the official commercial network and were able to screen films that were otherwise banned from commercial distribution. They were also a privileged venue for screening avant-garde film. In the interwar years, film clubs' activities were tolerated by French authorities, who perceived them as fashioning an aesthetic elite and not as competition to the mass market in either aesthetic or political terms. During the war and German occupation, ciné-clubs were completely prohibited, one of the many restrictions imposed by the Nazis, though there were still a few clandestine screenings.[27]

The explosive growth of ciné-clubs in the aftermath of the war shows the extent to which they were missed during the occupation. In 1944 there was only one ciné-club; in March 1945, six; in June 1945, twelve; in June 1946, eighty-three; in June 1947, one hundred thirty; and in June 1948, one hundred eighty-five. Throughout the 1950s, there were about two hundred ciné-clubs with an audience of sixty to eighty thousand.[28] According to a survey of one hundred thirty postwar ciné-clubs, the majority claimed as their purpose "to give the public a taste for good cinema . . . , so that it will reject sensationalist publicity, star worship, and vulgarity."[29] In pursuing this end, the ciné-club was no longer necessarily opposed to commercial cinema; its objective had become more subtle: "to form spectators at once conscious and passionate who continue to patronize commercial theaters . . . but with a different gaze [*regard*] and a refined sensibility."[30] Accordingly, in the 1950s, ciné-club culture helped to codify a specific practice of how to view and speak about film.

In April 1954, about two years after Lemaître's film and the publication of "Base d'une éducation cinématographique," André Bazin published the article "Comment présenter et discuter un film!" (How to Present and Discuss a Film) in a special issue of *Ciné-club*, which was published by the Fédération Française des Ciné-Clubs. Bazin begins by describing how ciné-club directors are more or less in agreement about how to provide a film with "appropriate commentary," noting that the "practical realization to date yielded unequal and uncertain results." He recommends that the presentation prior to the film be short, no more than ten minutes, given that "people go to the cinema to watch films, not to listen to lectures." The aim of the lecture should be to put the public "in a better position to receive the film with freshness and straight on [*de plein fouet*]." The best approach, he concludes, "is always to teach cinema by the cinema, to form sensitivity by means of sensitivity."[31]

For the discussion or debate after the screening, Bazin writes, much depends on "the personality of the speaker." The primary task, as he describes it, is "to leave the public . . . [with only] an illusion of critical freedom, while providing a minimum of security against the 'bores' [*raseurs*] and the perfectly superfluous digressions." He describes two principle methods for conducting a ciné-club discussion: the liberal and the authoritarian. In the liberal method, the film-presenter allows members of the public to speak. This entails certain risks, among them "intellectual disorder" and giving equal weight to interventions of differing quality. The authoritarian method, by contrast, entails a careful exposition of the film, isolating its important elements. This affords a chance for the lecturer to "indirectly impose through questioning previously chosen aspects of the work," and for listeners to gain "clarity."[32] Bazin confesses that he prefers the latter method but suggests striking a healthy balance between allowing viewers to say whatever they want, willy-nilly, and enforcing a strictly top-down model of communication.

Bazin's article emerges as a practical guide for leading ciné-club debates, whose common goal at the time was, according to one 1964 study, "to draw the viewer out of the hypnotic sleep in which the film plunged him, to transform passivity . . . into active attitude."[33] Bazin and ciné-club culture thus shared Lemaître's desire to cultivate the public's active reception. The differences in terms of how this was to be done reveal the discursive limitations regarding the conventional dichotomy between active and passive spectatorship, with Lemaître championing actual participation, while the film clubs promoted the knowledge one might gain through

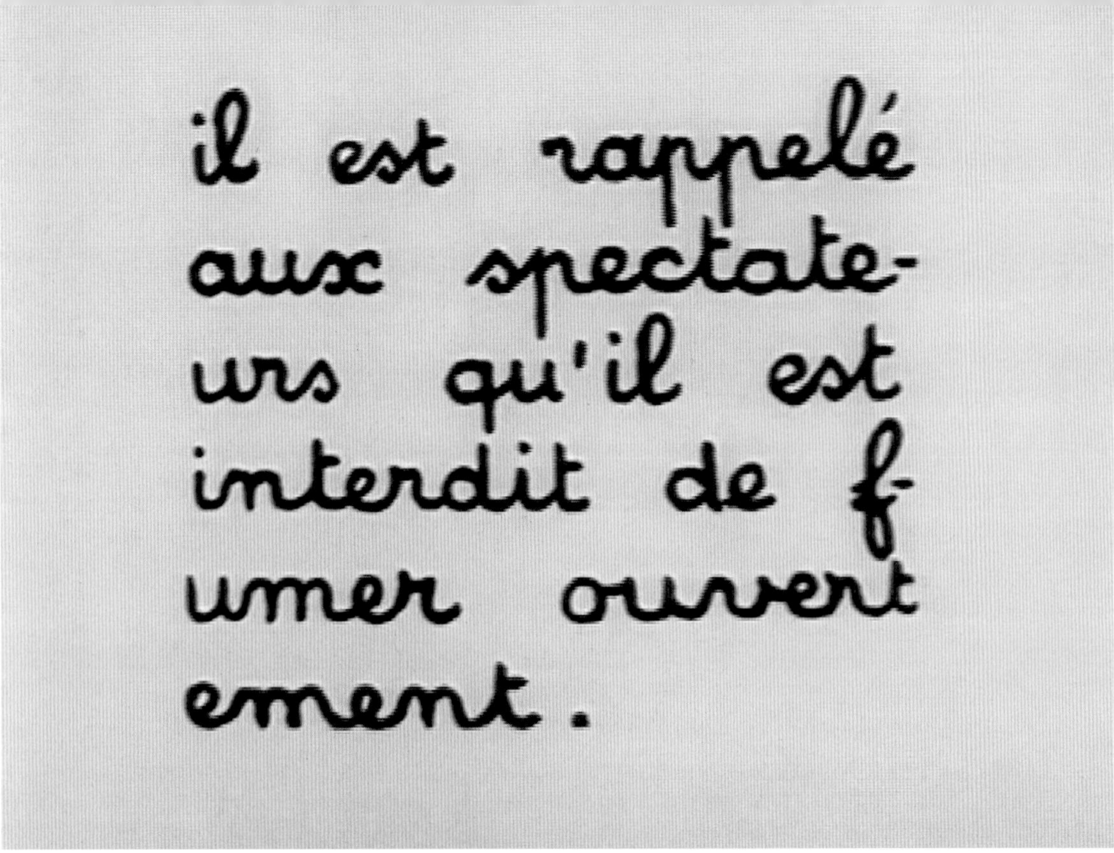

45. Maurice Lemaître, *Le film est déjà commencé?*, 1951. Frame enlargement.

contemplative modes of viewing.[34] That said, for Bazin and Parisian film-club culture in these years, debate as a social forum was largely attuned to the specificity of film aesthetics. Lemaître understands film as both an end and an explicit means of cultural critique; Bazin understands it as an end in itself. As a result, Bazin upholds a dialectic between quasi-mystical silence during the screening and the resonance and aesthetic appreciation of the film through guided conversation.

It is against the grain of the ciné-club's enforcement of silence and regulation of speech that Lettrist cinema and Lemaître's theory of cinematographic education must be understood. Lemaître's proposal for live and simultaneous critique through the use of professional spectators runs counter to the discussion format articulated by Bazin as well as its informational-educational conceit vis-à-vis the filmgoing public. Whatever the aesthetic of a particular film—whether it was best explained according to theories of montage or of realism—viewers were, in Bazin's view, to remain immobile and not to speak. The film audience, writes Serge Daney, had been "slowly trained to give up its 'bad' habits, to quit talking or interrupting the projection with cries." He continues, "What we call 'the history of cinema' is the history of the public's domestication, its 'immobilisation.' Broadly speaking: immobile people who became sensitive to the mobility of the world."[35] Apropos the taming of the public's bad habits, an intertitle in *Le film est déjà commencé?* rather cheekily calls attention to the emerging disciplinary regime: "il est rappelé aux spectateurs qu'il est interdit de fumer ouvertement" (spectators are reminded that smoking openly is prohibited; fig. 45).

If the professional spectator described in "Base d'une éducation cinématographique" also offers an alternative to the codified model of film club debate, Lemaître's film practice (his attention to the effects of sound-image relations; the incorporation of live elements, including debate) forms part of a larger strategy, whereby he subjects the visual image to a "discursive politics of appropriation and contextual transformation" through spoken language.[36] Yet his work on the voice of cinema and its public must be held apart from conceptions of language's transparency or originary innocence, just as his film counters the voice's ideological collusion with the image in narrative cinema or wartime propaganda. With *Traité*, Isou largely confined his work to the disjuncture of sound-image relations within film. In Lemaître's film, the critical import of *montage discrépant* was rerouted to take effect in the space between the voices and images of the film *and* the voices and action of and in the *salle*. Lemaître thereby refuses the regulation of silence and speech that contributed to the progressive homogenization of the cinematic public sphere. That such a project would necessarily move beyond the formal parameters of the voice in cinema to incorporate actual verbal interventions was prefigured in inchoate form in the final pages of Isou's "Esthétique du cinéma": "The debate [*discussion*], appendix of the show [*spectacle*], must become the real drama."[37]

Le film est déjà commencé? could not have been further from the modality of production and reception of the art films then circulating on the international festival circuit or being projected in Parisian *salles* such as the Cinémathèque Française. Indeed, in the pages of *Ion*, Marc'O (Marc-Gilbert Guillaumin) intimates that Lettrist cinema is likely to find the most resistance among the ciné-clubs:

> The avant-gardist will be the first to believe in an immutable cinema. He is the worst reactionary when faced with a new avant-garde. . . . The ciné-club intellectuals . . . will never accept the idea of a new cinema. . . . Ciné-club spectators—static mass of a given school—are, among the public, [responsible for] the main reaction against cinema's march toward unknown limits.[38]

It is worth noting that Henri Langlois regarded the didactic ciné-club tradition unfavorably. Hence for the members of the public and an emerging generation of filmmakers—most notably those who would later be affiliated with the Nouvelle Vague—Langlois's screenings at the

Cinémathèque Française offered an education in film history based exclusively on the study of film qua film.[39])

For Lemaître, the public was not to be treated as passive receptacle, as per Bazin, ready to "receive the film with freshness" and then be guided through a postscreening debate conceived as a one-way transfer of aesthetic knowledge. In the end, Bazin's cinematic pedagogy depends on the invisible authority of the debate leader; his proposed mode of collective viewing and discussion can also be read as a form of policing:

> an order of bodies that defines the allocation of ways of doing, ways of being, and ways of saying . . . ; it is an order of the visible and the sayable that sees that a particular activity is visible and another is not, that this speech is understood as discourse and another as noise.[40]

Lemaître proposes another means for the education and management of spectators in the cinema, and in so doing he imagines another type of governmentality, another way to conduct conduct, through film: a film "production" company, with its own rules, employees, and inspectors dedicated to the exercise of a pedagogical project premised on permanent critique.

Lemaître's proposal for a counter-conduct in cinema leads to an awareness of how the hypostatization of the medium when teaching film depends on the institutional and disciplinary constraints imposed on the viewing subject's right to speak. What is crucial in this context is not that Lemaître's project abandons authority, but rather how professional spectators' assault on the integrity of film and on the identifications film elicits presuppose the spectators' capacity to respond during the screening. Lemaître writes, "It is possible that during the interruptions an ordinary spectator voluntarily helps the professional spectators. The latter will encourage and praise him."[41] By clearly inscribing the filmgoing public within an art of permanent critique, Lemaître's theory of spectatorship calls to mind Foucault's subsequent theorization of the relation between power and the subject: "a relationship which is at the same time reciprocal incitation and struggle . . . a permanent provocation."[42] For Lemaître such a critical program finds its inspiration in the original contentiousness of ciné-club debates insofar as they present a supplementary history of film and cinematic modernity: the ciné-club was a site that provided the conditions of possibility for the discussion of what constituted the film medium, its "essence." Lemaître, in turn, upholds the ciné-club debate as part of the constitutive materials of film. Framed in this way, Lemaître's is less an aesthetic of shock than of a negotiation that emerges as immanent to the ciné-club as a social practice.[43] Lemaître's lesson is ultimately one in media literacy, a learning to see, but also to hear, that exposes and counters the politics of what Guy Debord would later designate as spectacle.

In 1954, the same year Bazin penned his essay, Lemaître circulated his "Les vrais et les faux pionniers du cinéma" (The Real and Fake Cinema Pioneers) in the pages of *Cahiers du cinéma*.[44] In this work, he tackles the problem of film distribution and recounts how he did not have the money to pay the required *taxe de sortie* (tax for release) for his film. He approached various ciné-clubs and specialized cinemas, such as Studio des Ursulines (historic site of interwar Surrealist scandals) and Studio 28, both of which refused to program his film. Consequently, he calls for changes in film distribution and criticism and concludes with this appeal: "It is now important that young filmmakers are offered that minimum chance that lies in the possibility to SHOW their film. This is the prerequisite for any honest critique and all progress in the cinema."[45] His critique of the alternate cinema network and the economic requirements that often restrict film's distribution eventually led to Lemaître's development of a counterinstitution: the Café-Cinéma.[46] Founded in 1967, Café-Cinéma was positioned against both the film industry and the Centre National du Cinéma; Lemaître claimed it as an alternative venue for engaging the *new* in cinema and unfailingly dedicated its programs to the work of young filmmakers.

For Lemaître, the ciné-club in the early 1950s still held the possibility of serving as a site for an alternative politics of cinematic reception and film distribution, at the precise moment when cinema was being consolidated as an industry, accompanied by a form of cinephilic culture dedicated to both upholding a canon of classic cinema and legislating a specific regimen of bodies, perception, and speech.[47] With *Le film est déjà commencé?*, film's outside folds into its inside: the space of cinematic reception becomes coterminous with the production of meaning, and the viewer—no longer a passive and idealist term in the functioning of the film apparatus—is placed in the complicated position of trying to comprehend how live performance and speech impinge on the images and speech emanating from the screen. In this way, Lemaitre's film, which is constantly beginning again both on and off the screen, constitutes one attempt to use this composite medium in the service of nonalienated and critical reception. Lemaître worked toward this end by enlisting live action and speech. With *L'anticoncept*, Gil J Wolman shifts toward another modality of film reception. By turning to sounds of the animal and nonhuman and dispensing with filmed images, Wolman provokes an ethical confrontation for the spectator by initiating what he calls cinema's *phase physique* (physical phase).

THREE

SPASMODIC SPURTS OF WHITE LIGHT ON A SPHERE

WE ARE WATCHING A FILM about the screening of another film. We see a man and woman sit smiling in the front row of a darkened room, where they also watch a film. In addition to seeing the audience, which numbers in the twenties, we see the projector, its alternating black-and-white rhythm of light, and the physical space in which the film-within-the-film unfolds. From the vantage point of the camera and the fixed-frame single take, extending to sixty-five minutes, we are not privy to any of the images projected on the screen. The film we watch is a film about the screening of a film whose cinematic image remains outside the frame.

Approximately seventeen minutes into the screening, we see two audience members exit the space in which the film-within-the-film is projected. Another person leaves at twenty-four minutes. At minute twenty-five, the man and woman in the front row gather their things and depart. At minute twenty-eight someone else takes off, while two others move to the front-row seats previously occupied by the man and woman. At minute thirty-one, two more people leave, and a minute later another pair slip out. By minute forty-five, those who remain seem likely to stay (fig. 46). At this point, fourteen minutes remain. The final three and a half minutes of the film-within-the-film's sound track are nauseating: growls, chokes, coughs, and burps.

When the film-within-the-film ends and the lights go on, one of the event's organizers explains to the audience that they have just seen *L'anticoncept* by Gil J Wolman and that during the screening Wolman simultaneously produced another film: namely, *L'anticoncept à New York*, in which all those in attendance that evening in 1990 played a role.[1] The film we watch documents the production of this film. By enacting a

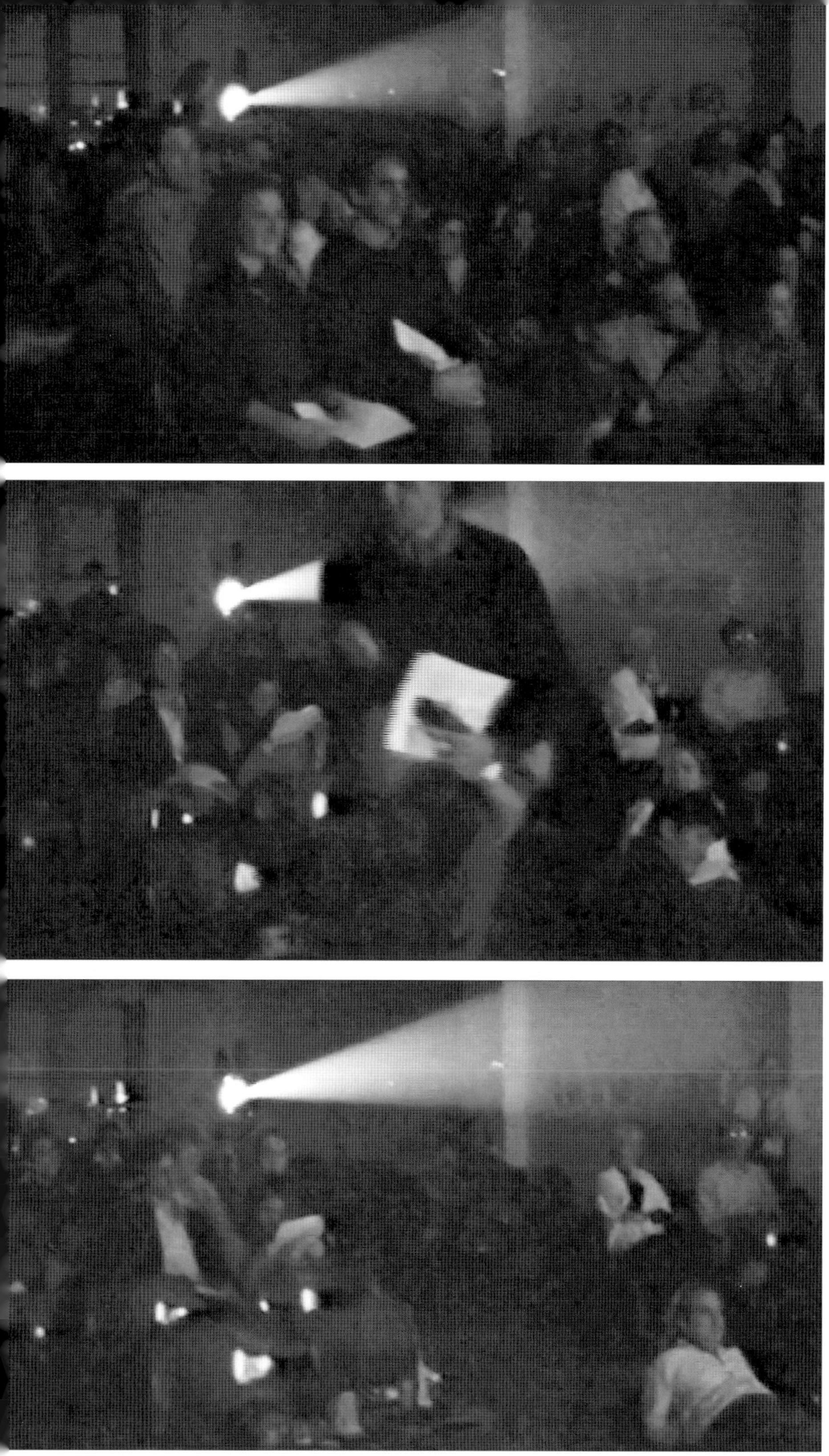

46. Gil J Wolman, *L'anticoncept à New York*, 1990. Frame enlargements.

displacement of attention from image and screen to audience and space, *L'anticoncept à New York* sets in relief the stakes of the original 1951 film for a contemporary viewer: *L'anticoncept*'s primary materials are its sound track and its alternating black-and-white rhythm of light.

Wolman completed *L'anticoncept* in September 1951, and it was first shown on February 11, 1952, at the Ciné-Club Avant-Garde 52 at the Musée de l'Homme in Paris. If Isidore Isou and Maurice Lemaître waged an attack on the traditional terms of spectatorship through markedly dissociative strategies—emphasizing disjunctures between speech and sound, sound and image, screen and space—Wolman similarly engaged the relation between speech and sound, screen and space. But he did so by totally abandoning the icono-indexical photographic image and altering the shape of the screen (fig. 47). Projected on a spherical, helium-filled weather balloon approximately two meters in diameter, *L'anticoncept* is a sound film without images: it alternates between brief black sequences and a white disk whose projected size matches as closely as possible the screen's circumference.[2]

L'anticoncept's sound track begins with a voice-over that invokes the history of moving images, starting with Emile Reynaud and the Lumière brothers sending Promio, their cameraman, to make the first traveling shots. To counter an understanding of film technology based on the "criterion of precision" and the reality effect produced in the wake of sound synchronization, the voice-over explains, "Isou destroyed photography in favor of sound; and one surprisingly saw, for example, how the most banal sea fishing takes on an unusual relief through a love story that unfolded on the sound track."[3] After describing the effect of a precise instance of *montage discrépant* (discrepant editing) in the second part of Isou's *Traité de bave et d'éternité* (On Venom and Eternity), the voice-over continues by differentiating Wolman's work:

> [*L'anticoncept*] produces an autonomous image that, beyond all symbolism, becomes the element that propagates movement external to photography. Asynchronous, with the unfolding atonic narration [*narration atonique*], this new antithetical movement counters each vocal inflection.

Part two of the sound track presents "TRITS," a Lettrist poem structured by a chorus (i.e., the repetition of "OVIL GTON"; fig. 48) and punctuated by whistling, phonemes, and other sounds pronounced by four superimposed voices, seemingly all Wolman's.[4] In part three, the longest part of the sound track, Wolman reads a disjointed story that he authored.[5] A female voice utters a few lines (e.g., "je voudrais courir toute la vie"; I would like to run endlessly), and one eventually hears the passing of

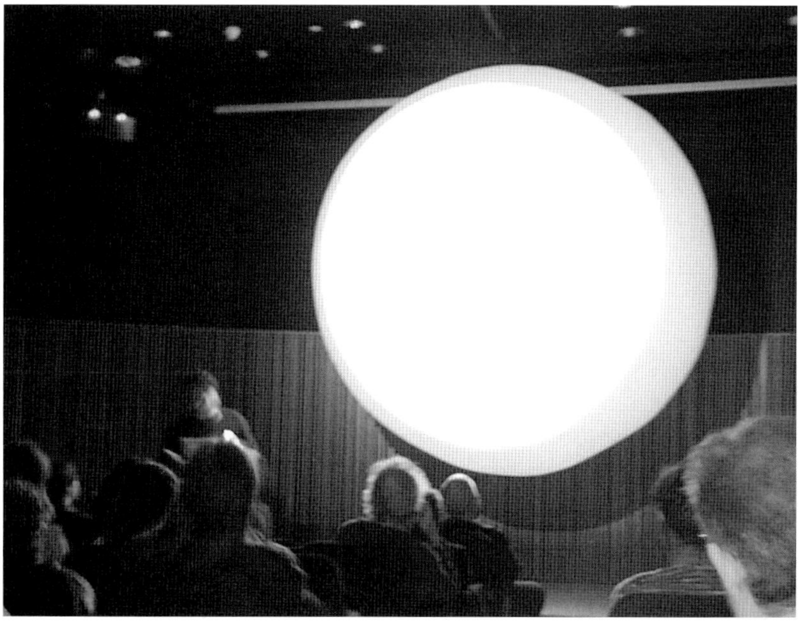

47. Gil J Wolman, *L'anticoncept*, 1951. Recreation at the Museu d'Art Contemporani de Barcelona, October 6, 2005. Photo: Jorge Ribalta.

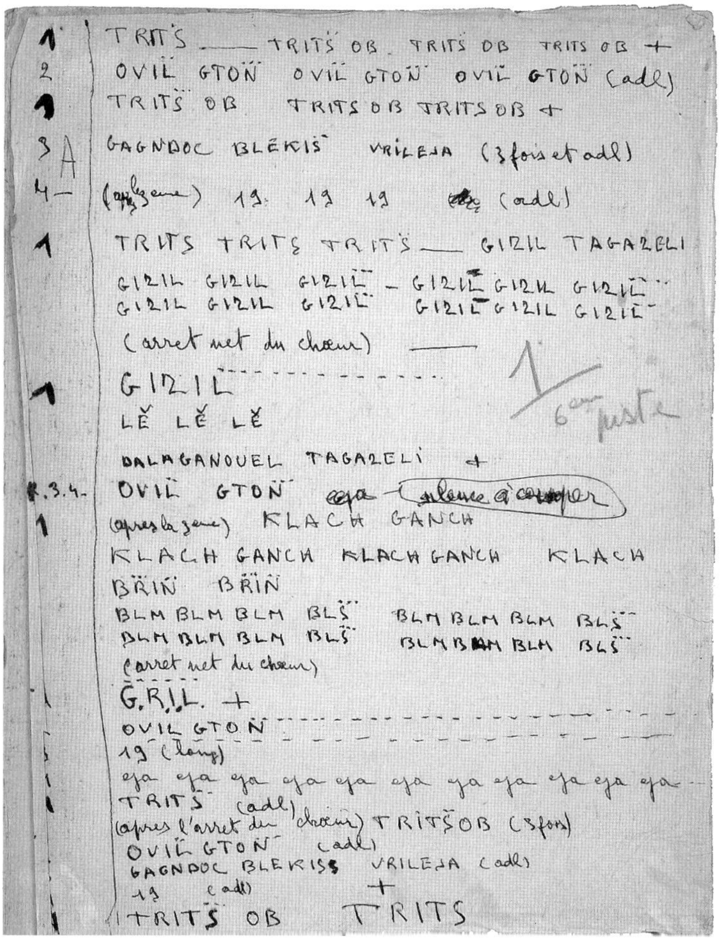

1 TRITS —— TRITS OB TRITS OB TRITS OB +
2 OVIL GTON OVIL GTON OVIL GTON (adl)
1 TRITS OB TRITS OB TRITS OB +
3 A GAGNDOC BLEKIS VRILEJA (3 fois et adl)
4 — (après 3ème) 19 19 19 (adl)
1 TRITS TRITS TRITS —— GIZIL TAGAZELI
GIZIL GIZIL GIZIL — GIZIL GIZIL GIZIL
GIZIL GIZIL GIZIL GIZIL GIZIL GIZIL
(arret net du choeur) ——
1 GIZIL
LĚ LĚ LĚ
DALAGANOUEL TAGAZELI +
.3.4. OVIL GTON silence à couper
1 (après la 3ème) KLACH GANCH
KLACH GANCH KLACH GANCH KLACH
BRIN BRIN
BLM BLM BLM BLS BLM BLM BLM BLS
BLM BLM BLM BLS BLM BLM BLM BLS
(arret net du choeur)
G.R.I.L. +
OVIL GTON
19 (long)
ga ga ga ga ga ga ga ga ga ga ga
TRITS (adl)
(après l'arret du choeur) TRITS OB (3 fois)
OVIL GTON (adl)
GAGNDOC BLEKISS VRILEJA (adl)
19 (adl) +
TRITS OB TRITS

48. Gil J Wolman, *TRITS*, 1951. Manuscript for *L'anticoncept*.

a train or subway, which creates the effect of a more extensive acoustic space. Finally, after a short "Post-scriptum," the film ends with approximately three and a half minutes of superimposed *mégapneumie*, what Wolman elsewhere describes as a *poésie physique* (physical poetry) that is based on breath, rather than on the letter as with Isou, and that explores the use of "all human sounds" (I return to this subject below).[6] Because it was recorded directly, the *mégapneumie* was not represented in the film's script, which was first published in *Ion* in April 1952. Moreover, in no part of the film does the rhythm of the alternating black-and-white sequences mimic or redouble the pacing of the sound track.

In 1952, *L'anticoncept*'s critical reception was as scant as it was varied. A writer for *Le Figaro* explained, "You suppress the image and you keep the sound, and what 'sound'! . . . sneers, strangulations, gurgles, onomatopoeia."[7] Five days later, again in the pages of *Le Figaro*, the same critic cites Woman's defense of his film following the public exodus from the initial screening:

> While it is true that the audience left the theater during the screening . . . this departure was motivated precisely by the physical intensity of my images [because] never were images and rhythms so flagrant as in *L'anticoncept*.[8]

The critic, though, takes issue with the artist's use of the term *images* to refer to what he calls "simple spasmodic spurts of white light on a sphere."[9]

In *Cinéma* 52, a certain "Dr. Philm" provided a more evenhanded account. He offered an overview of recent experimental films, making reference to both Isou's and Lemaître's work. With regard to *L'anticoncept*, he explains:

> A nonnarrative sound track, a kind of "interior monologue," including physiological noise and as if "musicalized"; an image track formed by the irregular alternation of black and white circles projected on a spherical screen. This "light music" bathes the theater and creates in the viewer a "physical movement." . . . To the objective and fixed concept, [Wolman] opposes the anticoncept "subjective and variable through the spectators' recations."[10]

Here the critic alludes to the final part of Wolman's "Avant propos" (in part one of the film's sound track), in which the filmmaker puts forth his theory regarding spectators' subjective response to his film. Nevertheless, Dr. Philm concludes, "visually insufficient, his experiment is to be resumed."[11]

Experienced as a beam of light intermittently interrupted by brief black sequences, *L'anticoncept*'s rhythm eventually includes short bursts of accelerated stroboscopic effects. Such effects, however, are not sustained in the way that would come to characterize the flicker films of the following decade.[12] The *Figaro* critic's "spasmodic spurts" are more like periodic disturbances to the steadier rhythm established at the film's outset, a rhythm more aligned with the blinking of an eye.

By negating the virtual space of diegesis as well as the icono-indexical images that remained in Isou's and Lemaître's work of the preceding months, *L'anticoncept* provided no alternatives to the space and time in which it unfolded. If one closed one's eyes or turned away from the screen, no part of the action or image would be missed. Like hearing something the source of which one cannot see, one can experience the rhythm of *L'anticoncept* with one's eyes shut. To this end, Wolman explains:

> The spectators who closed their eyes perceived the movement through the eyelids. Even those who turned around could not escape: the movement became one with the space [*le mouvement faisait corps à la salle*].[13]

In Wolman's final phrase, "le mouvement faisait corps à la salle," the use of the preposition *à* renders the phrase ambiguous, even grammatically incorrect. Had Wolman written, "le mouvement faisait corps *avec* la salle," the statement would have suggested something like *mouvement* and *salle* (theater) becoming one, a kind of unified body or *corps*. Whether *à* was used deliberately is less at issue than the fact that Wolman's phrase suggests that *salle* refers not only to the architectural space of the theater but also to the physical bodies (*corps*) that make up the *salle* (audience). In this way, the film's movement of light is posited as a direct contact with the spectators' bodies. This makes sense given how the visual field extends beyond the screen and toward a spatially enveloping condition: the light sequences pass through our eyelids and we experience the alternating rhythm, a movement external to film's usual photographic images, a movement that at once serves as filmic illusion's conditions of possibility.

In this context, I also want to draw attention to *L'anticoncept*'s actual filmstrip. When we examine the filmstrip we see a transparent disk framed in black (fig. 49). The circular composition mimics the framing of early cinema's peephole shots. Peephole films constituted one of the many steps along the way toward the centering of the cinematic spectator. As Noël Burch explains, "Through the alternation of views of the watcher and the watched, spectators were given their first, very simple lesson . . . in identifying with the camera, since the voyeur on the screen is the spectator's obvious surrogate."[14] Keyholes, telescopes, magnifying lenses, and other optical devices made frequent and flagrant film appearances

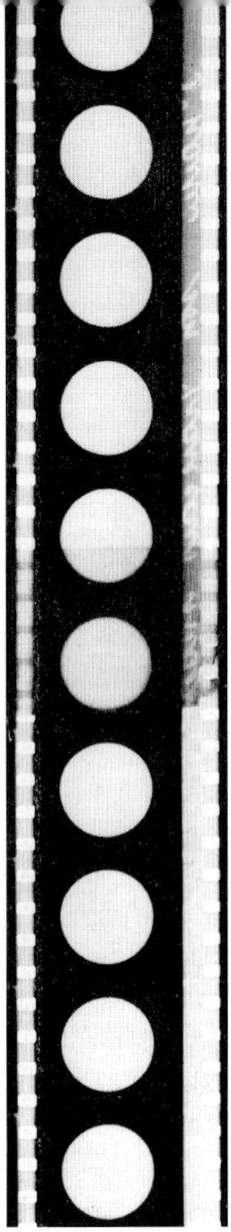

49. Gil J Wolman, *L'anticoncept*, 1951. Filmstrip detail.

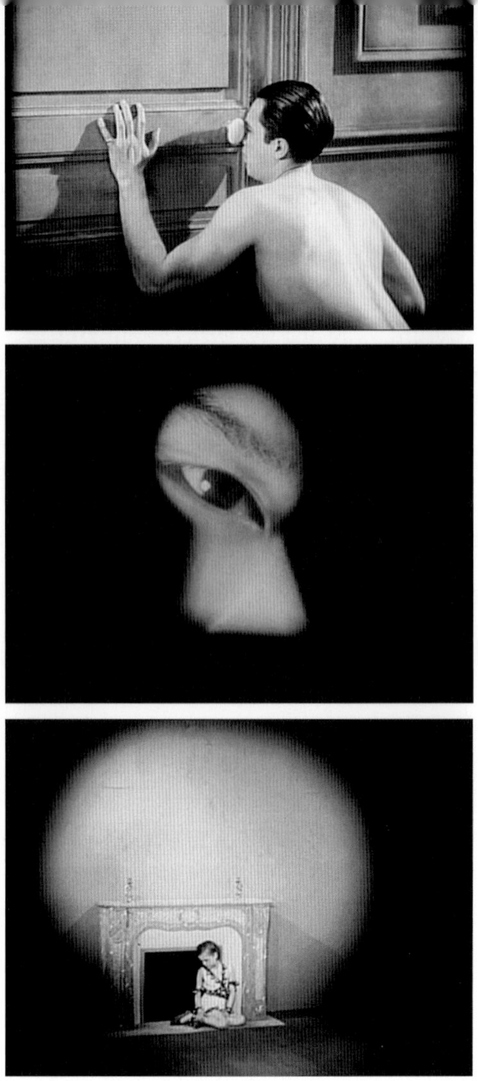

50. Jean Cocteau, *Le sang d'un poète*, 1930. Frame enlargements.

in the years 1901–1906, and the voyeuristic principle instituted by these sequences eventually became embedded in the cinematic apparatus and in the very syntax of narrative film. Elsewhere Burch writes, "The primitive cinema often said out loud what the IMR [institutional mode of representation] would contrive to say *sotto voce*."[15] The dominant mode of film production eventually secured a subject position in concert with the model of the Cartesian camera obscura, whereby the spectator observes a projection that is taken to be exterior and to exist independent of herself or himself. In short, the projection does not implicate the spectator's bodily subjectivity.

Avant-garde filmmakers such as Jean Cocteau, whose work Wolman would have undoubtedly known, would mine the devices and images of early cinema as a way to counter dominant narrative trends in the interwar years.[16] For instance, Cocteau includes a keyhole sequence in the second part of *Le sang d'un poète* (The Blood of a Poet, 1930; fig. 50). During the protagonist's journey in the hall of the Hôtel des Folies-dramatiques, he peeks into various rooms whose scenes recall the images of early cinema.[17] *L'anticoncept*'s "peephole," whose transparency allows light to pass through the filmstrip and flash into the theater, goes beyond mere morphological resemblance to the circular and keyhole frames of these earlier shots. Wolman's use of a weather balloon, together with a palpitating rhythm of light that evokes a blinking eye, relates his film to the militarized perception that weather balloons, and balloons more generally, represent. As a result, the film's circular frame evokes another type of peephole, one inscribed with cross-hair marks.

EYELESS VISION

Balloons have a long history in relation to visual imaging and war, forming part of what Paul Virilio identifies as the development of an "eyeless vision" that has used as its support various platforms, including camera-kites, camera-pigeons, and camera-balloons, all of which predate the use of cameras on reconnaissance aircraft.[18] Such an eyeless vision, Virilio maintains, developed from the military line of aim: "the ideal alignment of a look which, starting from the eye, passes through the peep-hole and the sights and on to the target object."[19] Aerial observation balloons were used in World War I, where they facilitated observation behind enemy lines (World War I was the last conflict to use manned observation aerostats). During both world wars, barrage balloons were deployed for antiaircraft defense operations, and in the 1940s the British and Japanese further experimented with the use of balloons for offensive bombing operations (fig. 51).

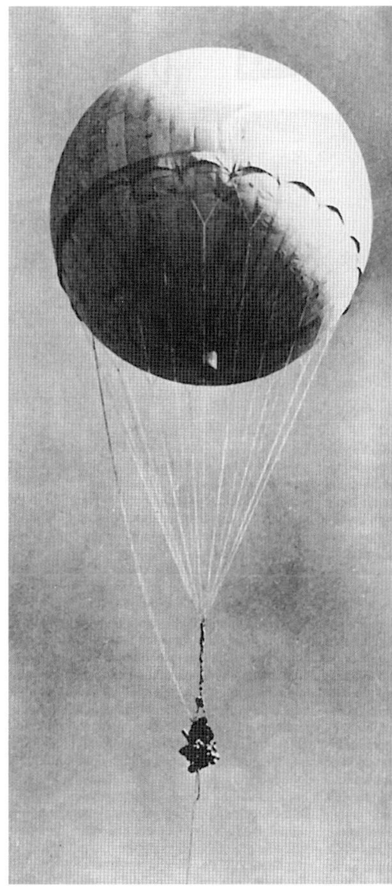

51. World War II Japanese balloon bomb reinflated at Moffett Field, California, after having been shot down by a US Navy aircraft, 1945. Image: US Army.

Weather balloons (or sounding balloons), one of which formed the actual screen support for Wolman's film, also form part of the history of the military's use of aerostats.[20] Beyond the meteorological data they collect, the weather balloon's material form—a sphere generally made

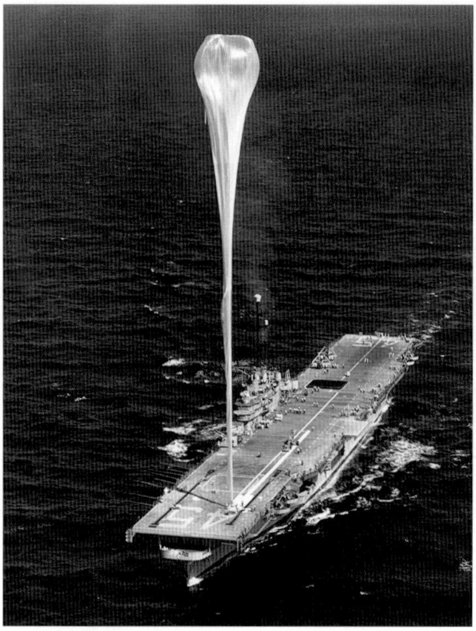

52. USS *Valley Forge* (CVS-45). Ten-million-cubic-foot Winzen research balloon on the carrier's flight deck just prior to launching, during Operation Skyhook, Refly "B," January 30, 1960. The balloon carried scientific devices to measure and record primary cosmic rays at altitudes of eighteen to twenty-two miles. Photo: US Navy.

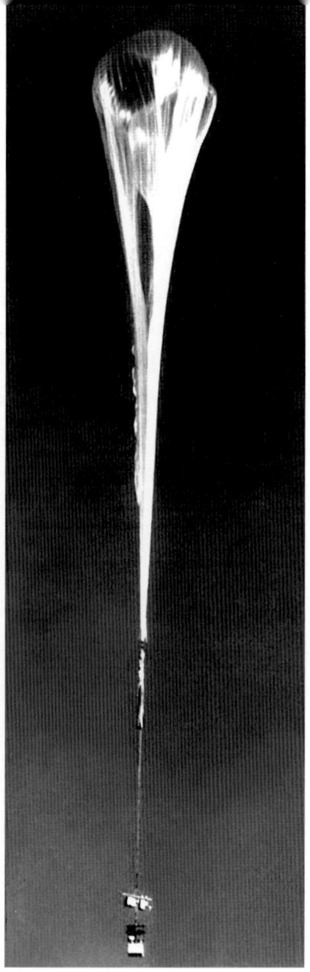

53. High-altitude reconnaissance balloon with HYAC panoramic camera. National Reconnaissance Office, Image 1400041726.

of flexible latex rubber and filled with hydrogen or helium—has been used for reconnaissance, gathering both aural and visual information. For example, in 1947 the US Air Force's Project Mogul used weather balloons for the long-distance detection of sound waves generated by nuclear blasts. Not successful in practice, the Mogul balloons also resulted in various reports of UFO sightings by the public. At the time that Wolman produced *L'anticoncept*, also coincident with the Korean War, the RAND Corporation was steeped in research on balloon observation systems.[21] RAND's development of unmanned balloons contributed to various other US Air Force projects, including Gopher, Moby Dick, and Genetrix, in which weather balloons were outfitted with cameras and repurposed as reconnaissance platforms (figs. 52–53). In the case of Genetrix, the air force launched actual balloon operations over the Soviet Union in the fraught context of the Cold War.[22]

L'anticoncept exceeds the materials of cinema as an art and the disciplinary dimension of its architecture. Wolman's film thus goes beyond the institutional forums and related concerns that drive Lemaître's practice. More specifically, Lemaître's *syncinéma* worked to dissolve the distinction between the space of the theater and the space of/in the screen through the spectators' and cinema staff's participation. But the projected image still maintains the frontal subject-object relation that defines the primary axis of conventional theater and cinema. Consequently, the direction and placement of the image is experienced as consistent with a cinematic convention: theatrical projection. By using a weather balloon as a screen, Wolman engages the history of a militarized perception that forms cinema's dialectical counterpart. Where classical cinema displaces bodily reception through the spectator's diegetic absorption in narrative and illusionism, the weather balloon's "eyeless vision" similarly uncouples vision from the body, but here the camera sees in one's stead.[23] In short, traditional cinematic reception and militarized vision each derealize bodily and embodied perception, albeit to distinct but at times interrelated ends.

I would like to return to Wolman's phrase regarding how his film's movement *faisait corps à la salle*, as well as his unconventional use of *à* in this context. The French language employs the preposition *à* together with *corps* in the context of the colloquial phrase *corps à corps*: body-to-body or hand-to-hand. Describing physical aggression and the contact between bodies, *corps à corps* is primarily used in the context of fighting and combat.[24] Wolman's use of *à* rather than *avec* may be deliberate given the weather balloon's military resonances. With *L'anticoncept* Wolman achieves body-to-body physical proximity by using a spherical screen that pushes the surface of projection in the spectator's direction and encourages physical confrontation rather than diegetic absorption.[25] Rather than constitute the enabling technology for vision at a distance, Wolman redirects his screen toward bodies that see, occupying the space in front of the conventional screen. *L'anticoncept* inaugurates what Wolman designates as cinema's *phase physique* (physical phase).[26]

If the rhythm of the palpitating light, together with the weather balloon/eye, engaged in a type of body-to-body contact with the viewing public, the attendant sound track put another type of bodily contact, and another understanding and experience of the body, into play.[27] How effectively *le mouvement faisait corps à la salle* depends not only on the light projection and the physicality of the screen, but also on the sonic component of the visual-acoustic envelope the film creates. Recall the words of the *Figaro* critic: "You suppress the image and you keep the sound, and what 'sound'!" It is to the sounds of *L'anticoncept* that I will now turn.

ATTACK THE LETTER

Alongside his fellow Lettrists, Wolman does not locate the voice in an image of a body on the screen, nor does he inscribe within it the grammatical rules and prosody that govern and motivate speech. After the initial "Avant-propos" and "TRITS," *L'anticoncept* launches into approximately forty-six minutes of narrative fragments. The voice-over's incessant speech—the verbal bursts, abrupt shifts in volume and pace, and atonic delivery—contributes in large measure to the sense of an aural assault. Wolman introduces gaps between a phrase (*énoncé*) and its expected emotional inflection (*énonciation*), violently separating the conceptual content of language from the rhythm, stress, and intonation that usually connect speech. Such disjunctions are marked by the words' spatialized distribution in the film's script (fig. 54). Moreover, the voice-over inserts gaps between smaller linguistic units, such as syllables. In so doing, it engenders semantic confusion (i.e., do the words represent a question or a command?) as well as uncertainty at the level of communicative intent (is the speaker ironic or sarcastic, angry or moved?).

Approximately forty-nine minutes into the film, Wolman further disavows the prosodic context of speech by emphasizing the materiality of recording. The sound track seems to have been repeatedly slowed down and then sped up. If Isou, in *Traité*, exploited the faulty transfer of sound from vinyl disks to the optical sound track, and Lemaître played sound in reverse, Wolman here deploys the variability of the Magnetophone to foreground technological reproduction through distortions in pitch and speed. He further demonstrates that sound recording does not faithfully reproduce the original acoustic event or its unique spatiotemporal perception. These forty-some seconds of tape manipulation apparently constitute the sole known instance in which Wolman deploys the Magnetophone for experimental-productive ends.[28] Even so, the cumulative effect of the sound track's parts establishes an acoustic representation of space, wherein variations in the microphone's distance from a recorded sound source prove key to our perception of the recorded sound's spatial effects.[29] The four voices in "TRITS," the dialogic inscription of a female voice, and the sound of a passing train combine to produce the aural perception of a broader acoustic surround, thereby establishing a conceptual distance between the listener-spectator and the sound track. With the concluding *mégapneumie*, however, we hear the emphatic movement of lips in the act of pronunciation, the rumbling

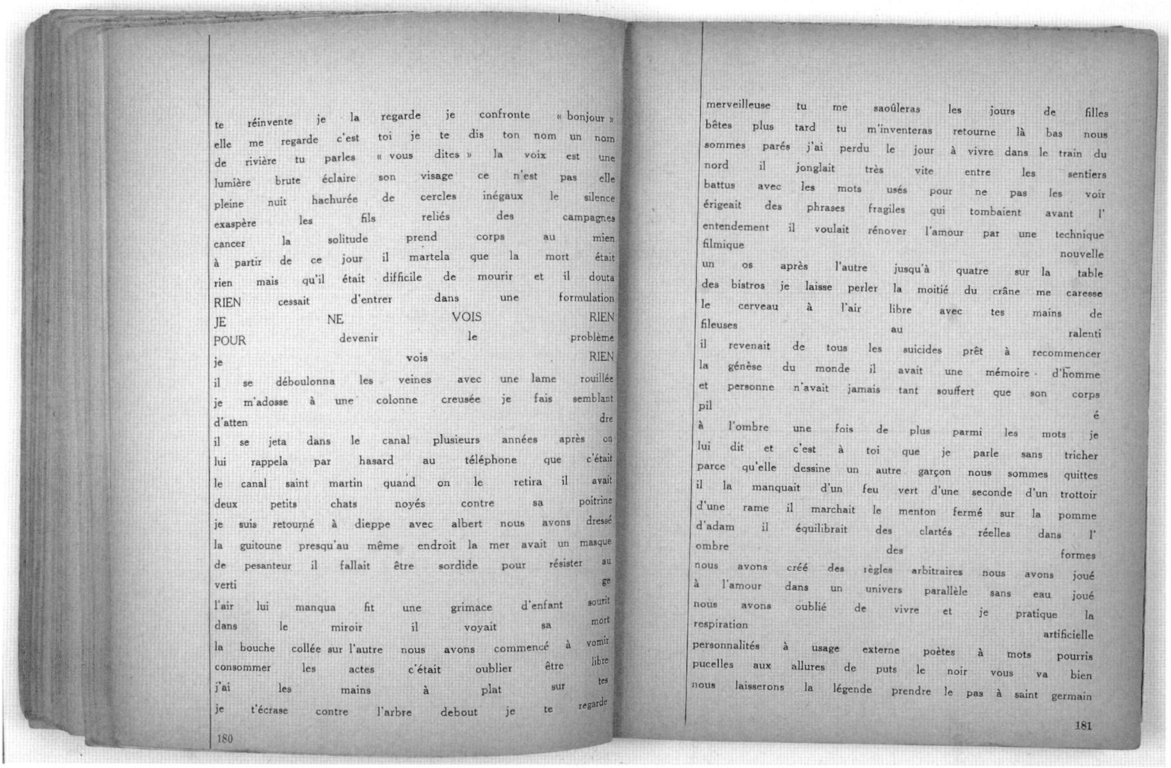
te réinvente je la regarde je confronte « bonjour »
elle me regarde c'est toi je te dis ton nom un nom
de rivière tu parles « vous dites » la voix est une
lumière brute éclaire son visage ce n'est pas elle
pleine nuit hachurée de cercles inégaux le silence
exaspère les fils reliés des campagnes
cancer la solitude prend corps au mien
à partir de ce jour il martela que la mort était
rien mais qu'il était difficile de mourir et il douta
RIEN cessait d'entrer dans une formulation
JE NE VOIS RIEN
POUR devenir le problème
je vois RIEN
il se déboulonna les veines avec une lame rouillée
je m'adosse à une colonne creusée je fais semblant
d'atten dre
il se jeta dans le canal plusieurs années après on
lui rappela par hasard au téléphone que c'était
le canal saint martin quand on le retira il avait
deux petits chats noyés contre sa poitrine
je suis retourné à dieppe avec albert nous avons dressé
la guitoune presqu'au même endroit la mer avait un masque
de pesanteur il fallait être sordide pour résister au
verti ge
l'air lui manqua fit une grimace d'enfant sourit
dans le miroir il voyait sa mort
la bouche collée sur l'autre nous avons commencé à vomir
consommer les actes c'était oublier être libre
j'ai les mains à plat sur tes
je t'écrase contre l'arbre debout je te regarde
180

merveilleuse tu me saoûleras les jours de filles
bêtes plus tard tu m'inventeras retourne là bas nous
sommes parés j'ai perdu le jour à vivre dans le train du
nord il jonglait très vite entre les sentiers
battus avec les mots usés pour ne pas les voir
érigeait des phrases fragiles qui tombaient avant l'
entendement il voulait rénover l'amour par une technique
filmique nouvelle
un os après l'autre jusqu'à quatre sur la table
des bistros je laisse perler la moitié du crâne me caresse
le cerveau à l'air libre avec tes mains de
fileuses au ralenti
il revenait de tous les suicides prêt à recommencer
la génèse du monde il avait une mémoire d'homme
et personne n'avait jamais tant souffert que son corps
pil é
à l'ombre une fois de plus parmi les mots je
lui dit et c'est à toi que je parle sans tricher
parce qu'elle dessine un autre garçon nous sommes quittes
il la manquait d'un feu vert d'une seconde d'un trottoir
d'une rame il marchait le menton fermé sur la pomme
d'adam il équilibrait des clartés réelles dans l'
ombre des formes
nous avons créé des règles arbitraires nous avons joué
à l'amour dans un univers parallèle sans eau joué
nous avons oublié de vivre et je pratique la
respiration artificielle
personnalités à usage externe poètes à mots pourris
pucelles aux allures de puts le noir vous va bien
nous laisserons la légende prendre le pas à saint germain
181

54. Gil J Wolman, film script for *L'anticoncept*, 1951, published in *Ion*, April 1952.

current of breath as it hits the microphone. We also hear Wolman gag, pant, vomit, and screech.

The *mégapneumie* are central to understanding the uniqueness of Wolman's film. Its distinction from the work of Isou and Lemaître does not rest solely on the absence of images or the use of a spherical screen. Wolman began to develop his *mégapneumie* in 1950 and publicly asserted the originality of his poetic work through declarations such as: "Isou was an end. / In the beginning there was Wolman."[30] This claim begins his essay "Introduction à Wolman," which was published in the first volume of *Ur: Cahiers pour un dictat culturel*, a magazine edited by Lemaître. It evokes the opening of Genesis, as well as the first line of the Gospel of St. John: "In the beginning was the Word, and the Word was with God, and the Word was God." Ironically the Lettrists, like the Dadaists before them, countered the logocentricism of speech, as well as the word's onto-theological underpinnings, even as they aspired to harness all types of writing and sound in the service of a communicative immediacy beyond mediation.[31] Indeed, Isou considered the word "the first stereotype," claiming the letter as the new ground by which to achieve true communication.[32]

With his development of *mégapneumie*, Wolman called into question Isou's valorization of the letter and argued that Isou's poetic system—as first published in his *Introduction à une nouvelle poésie et à une nouvelle*

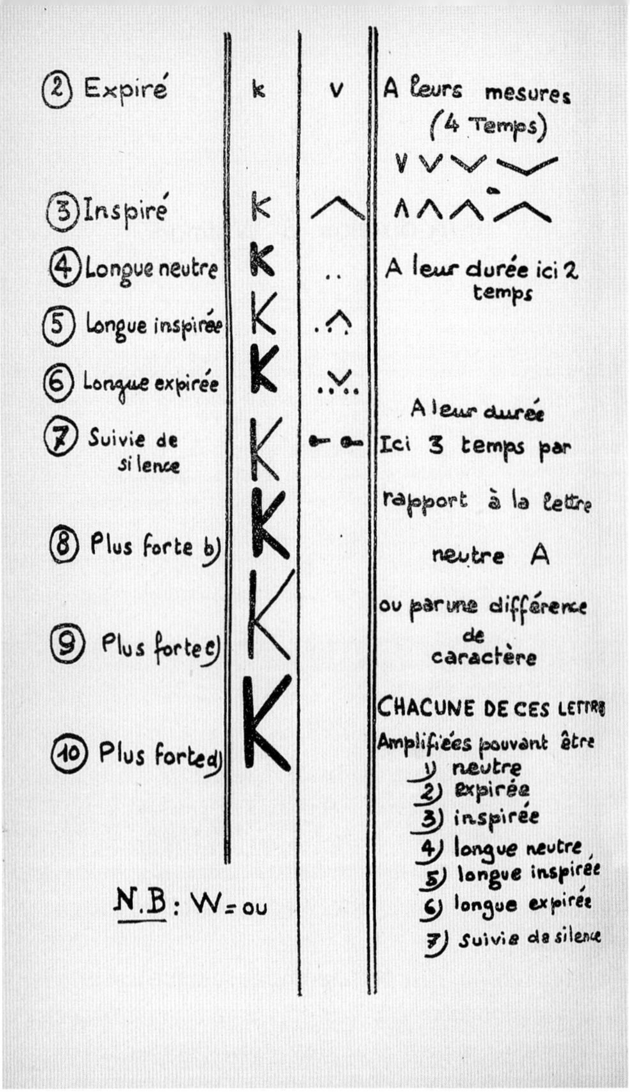

55. Gil J Wolman, "Introduction à Wolman," *Ur*, no. 1 (Paris, 1950).

musique (Introduction to a New Poetry and New Music, 1947)—remained tethered to the nineteen letters of the Greek alphabet. "One must attack the letter," he insists.[33] At the precocious age of twenty-one, like many of his cohort, Wolman theorizes a new poetry based on breath (*souffle*) that also explores the use of "all human sounds."[34] In "Introduction à Wolman," he describes how to separate vowels from consonants and consonants from their "breath," which he proposes to "structuralize." With vowels, he proposes to invert the process: "breath becomes structural, an *in-itself* vis-à-vis the vowel."[35] Wolman's graphic notation for his new system represents the acoustic possibilities for what he calls *consonnes désintégrées* (disintegrated consonants) as well as vowels, each inflected by a different quality of breath. For example, the conventional phonetic transcription of *k* is *ka*. In order to obtain a neutral *k*, Wolman segregates the *a* by inventing the notation *k (a)*. The adjacent table represents how the neutral *k* may be modified by the particular quality of breath with which it is enunciated—from short expiration to long expiration, from short inspiration to long inspiration (fig. 55).[36] Wolman thereby rids the consonant of the vowel that usually accompanies its phonetic pronunciation and transcription.

By insisting on a model of breath (*pneuma*), the *mégapneumie* may seem to seek the purity of voice prior to language's articulation and linguistic dispersion. Echoing this end, Wolman explains, "Before becoming sonically modified and fully defined, phonemes are nothing but columns of air. / Vibrating movement is therefore not the first agent exciting tone (*timbre*): this function belongs to the air current."[37] Yet Wolman's breath is one that takes place.[38] If "in the beginning there was Wolman," Wolman's originary speech is always already marked by the body and addressed to another's body. Rather than unite breath to voice and voice to spirit, Wolman's *poésie physique* takes the listening subject to the body, to the seemingly animal and nonhuman.[39]

With *L'anticoncept*, Wolman deviates from his pneumatic writing system, which codified *mégapneumie* production, in order to produce the "Improvisations—mégapneumes" with which he ends the film.[40] Because of his insistence on the body and the force of bodily sounds, he abandoned the graphic representation provided by written poetic scores, which were so indispensable to Isou, Lemaître, and François Dufrêne (who in these years was still writing down his poems).[41] Wolman's mature *mégapneumie* abandon written notation and in so doing further reject the propositional content (i.e., concepts) and conceptual understanding usually granted to the production and reception of speech. Wolman explains in a passage worth citing in full:

> Sound-language establishes a conceptual correspondence. The *mégapneumie*, which is a-linguistic, also refuses the tone [*sonorité*] of human language commonly used at present. It searches for the maximum nonconceptual possibilities and opposes sound-language correspondence in order not to target only hearing, not to strike the intellect but the nervous system.[42]

In denaturalizing the correspondence between concept and sound, sense and phonic signifier, the *mégapneumie* insist on speech's materiality, aiming to strike the nervous system directly, through the vibrations of sound.

As discussed in this volume's introduction, Lettrist poetry devised multiple ways to intone speech: with tongue clicks, hiccups, coughs, growls, and lisps. Isou and Lemaître each developed a bodily alphabet and at times indicated how a foot (for example) could produce the sound of a letter. They codified their alphabets through complex notation systems, which not only had recourse to international phonetic symbols but also incorporated original graphic signs.[43] While Isou and Lemaître at times used the body's extremities (e.g., arms, legs, feet) to create the sound of a new letter, Wolman's *mégapneumie* externalize sounds whose delivery begins within the body, and thus anterior to the modulation provided for by the organs of speech, the technical site of mediation between language and the body. Nevertheless, Isou would disavow the *mégapneumie*'s innovation vis-à-vis his own poetic conception, claiming that Wolman's work "did not lead to any novelty in the aesthetic manners of our territory" and "remains within the chiseling [i.e., Isou's] framework."[44] Yet Isou gives the lie to his attempt to discredit Wolman's poetic achievement when he recalls that, among the Lettrists, Wolman was "the most unpleasant, most ridiculed in the spaces, the one that was most despised."[45] Lemaître would also affirm, "Wolman justified, at the same time, the accusations of 'beautiful lettrism' made against Isidore Isou by certain among us."[46] Dufrêne echoes these words when he writes, "[Wolman] knew and wrote in spite of Isou: only breath founds the poem—rhythm and cry, the cry, content contained, until here, of the poem; of joy, love, anguish, horror, hatred, but a scream."[47]

Through his insistence on the bodily materiality of the acoustic signifier's production, Wolman produced a *poésie physique* that, I argue, was informed by the late work of Antonin Artaud. Whether Wolman was reading Artaud directly or having his ideas filtered through his friends Jean-Louis Brau and Dufrêne, there is no doubt that Wolman contrived his *mégapneumie* in the wake of the howls, cries, screams, and glossolalia that interrupted not only Artaud's final public performance, "Histoire

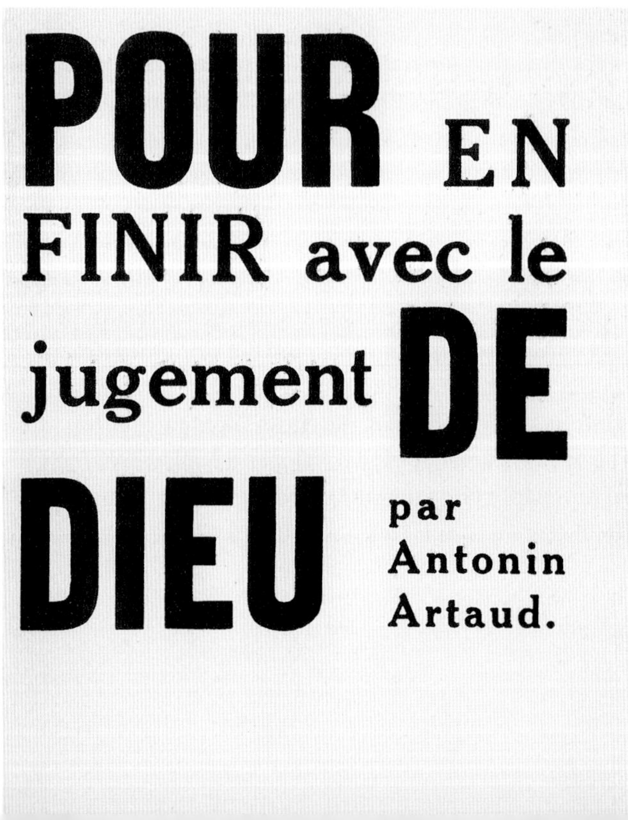

56. Antonin Artaud, *Pour en finir avec le jugement de Dieu* (Paris: Éditions K, 1948).

vécue d'Artaud-Mômo" (The History Lived by Artaud-Mômo) at the Théâtre du Vieux-Colombier on January 13, 1947, but also his sound recordings for radio.[48]

In November 1947, Artaud received an invitation from Radiodiffusion Française to prepare a broadcast for a new program titled *La voix des poètes* (The Voice of Poets), under the direction of Fernand Pouey. Artaud's now infamous *Pour en finir avec le jugement de Dieu* (To Have Done with the Judgment of God; fig. 56) was recorded in two sessions with the collaboration of Maria Caserès, Roger Blin, Paule Thévenin, and a *bruitage* of percussion instruments. Its broadcast was scheduled for February 2, 1948. Taking up subjects from American capitalism to Tarahumara Indian dance, the work's five parts were interspersed with various noise effects, resulting in a cacophony of language, screams, and outbursts.

Given *Pour en finir*'s vitriolic critique of rationality, militarism, and bourgeois society in the wake of World War II, Wladimir Porché (Pouey's boss) banned the radio poem the day prior to transmission.[49] On account of the ban, Artaud wrote to Jean Paulhan:

> the sounds will not be heard
> the resounding xylophony,
> the screams, guttural noises and the voice,
> all of which would have at last constituted a first grinding-over of the Theater of Cruelty.
> This is a DISASTER for me.[50]

Pour en finir develops in radio Artaud's declarations from some twenty years earlier about what he called a Theater of Cruelty. His attempt to transform word into action is key to an understanding of his legacy. The primary objective for theater as for poetry, on which their effectiveness depends according to Artaud, is their condition of possibility: "the action of movement and spoken things, *never reproduced twice*."[51] For Artaud language's *force* derives not from the successful fulfillment of conventions but from a dogged attempt to embody language in gesture, to harness graphic traces toward performative ends.[52] He hoped to reduce the difference between speech and bodily gesture, force and form.[53] By the time of his final interview on February 28, 1948, Artaud confessed, "I have been haunted for so long, *haunt-ed* by a kind of writing that is not the norm. I would like to write outside of grammar, to find a means of expression beyond words. And I occasionally believe that I am very close to that expression . . . but everything pulls me back to the norm."[54]

In Wolman's early notes and essays, writing, words, letters, and phonemes take on the oppressive role they also held for Artaud. In an unpublished manuscript dating from the early 1950s, Wolman maintains:

Writing is approximative
A word lying down dead
Writing codifies symbols
Mégapneumie achieves the impossible:
Transmutation of the primary matter of sound in sonic primary matter[55]

With his *mégapneumie*, Wolman produced singular somatic sounds that interrupt discursive language and its indicative function through a concerted desublimation. Yet when one considers the recordings of the *mégapneumie* in relation to Artaud, one encounters a significant difference. With machine recording, the minimization of the difference between word and gesture (essential to Artaud's poetics) confronts its opposite: the separation of voice from the body. Artaud continually struggled against the appropriation of his speech, even when the voice of the body, his body as a ghost, returned through his recorded voice in *Pour en finir avec le jugement de Dieu*. The *mégapneumie* similarly produce an exteriorization of the voice: their recording entails the "theft of the voice and a disappearance of the body."[56] If Artaud pushed language toward embodiedness, one paradoxical aspect of his spectral legacy is the experimental recording of unconventional bodily sounds.[57] In the case of *L'anticoncept*'s concluding minutes, the effect of the superimposed *mégapneumie* is exacerbated by the microphone's technological mediation, which picks up bodily sounds and amplifies them. The illusion of spatial distance between the listener and the recorded speech event is effectively breached: Wolman vomits into our ear as he vomits into the microphone.

ANTICONCEPTUAL ART

The Commission de Contrôle des Films Cinématographiques banned *L'anticoncept* on April 2, 1952. An official form letter in Wolman's archive, on which the handwritten traces "*Non Commercial*" (noncommercial) and "*Interdit*" (banned) can be read, is the only public record that documents the ban (fig. 57). The film remains, in accordance with the law, prohibited to this day.[58] A year after the film's premiere, Guy Debord writes, "*L'anticoncept* could not be screened since, even in noncommercial venues."[59] He observes that the film is "more offensive today than the images of Eisenstein, which frightened Europe for so long."[60] Around that time Debord also created a poster proposal for the film, of which only a photocopy remains (fig. 58).

Beyond its status as an imageless film, *L'anticoncept* was more than likely banned on account of Wolman's refusal of language's communicative function, as well as his use of disgusting bodily sounds. Wolman

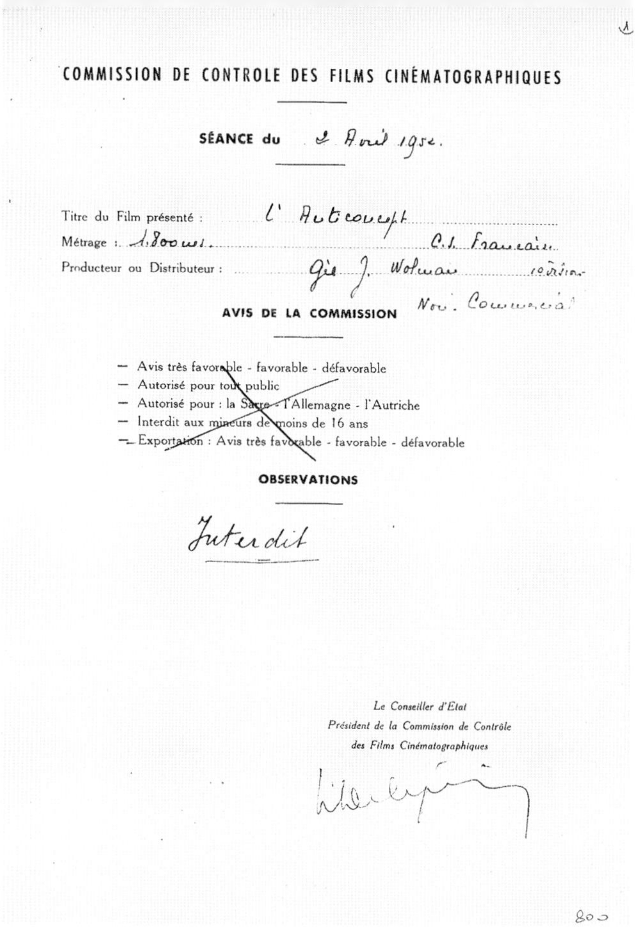

COMMISSION DE CONTROLE DES FILMS CINÉMATOGRAPHIQUES

SÉANCE du 2 Avril 1952.

Titre du Film présenté : L'Anticoncept

Métrage : 1.800 m.

Producteur ou Distributeur : Gil J. Wolman

AVIS DE LA COMMISSION

— Avis très favorable - favorable - défavorable
— Autorisé pour tout public
— Autorisé pour : la Sarre - l'Allemagne - l'Autriche
— Interdit aux mineurs de moins de 16 ans
— Exportation : Avis très favorable - favorable - défavorable

OBSERVATIONS

Interdit

Le Conseiller d'Etat
Président de la Commission de Contrôle
des Films Cinématographiques

57. Official form of the Commission de Contrôle des Films Cinématographiques, signed April 2, 1952.

further compounded such offenses to propriety by disavowing the "proper" conceptual distance that would conventionally separate a listener from such recorded sounds. In parallel with his *mégapneumie*, which ground poetry in the physicality of the body and liberate sound from the conceptual confines of language, *L'anticoncept* insists on an anticonceptual production and reception of language. On this point, Wolman is consistently clear: "Je n'ai guère quitté l'obsession d'attenter le concept" (I very rarely gave up the obsession of attacking the concept).[61]

What is exposed in the final minutes of the *L'anticoncept*'s sound track is a vocal experimentation that brings performative language back not to speech or even to writing (as in the work of Jacques Derrida) but to the body. It follows that Wolman's speechless voice does not claim the status of a sovereign subject, but rather, as evoked above, his nonspeaking body upsets the metaphysical dichotomies between body and spirit, the physical and the mental, on which an understanding of language and the performative traditionally depend. Wolman demonstrates how in

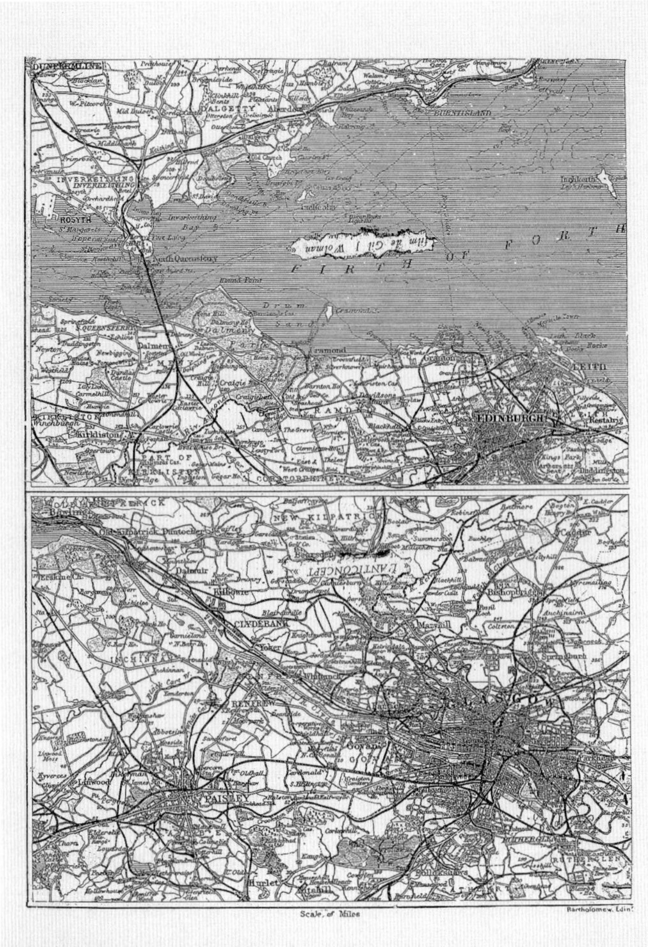

58. Guy Debord, proposal for a poster for *L'anticoncept*, n.d. Scan from copy; location of original unknown.

performance the body constitutes the organic basis of utterances, but he does so by casting the "speaking body" as one that resists verbalization through the *mégapneumie*'s sustained rejection of phonemes and words.[62] The film's sound track was offensive not only due to its content (which includes references to urine, foul smells, and corpses) but on account of the irruption of the body in the public space of cinema. At issue, then, is not only what kind of speech was censored, but how the very operation of the film's ban determined that the concluding *mégapneumie* should not be heard, based on certain norms that govern speech and secure one's status as a subject.[63]

In the case of film, the domain of speakability for the "voice in cinema" includes the conventions of voice-over in propaganda and newsreels as well as the dialogue and narrative in Hollywood films. The conventions also depend on a conceptual distance between the live body that hears and the voice in reproduction that produces speech.[64] Indeed, such sound-image relations in film secure the spectators' visual interpellation by reducing the noise of the apparatus, as well as omitting any voice that is "not pleasing to the ear."[65] Wolman's *mégapneumie* test the material and representational limits of the voice in cinema by insisting that the listening viewer recognize a voice outside the domain of legislated, conceptual, and commodified speech. Reflecting on instances of what she calls "impossible speech," Judith Butler explains, "To move outside the domain of speakability is to risk one's status as a subject." Such speech, she continues, includes "precisely the ramblings of the asocial, the rantings of the 'psychotic' that the rules that govern the domain of speakability produce, and by which they are continually haunted."[66] The scandal of Wolman's nonspeaking body thus arises more precisely from the tension between the recording's affirmation of the body and the politics of what it might have meant in 1952 to recognize this speechless voice of the other. To this end, Jacques Villeglé recalls Wolman's work and avows, "Wasn't the *détournement* of language's tonality the most effective synthetic attitude of a poet feeling the impossibility of writing poems after Auschwitz?"[67]

With *L'anticoncept*, the body and its speechless voice become the site of a release from representation (e.g., from writing, narrative, articulate speech), while demanding the cinema spectator's recognition of a voice that is exterior, different, other. Yet this voice penetrates them by infiltrating their bodies, their nervous system, literally, through the ear. By affirming a speech otherwise excluded from the realm of officially recognized speech, Wolman's improper use of the voice in cinema remains no less scandalous today. The *mégapneumie* institute a relation between a subject whose speech is excluded from the domain of speakability and a spectator who hears the monstrous gags, cries, and suffocations, which are reciprocated by the spectator's own bodily nausea at hearing these sounds.The concluding minutes of *L'anticoncept* thereby insist on a "common" corporeality that subtends speech and the subject and at once suggests that such sounds not be banished from the realm of recognizability or historical memory.[68]

L'anticoncept registers a specific set of historical and aesthetic stakes in relation to language. The sound track creates a breach in language, enacting a failure to effectively communicate, while its final minutes assert the voice of the body. Together with the flashing light and spherical screen, Wolman's nonspeaking voice challenges the epistemological comfort of the camera-obscura setting in cinema, further deconstructing its frontal subject-object relation by means of amplified bodily sounds. So, too, does the resulting lack of conceptual distance between the listener and

Wolman's nonspeaking voice differentiate his work from Debord's films, a subject I take up in the next chapter.[69] By the final minutes of *L'anticoncept*, the *mégapneumie* divest language of its conceptual meaning while maintaining its performative force. Under the guise of a *poésie physique*, Wolman demonstrates how to do things without words.[70]

FOUR

EROTICISM SHOULD OCCUR IN THE AUDIENCE

A SOUND FILM WITHOUT IMAGES: when someone speaks, the screen is white and filled with light; when no one speaks, the screen remains dark. Of the total running time, seventy-five minutes, only twenty minutes contain light and speech. The film is Guy Debord's *Hurlements en faveur de Sade* (Howls for Sade, 1952). And on this particular day, Sunday, March 1, 2009, I imagine that the grandeur of Lincoln Center's Walter Reade Theater is decidedly at odds with the ambiance of the Parisian ciné-clubs in which the film was originally shown.[1] At the Walter Reade, during *Hurlements*' black sequences, members of the audience begin to talk (myself and Ryan Holmberg included). Everyone talks at a moderate volume, except during the sequences of light and speech. During one black sequence, a member of the audience—frustrated, I gather, by the acoustic disturbances interrupting his aesthetic contemplation of the darkened screen—tells two men on the front left side of the auditorium to "shut up." Needless to say, his act of censure is not welcomed by others in attendance, who accost him with questions along the lines of "Do you really think an attitude of reverential silence is the best way to approach this film?"[2]

Thus my fellow viewers attempt, inevitably, to recapture what Debord once referred to as the first "very tumultuous showing of this film."[3] At some point during the screening, an audience member mobilizes the admittedly scant public to engage in song; they sing everything from the "Internationale" to "Born in the USA." Given *Hurlements*' notorious reception both then and now, one reviewer writes, "How can one recreate a scandal when the whole story is already known? Why replay a role that an audience had already played fifty years earlier?"[4] Another reviewer reports that the screening "came as close to inciting a riot as any movie

I have ever seen play out before an audience."[5] As the extemporaneous behavior continued, I could not help but think that what was being enacted was a desire for a lost avant-garde project. The spontaneity was decidedly forced.[6]

Shortly after I had these thoughts, a security officer from the Walter Reade entered and demanded that the impromptu actions be quelled; otherwise, the culprits would be asked to leave. From forced spontaneity to the enforcement of silence, I wondered whether the guard's appearance was a hoax: was she really invested with power, or was her entrance staged, an act scripted to recall *Hurlements*' first screening (or an intervention along the lines of Maurice Lemaître's professional spectators)? Either way, the historical specificity of the first screening's reception was reversed: in 1952, the ciné-club management stopped the film due to public outcry directed against it; in 2009, the film's devotees were reproached so as to maintain the film's integrity. But beyond the public's attempt to reproduce the contentious reception of a film they already supported, what the 2009 screening reveals is the active reception the film inevitably provokes. At the Walter Reade, the public felt they needed to "*do* something."[7] In this way, the event of *Hurlements* is less its imageless status than the historical discontinuities revealed at the moments of its reception, as well as the various scripted and unscripted actions that occurred on account of the film's first two screenings. It is to the historical context of *Hurlements*' emergence that I now turn.

ION TO *LES LÈVRES NUES*

Debord's first public appearance in print was his "Prolégomènes à tout cinéma futur" (Prolegomena to Any Future Cinema), which was included as a preface to the original script for his film *Hurlements en faveur de Sade* in the pages of *Ion*. At this point the script also included an image track (fig. 59). Published alongside other Lettrist writing on cinema, as well as the scripts for three other films, the short half-page prolegomena situates *Hurlements* within the Lettrist aesthetic in cinema as put forth primarily by Isidore Isou. Debord writes, "My film will remain among the most important in the history of the reductive hypostasis of cinema through the terrorist disorganization of the discrepant [editing]."[8] With the invocation of the "discrepant," Debord acknowledges his film's recourse to *montage discrépant* (discrepant editing), or what Isou first theorized as the purposeful nonsynchronization of sound and image in film in the pages of "Esthétique du cinéma" (which I address in the introduction and chapter 1).[9] While Debord's affiliation with Isou and the Lettrists often constitutes little more than a passing reference in the critical literature

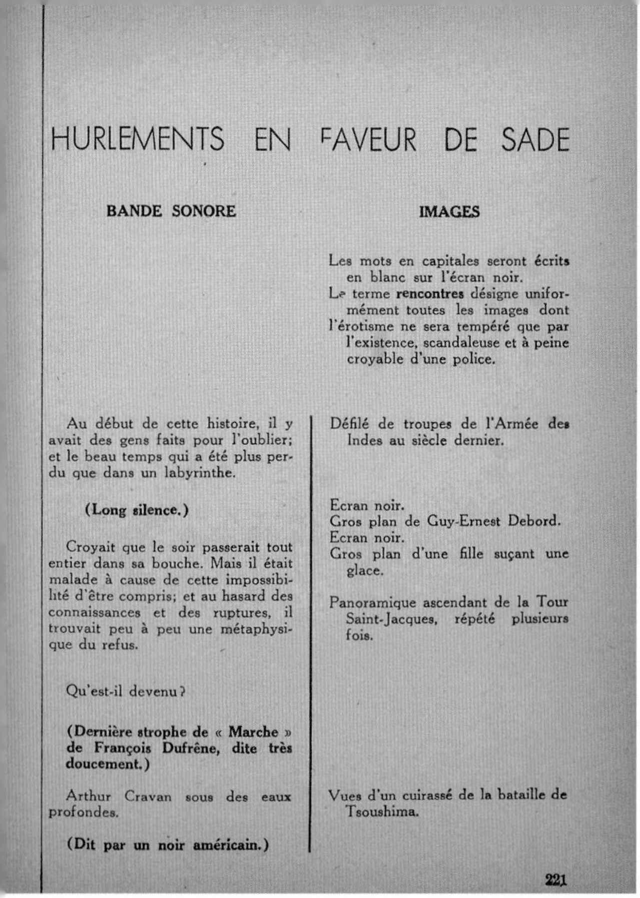

HURLEMENTS EN FAVEUR DE SADE

BANDE SONORE	IMAGES
	Les mots en capitales seront écrits en blanc sur l'écran noir. Le terme **rencontres** désigne uniformément toutes les images dont l'érotisme ne sera tempéré que par l'existence, scandaleuse et à peine croyable d'une police.
Au début de cette histoire, il y avait des gens faits pour l'oublier; et le beau temps qui a été plus perdu que dans un labyrinthe.	Défilé de troupes de l'Armée des Indes au siècle dernier.
(Long silence.)	Ecran noir. Gros plan de Guy-Ernest Debord. Ecran noir. Gros plan d'une fille suçant une glace.
Croyait que le soir passerait tout entier dans sa bouche. Mais il était malade à cause de cette impossibilité d'être compris; et au hasard des connaissances et des ruptures, il trouvait peu à peu une métaphysique du refus.	Panoramique ascendant de la Tour Saint-Jacques, répété plusieurs fois.
Qu'est-il devenu ?	
(Dernière strophe de « Marche » de François Dufrêne, dite très doucement.)	
Arthur Cravan sous des eaux profondes.	Vues d'un cuirassé de la bataille de Tsoushima.
(Dit par un noir américain.)	

221

59. Guy Debord, opening page of the script for *Hurlements en faveur de Sade*, published in *Ion*, April 1952.

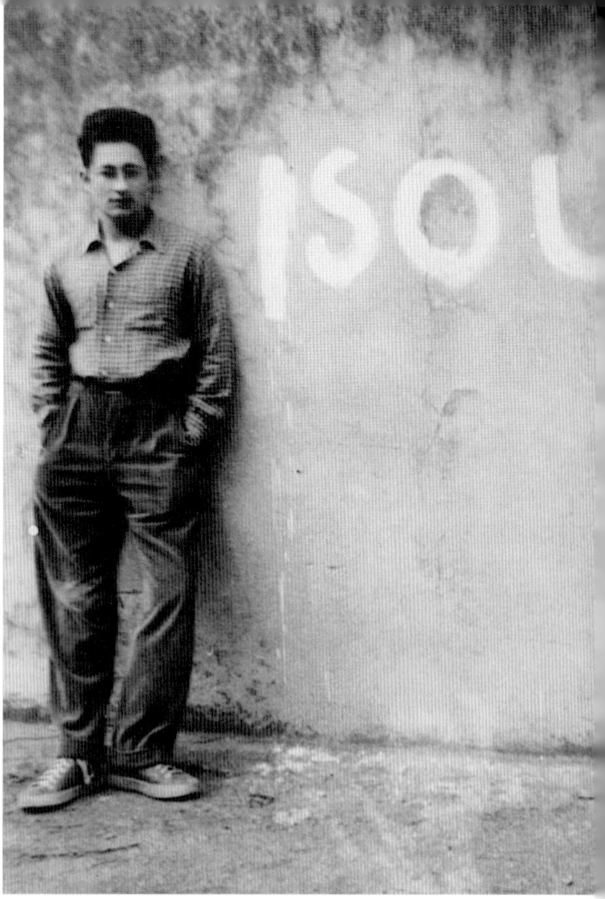

60. Guy Debord in front of the name Isou written on a wall, early 1950s. Photographer unknown.

on Debord, a photograph from the time makes the identification explicit: a young Debord stands in front of a wall on which "ISOU" is written in white paint (fig. 60).

Hurlements' original script, which was elaborated in the winter of 1951–1952, further demonstrates its indebtedness to a Lettrist film aesthetic. The image track lists shots of military troops, erotic scenes, riot scenes, a boxing match, views of St. Germain-des-Prés, and the clientele at Mabillon café. Debord mentions six images of himself, images of Isou and Marc'O (Marc-Guilbert Guillaumin), sequences of *pellicule brossée* (painted filmstrip), and the black sequences that would come to define the completed film. The mixing of original shots with preexisting footage, as well as the painted filmstrip and sequences of pure color, explicitly recall the visual aspects of Isou's and Lemaître's films. Meanwhile, the sound track proposed to trace a poetic of refusal from the Dadaists to the Surrealists and was interspersed with Lettrist sounds: François Dufrêne's poems "Marche" (March) and "J'interroge et j'invective" (I Question and I Accuse; also featured in Isou's film *Traité de bave et d'éternité* [On Venom and Eternity]), a Lettrist chorus with background cries and whistles (similar sounds are heard in previous Lettrist films), glossolia-graphic transcriptions such as "KWORXKE KOWONGUE KKH," and "violent screams in the darkness" (des cris très violents dans le noir) during the final black sequence.[10]

Among the documentation of this moment available in Debord's archive, one finds three martini napkins on which Isou has written descriptions of scenes from *Traité*, along with the time and place of a meeting. One of these curious vintage napkins reads, "A young man exits a ciné-club where he presented new ideas on the art of film. The first part is also composed of a manifesto against contemporary cinema" (fig. 61).[11] That Debord was in coversation with Isou and also working through Isou's theory of cinema is further evinced by his copy of two published diagrams

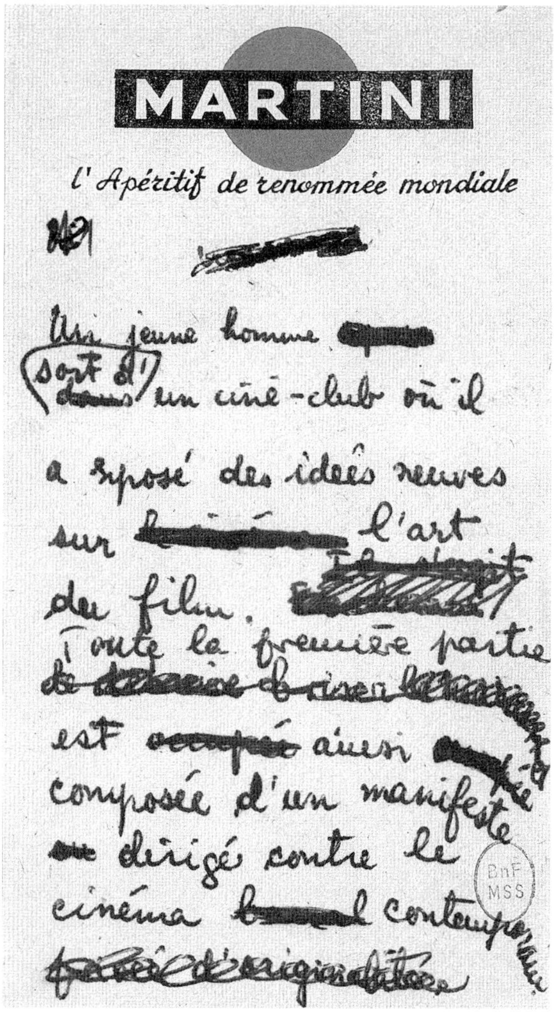

61. Isidore Isou, description of a scene from *Traité de bave et d'éternité* (1951), 1951. Martini napkin. Fonds Guy Debord, Bibliothèque Nationale de France, Paris.

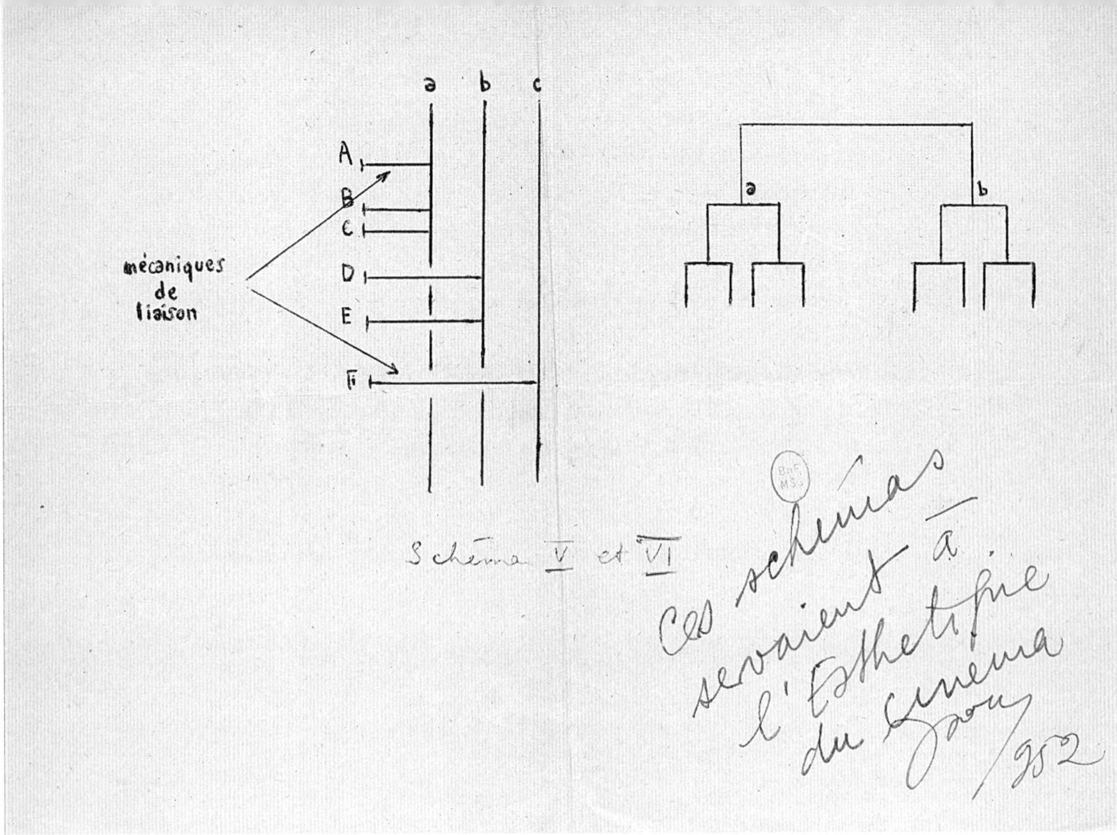

62. A diagram of Isidore Isou's system of *montage discrépant* (discrepant editing), 1952. Fonds Guy Debord, Bibliothèque Nationale de France, Paris.

that refer to Isou's "Esthétique." According to Isou, one of the diagram's (fig. 62, left) schematizes how technology combines toward a realist aesthetic, while the other (fig. 62, right) proposes the "desired situation" that enables the development of *montage discrépant*.[12]

Between the publication of *Hurlements*' script in *Ion* in April and the film's debut two months later in June, Debord's film was transformed. It was neither shot nor printed; instead it was constructed using clear and opaque leader, thereby negating the filmed image.[13] As noted in my account of the Walter Reade screening, when someone speaks on the sound track, the screen remains white; otherwise it remains dark. For the final twenty-four minutes, the viewer sits in darkness and silence. The realized sound track preserves only about half of the original script's text.[14] The five voices one hears utter citations from letters, books, and newspapers and repeat everyday conversations, which are at times punctuated by Debord's observations (e.g., "The arts of the future will be nothing less than disruptions of situations," "I made this film while there was still time to talk about it"). The voices deliver their texts with minimal tonal variation. Other than these spoken snippets of original and appropriated language, there is nothing of the sound or aural accompaniment listed in the script: no Lettrist poetry or chorus, no cries, no whistles or screams.

Debord published the final script for the realized version of the film three and a half years later, in December 1955, in *Les lèvres nues*, a magazine edited by the Belgian Surrealist (later Situationist) Marcel Mariën (fig. 63). The various voices are identified in a note: Gil J Wolman (Voice 1), Debord (Voice 2), Serge Berna (Voice 3), Barbara Rosenthal (Voice 4), and Isou (Voice 5). The script also notes the lengths of the fourteen dark sequences, which range from thirty seconds to the final twenty four minutes, as also seen in the maquette for publication (fig. 64). Debord's introduction, "Grande fête de nuit" (Great Night Party), describes the actual film:

> The sound track lasted only about twenty minutes . . . the interruptions of the sound, always quite long, left the screen and theater in absolute darkness. The replies were substituted for by nonhabitual voices that were resolutely monotone. The almost constant use of press clippings, law texts, and citations with a detourned meaning made understanding the dialogue all the more difficult.[15]

Debord here invokes what would become the principle Situationist aesthetico-political strategy, *détournement*, whereby "any elements, no matter where they are taken from, can serve in making new

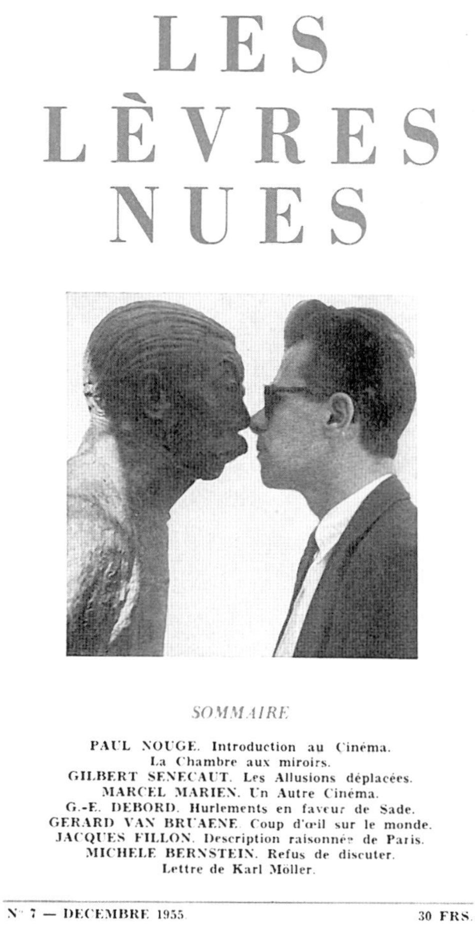

LES LÈVRES NUES

SOMMAIRE

PAUL NOUGE. Introduction au Cinéma.
La Chambre aux miroirs.
GILBERT SENECAUT. Les Allusions déplacées.
MARCEL MARIEN. Un Autre Cinéma.
G.-E. DEBORD. Hurlements en faveur de Sade.
GERARD VAN BRUAENE. Coup d'œil sur le monde.
JACQUES FILLON. Description raisonnée de Paris.
MICHELE BERNSTEIN. Refus de discuter.
Lettre de Karl Möller.

N° 7 — DECEMBRE 1955 30 FRS.

63. *Les lèvres nues*, no. 7, December 1955. Cover.

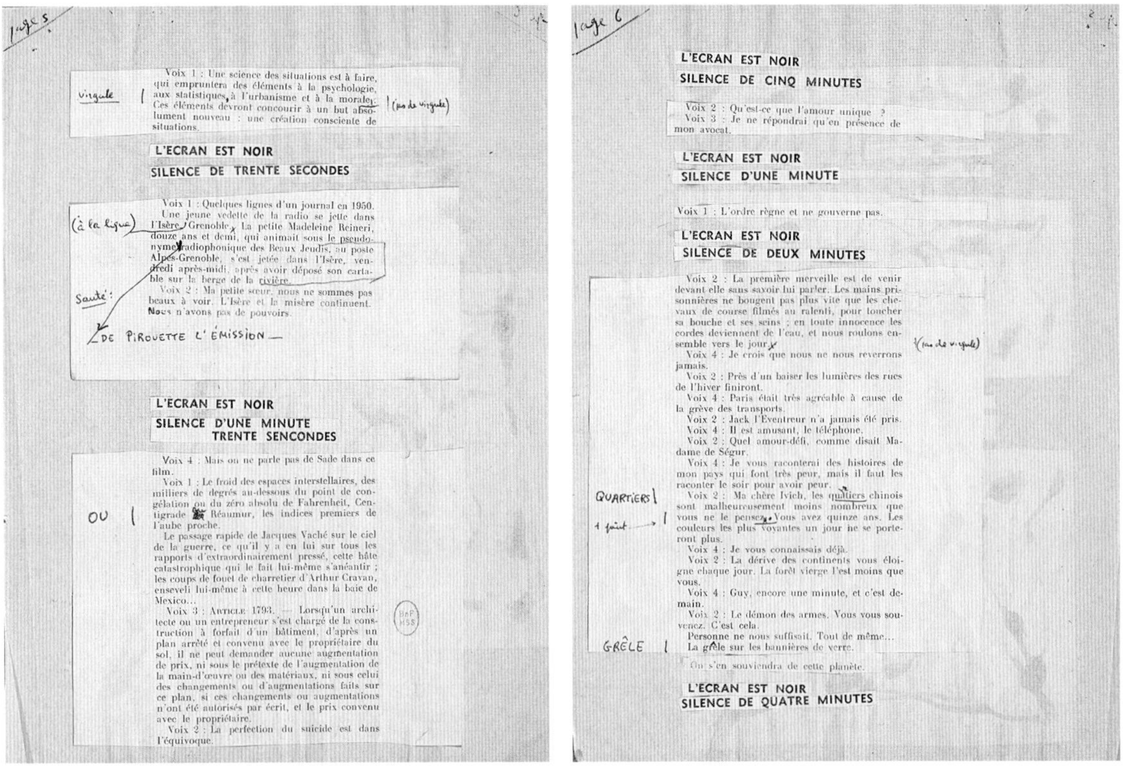

page 5

Voix 1 : Une science des situations est à faire, qui empruntera des éléments à la psychologie, aux statistiques, à l'urbanisme et à la morale. Ces éléments devront concourir à un but absolument nouveau : une création consciente de situations.

virgule — (pas de virgule)

L'ECRAN EST NOIR
SILENCE DE TRENTE SECONDES

Voix 1 : Quelques lignes d'un journal en 1950.
Une jeune vedette de la radio se jette dans l'Isère. Grenoble. La petite Madeleine Reineri, douze ans et demi, qui animait sous le pseudonyme radiophonique des Beaux Jeudis, au poste Alpes-Grenoble, s'est jetée dans l'Isère, vendredi après-midi, après avoir déposé son cartable sur la berge de la rivière.
Voix 2 : Ma petite sœur, nous ne sommes pas beaux à voir. L'Isère et la misère continuent. Nous n'avons pas de pouvoirs.

(à la ligne) — Sauté : — DE PIROUETTE L'ÉMISSION —

L'ECRAN EST NOIR
SILENCE D'UNE MINUTE
TRENTE SENCONDES

Voix 4 : Mais on ne parle pas de Sade dans ce film.
Voix 1 : Le froid des espaces interstellaires, des milliers de degrés au-dessous du point de congélation ou du zéro absolu de Fahrenheit, Centigrade ou Réaumur, les indices premiers de l'aube proche.
Le passage rapide de Jacques Vaché sur le ciel de la guerre, ce qu'il y a en lui sur tous les rapports d'extraordinairement pressé, cette hâte catastrophique qui le fait lui-même s'anéantir ; les coups de fouet de charretier d'Arthur Cravan, enseveli lui-même à cette heure dans la baie de Mexico…
Voix 3 : Article 1793. — Lorsqu'un architecte ou un entrepreneur s'est chargé de la construction à forfait d'un bâtiment, d'après un plan arrêté et convenu avec le propriétaire du sol, il ne peut demander aucune augmentation de prix, ni sous le prétexte de l'augmentation de la main-d'œuvre ou des matériaux, ni sous celui des changements ou d'augmentations faits sur ce plan, si ces changements ou augmentations n'ont été autorisés par écrit, et le prix convenu avec le propriétaire.
Voix 2 : La perfection du suicide est dans l'équivoque.

OU

page 6

L'ECRAN EST NOIR
SILENCE DE CINQ MINUTES

Voix 2 : Qu'est-ce que l'amour unique ?
Voix 3 : Je ne répondrai qu'en présence de mon avocat.

L'ECRAN EST NOIR
SILENCE D'UNE MINUTE

Voix 1 : L'ordre règne et ne gouverne pas.

L'ECRAN EST NOIR
SILENCE DE DEUX MINUTES

Voix 2 : La première merveille est de venir devant elle sans savoir lui parler. Les mains prisonnières ne bougent pas plus vite que les chevaux de course filmés au ralenti, pour toucher sa bouche et ses seins ; en toute innocence les cordes deviennent de l'eau, et nous roulons ensemble vers le jour.
Voix 4 : Je crois que nous ne nous reverrons jamais.
Voix 2 : Près d'un baiser les lumières des rues de l'hiver finiront.
Voix 4 : Paris était très agréable à cause de la grève des transports.
Voix 2 : Jack l'Eventreur n'a jamais été pris.
Voix 4 : Il est amusant, le téléphone.
Voix 2 : Quel amour-défi, comme disait Madame de Ségur.
Voix 4 : Je vous raconterai des histoires de mon pays qui font très peur, mais il faut les raconter le soir pour avoir peur.
Voix 2 : Ma chère Ivich, les quatiers chinois sont malheureusement moins nombreux que vous ne le pensez. Vous avez quinze ans. Les couleurs les plus voyantes un jour ne se porteront plus.
Voix 4 : Je vous connaissais déjà.
Voix 2 : La dérive des continents vous éloigne chaque jour. La forêt vierge l'est moins que vous.
Voix 4 : Guy, encore une minute, et c'est demain.
Voix 2 : Le démon des armes. Vous vous souvenez. C'est cela.
Personne ne nous suffisait. Tout de même…
La grêle sur les bannières de verre.
On s'en souviendra de cette planète.

(pas de virgule) — QUARTIERS — 1 point — GRÊLE

L'ECRAN EST NOIR
SILENCE DE QUATRE MINUTES

64. Guy Debord, pages 5 and 6 of "Maquette pour une publication, 24 décembre 1952." Fonds Guy Debord, Bibliothèque Nationale de France, Paris.

combinations."[16] Yet what remains outside the purview of Debord's account of the film and the final script is the approximately twenty-five seconds of Wolman performing *mégapneumie* with which *Hurlements* begins. These recorded *mégapneumie* recall the concluding minutes of Wolman's own film, *L'anticoncept*, which, like *Hurlements*, is a sound film without images. And similar to the other Lettrist films that precede it, *Hurlements* opens with a short history of film, a genealogy in which Isou's, Wolman's, and Debord's films all form a part:

> 1902: *A Trip to the Moon*. 1920: *The Cabinet of Dr. Caligari*. 1924: *Entr'acte*. 1926: *Potemkin*. 1928: *An Andalusian Dog*. 1931: *City Lights*. Birth of Guy-Ernest Debord. 1951: *On Venom and Eternity*. 1952: *The Anticoncept*. *Howls for Sade*.[17]

Despite the explicit lineage uttered by Voice 1, critics often fail to mention *L'anticoncept* among the Lettrist work with which Debord was involved.[18] Consequently, the specificity of each imageless film remains unresolved and unremarked in the increasingly expansive literature on the Situationists and amid the hagiographic adulation so often conferred on Debord.

EVERYTHING THAT I OWE YOU

In October 1952, Charlie Chaplin arrived in Paris to support his latest film, *Limelight*. The various promotional events included a press conference at the Ritz Hotel, which Wolman and Jean-Louis Brau sabotaged, distributing leaflets that stated, "We hope that your last film really will be your last." Signed by Serge Berna, Brau, Debord, and Wolman, the last line of its text insisted, in English, "Go home Mister Chaplin." Isou, Lemaître, and Gabriel Pomerand publically distanced themselves from the hostile action, publishing a letter in *Combat* that affirmed, "We dissociate ourselves from our friends' leaflet, and we associate ourselves with the homage paid to Chaplin by all of the population."[19] The Lettrists' public rebuff helped to consolidate the formation of a splinter group, the Lettrist International (LI), which in turn disavowed Isou, Lemaître, and Pomerand in their text "Position de l'International lettriste," which was published and signed by Berna, Brau, Debord, and Wolman.[20] As is now well known, the LI increasingly separated itself from the Lettrists, and in the course of the 1950s merged with other avant-garde groups, including the International Movement for an Imaginist Bauhaus and the London Psychogeographical Committee, forming the Situationist International (SI) in 1957—although by that time initial alliances had shifted again.

Wolman, for one, never became a Situationist, though his name is often associated with the Situationist International today. Six months prior to the foundation of the SI, Wolman was barred from the LI. A notice, tellingly titled "La retraite," in the May 1957 issue of *Potlatch* explains: "Fillon and Wolman were excluded from the Lettrist International on January 13. They were accused for quite some time of a ridiculous way of life, cruelly underwritten by increasingly weak and petty thinking."[21] The unsigned notice remains vague as to the motivation behind the expulsion. But lest Wolman's participation in the LI be discounted *tout court*, the text continues:

> Wolman had an important role in the organization of the Lettrist left in 1952, and then in the foundation of the LI. Author of *mégapneumique* poems, a theory of *cinématochrone*, and a film, he had been Lettrist delegate to the Alba conference in September 1956.[22]

The notice ends like an obituary: "He was twenty-seven."[23]

Just prior to Wolman's "retirement" and the rupture of his friendship with Debord, the latter had written the following to his friend:

> I am satisfied to have been part of the Chaplin affair (although held back in the shadowy periphery) and to have made *Hurlements*. In this regard I know everything that I owe you [*A ce propos je sais tout ce que je te dois*].[24]

What exactly does Debord "owe" to Wolman? As we know, *L'anticoncept*'s black-and-white rhythm and concluding gurgles lived on in *Hurlements*, just as Wolman introduces its only credit line: "A film by Guy-Ernest Debord, *Howls for Sade*." This is followed by Debord's dedication: "*Howls for Sade* is dedicated to Gil J Wolman." As to what Debord may have meant when writing "je sais tout ce que je te dois," Jean-Michel Bouhours suggests that Wolman probably recommended the formal radicalization of Debord's film as a way of circumventing the costs involved in shooting, purchasing stock shots, and recording poems.[25] If this is true, *Hurlements* was born on account of financial constraints and Wolman's recommendation.

More than a decade after the film's premiere, Debord cast a retrospective glance on the historical specificity of *Hurlements*' making:

> The content of the film must first be connected to the context of the Lettrist avant-garde of the time: both on a more general level, whereby it appears as a negation and supersession of Isou's conception of *cinéma discrépant*, and on an anecdotal level, after the trend in double first names that so characterized this group . . . up to the dedication to Wolman, author of the previous Lettrist film, the admirable *Anticoncept*. The other aspects are to be considered in the context of Situationist positions that are defined since: first among them, the use of *détourned phrases*.[26]

Both *L'anticoncept* and *Hurlements* reject the language of cinematic realism, and both conjure the origins of cinema through their alternating black-and-white rhythm. Moreover, each film owes something in spirit and in fact to the Lettrist work of Isou. At issue is not whether Wolman had the initial idea that drove *Hurlements*' subsequent material realization but the divergence in film production and ultimately film reception between *L'anticoncept* and *Hurlements*, and also between *Hurlements* and Debord's later films. To be sure, the difference from *L'anticoncept* does not rest on the use of détourned passages alone.

The first screening of *Hurlements* took place on June 30, 1952, at the Ciné-Club Avant-Garde 52 in the Musée de l'Homme. From the outset, audience members disrupted the screening, audibly expressing their discontent,

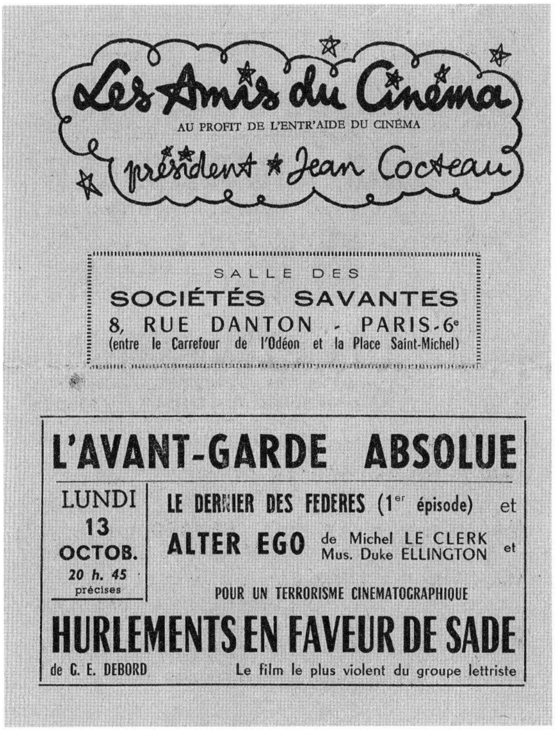

65. Flyer for the screening of *Hurlements en faveur de Sade* at the Ciné-Club du Quartier Latin on October 13, 1952. Fonds Guy Debord, Bibliothèque Nationale de France, Paris.

such that the film club management stopped the film shortly after it began. According to Debord, "Several lettrists then dissociated themselves from such a crudely extremist film."[27] Just three days after the film's failed screening, Isou wrote to Debord. His letter supports Debord's claim as to the Lettrists' unsupportive response. Isou cautions:

> Your film was poorly done. Such things make us temporarily lose what has been gained. (Cauliez stopped your film in the middle. Wolman had at least entirely screened his film. Maurice had even been paid, etc.)
>
> This comes from the speed with which you enter into the race. I know the risk, but I also know that *with practice itself* you develop more quickly and you reach, through acting, a quicker mastery.[28]

Combining critique with a healthy dose of support, Isou also writes:

> Your aloofness [*solitude*] toward Marc'O was desired by you. You made a separate group with Wolman and Serge. Things are in order on account of the lack of reciprocal kindness (which has its advantages and disadvantages).[29]

Isou here evokes an initial break between Debord and the Lettrists, one that occurred prior to the Chaplin affair: in Brussels in May and June of 1952, Debord and Wolman had indeed conceived of a dissident group. Yet at the time of *Hurlements*' first screening, the schism had not been formalized.

On October 13, 1952, almost four months after the screening at the Musée de l'Homme, *Hurlements* was finally shown in full at the Ciné-Club du Quartier Latin in their program on avant-garde film (fig. 65). The few published eyewitness accounts reveal the various extrafilmic elements designed for the occasion, as well as the participation of competing Lettrist groups. Jean-Michel Mension (who was briefly an LI member) and Maurice Rajsfus (historian and French militant) offer the most detailed observations.[30] Mension recounts how the LI and its supporters sat in the balcony, while affiliates of Soulèvement de la Jeunesse, including Dufrêne, Marc'O, and Yolande du Luart, were seated in the orchestra below. Prior to the screening and in true ciné-club format, a professor from the "Cinémathèque of Lausanne" introduced the film. But like the fake press that reviewed Lemaître's film on the sound track of *Le film est déjà commencé?* (Has the Film Already Started?), the "professor" was a fake film club lecturer. Using a thick Belgian-German accent, Berna gave a lengthy opening presentation in which he described an "erotic tension" in the film that would eventually become "all-consuming."[31] According to Rajsfus, one Lettrist cheekily proclaimed, "The eroticism should occur in the audience."[32] He also explains how the order of the day was "*amuser, après théoriser*" (to amuse, then theorize).[33]

Mension's account details other staged disturbances and how the Lettrists "started shouting, crying scandal, insulting us. . . . We [the LI] responded in kind from the balcony."[34] Michèle Bernstein recalls that within this seemingly contentious context the exchanges were "tout à fait joyeux" (quite joyous) and that a scandal among "complices" (accomplices) has nothing "méchant" (mean) about it.[35] What is more, Bernstein remembers a series of "Hurlements en faveur de vous," whereby Debord would make a sign to prompt someone to scream. Bernstein responded to the prompt with her own "Hurlements en faveur de Guy."[36]

Reporting on the notorious final sequence of twenty-four minutes of darkness, as well as the postscreening ciné-club debate, Rajsfus recalls in a passage worth citing at length:

> The last minutes of the film consisted of total darkness. No one had walked out. The show had begun about nine, and at ten-thirty the lights went up definitively to the catcalls of a frenzied public. The master of ceremonies seized on a brief moment of respite to announce question-and-answer time [i.e., the scheduled time for a film club debate]. Ever

> serious, Serge Berna spoke, developing a few complimentary thoughts concerning Guy-Ernest Debord and his œuvre. One spectator, trembling with rage, demanded an explanation of the filmmaker's reasons for entitling his film *Hurlements en faveur de Sade*. Completely straight-faced, Berna responded that there was a misunderstanding and that the film was really dedicated to a friend of Debord's, one Ernest Sade, currently engaged in the worthy trade of procurer in the Rue Nicolas-Flamel.[37]

Such proceedings—that is, the tripartite structure of lecture, screening, and postscreening debate—uphold ciné-club conventions that emerged in the 1920s. Rajsfus also remembers that he was invited to the screening precisely because they needed live *figurants* (extras).[38] But Debord makes no mention of any of the above in the technical notes on the film or in his various references to it.

In the pages of Isou's "Esthétique du cinéma," one finds the following:

> Marc-Gilbert Guillaumin [Marc'O] and Guy-Ernest Debord would have concretely and willingly realized this lack. They had planned to speak to a director of a ciné-club that had shown a number of works of our group and to announce an even more sensational creation. The title was already set: *Hurlements en faveur de Sade*. They would have sent out invitations, made posters, and called the journalists. They would have then brought the reels from another film in order to reassure the director who, by the way, had taken us at our word. At the point when the projection was to have begun, Debord would have gotten up on stage in order to say a few words of introduction. He would have simply said, "There is no film." I thought I would get involved and link up their destructive scandal with the theory of the constructive pure debate. Debord would have said, "The cinema is dead. There can be no more film. Let us proceed, if you like, to the debates."[39]

It remains unclear whether the events Isou narrates actually took place or represent a hypothetical scenario. Nevertheless, elements from this scene, which was published in April 1952, more than five months prior to *Hurlements*' second screening, may inform *Hurlements*' various scripted and impromptu actions, thereby keeping it firmly within the purview of early Lettrist experiments in cinema. Furthermore, Debord's purported declaration that "the cinema is dead" and that one should move on "to the debates" eventually found its way into the sound track of his realized film, in which Voice 5 (Isou) utters these very words. With his nod to the importance of ciné-club debate, Isou's account also anticipates his own *Film-débat* (1952), which was produced later that year. Sometime between May and December at the Musée de l'Homme,

Isou proclaimed that cinema was dead and that the debate itself constituted the film.[40]

It is undeniable that Lettrist strategies survive in both the LI and early Situationist practice. Take, as another example, one early account of a *dérive*. Published in *Potlatch* in 1955, the unidentified author suggests:

> In the dark theaters where the *dérive* can traverse, one should stop for at least an hour and [oneself] interpret the adventure films that play: let the heroes be some more or less historical characters who are close to us, connect the events of the inept scenario to the real reasons which we understand are behind the actions, and connect them also to the events of the current week. Here you have an acceptable collective distraction.[41]

The proposal combines the surrealist meanderings of film viewing proposed by André Breton with the exemplary activity of Lemaître's professional spectator. The LI also reelaborated the latter activity in relation to speech-on-film through a proposal to add a sound track to D. W. Griffith's silent *The Birth of a Nation* (1915) in order to reveal the film's racism without altering the montage. This example counts among the various possible uses of *détournement*, which would here keep the film's visual innovations intact while exposing its ideological meaning.[42]

Debord's specific deployment of appropriated language—to the exclusion of cries, whistles, and screams—at the same time aligns *Hurlements*' sound track with his later work. Like *Hurlements*, all of Debord's later films privilege the sound track over the image. More specifically, they privilege speech—as voice-over or as manifested graphically through subtitles and intertitles. Yet in all of his subsequent films, Debord reintroduces the filmed image, combining appropriated shots with shots taken by his cameraman. Debord radicalizes the *détournement* already present in *Hurlements*' sound track in order to insist on the critical refusal of language (both visual and verbal). Applied as much to texts and words as to images, *détournement* is a procedure of quotation and reuse of an original element in a new context so as to reclaim a different and noncommodified meaning. After 1962, *détournement* became a primary technique for contesting spectacle, a strategy more prominent in the SI's discourse than the more spatialized and aleatory *dérive*. In addition to the use of preexisting footage, Debord deploys other strategies to interrupt visual illusionism, narrative continuity, and spectatorial absorption, such as refilming still images (e.g., photographs, comics, newspaper clippings) and including shots of the film crew and clapper that avow his later films' constructed status.

An extended analysis of all of Debord's films is beyond the scope of the present study and is otherwise available in the current literature.[43] Nevertheless, I would like to draw attention to aspects of both *Sur le passage de quelques personnes à travers une assez courte unité de temps* (On the Passage of a Few Persons through a Rather Brief Unity of Time, 1959) and *Critique de la séparation* (Critique of Separation, 1961), so as to put in sharper relief the specificity of *Hurlements*.[44] *Sur le passage* is often described as Debord's most melancholic film: views of St. Germain-des-Prés are coupled at times with wistful voice-over that describes the neighborhood, or what is called the "external setting of our story." In the film's technical specifications, Debord assigns the three voices specific tonal inflections: Voice 1 (Jean Harnois) speaks in the tone of a radio or *actualité* (newsreel) announcer; Voice 2 (Debord) is more sad or muted; and Voice 3 (Claude Brabant) is described as that of a young girl.[45] The film includes original shots of Debord and his cohort as well as various appropriated shots, from a Monsavon soap ad to newsreel footage (fig. 66). It also uses appropriated language (from classical thinkers to science fiction) interspersed with Debord's own reflections.

Like *Hurlements*, *Sur le passage* employs clear leader, and thus a blank screen, with voice-over to critical effect. For example, at around nine minutes, Voice 1 explains:

> What makes most documentaries so easy to understand is the arbitrary limitation of their subject matter. They confine themselves to depicting fragmented social functions and their isolated products. In contrast, imagine the full complexity of a moment that is not resolved into a work, a moment whose development contains interrelated facts and values and whose meaning is not yet apparent. This confused totality could be the subject matter of such a documentary.

In such sequences, the communicative function of language problematizes documentary practice and the purported self-evidence of documentary images, a criticism that is sustained in the course of the film.[46] Subsequent views of the Rue des Écoles and Rue Montagne Sainte Geneviève are coupled with Debord's voice, which muses, "We wanted to break out of this condition, in search of different uses of the urban landscape, in search of new passions." Following the references to a "confused totality" and the desire for "new passions," the film continues with visual and verbal images of the LI, just as it contests the reification of everyday life in advanced capitalism.

I would like to further emphasize in this context the images of power that take on an increasingly decisive role in Debord's films. *Critique de la séparation* abandons the nostalgic tone of *Sur le passage* and offers a critique of everyday life and the historical context of the Cold War. Approximately nine minutes into the film, one sees a sequence that includes shots of the United Nations Security Council; Nikita Khrushchev with Charles

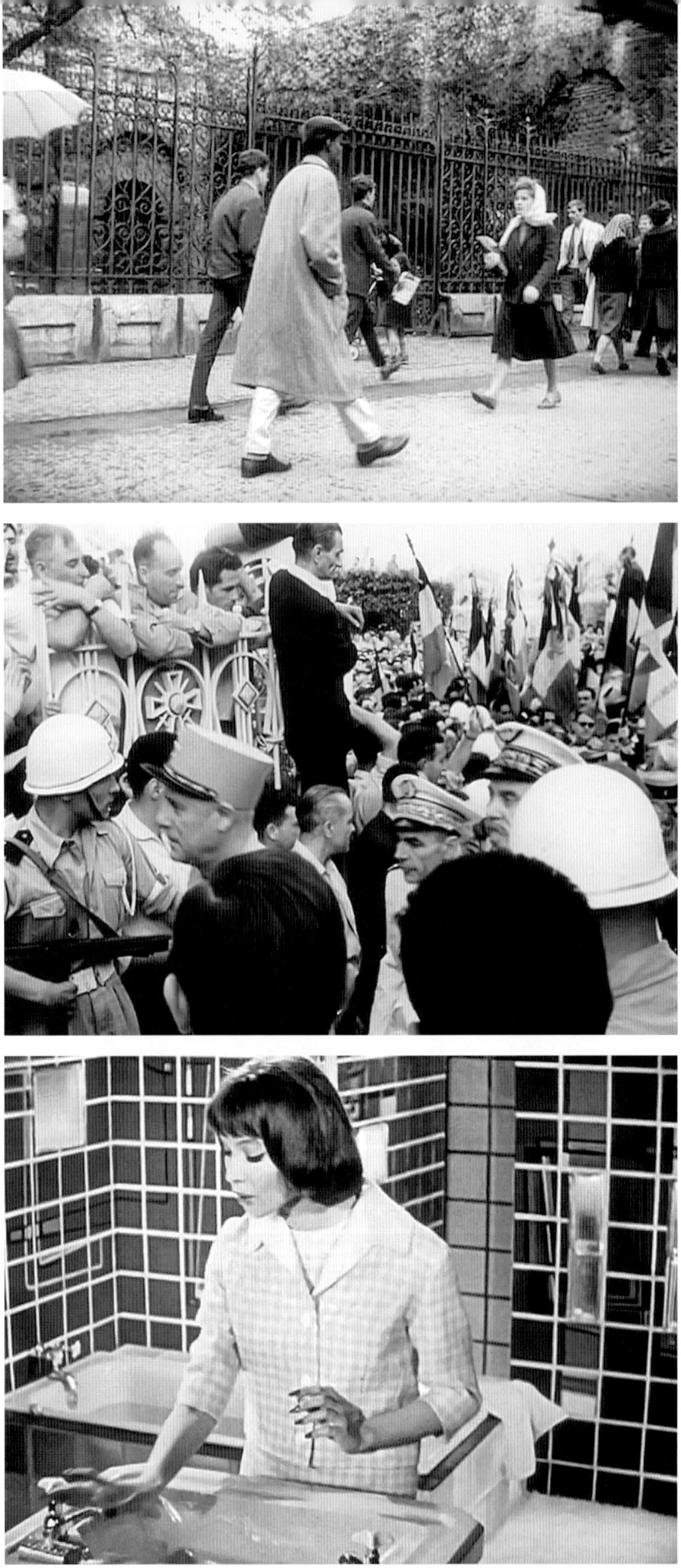

66. Guy Debord, *Sur le passage de quelques personnes à travers une assez courte unité de temps*, 1959. Frame enlargements.

de Gaulle; Dwight Eisenhower welcoming de Gaulle; a patriotic ceremony at the Arc de Triomphe; de Gaulle and Khrushchev standing at attention; and Eisenhower with the pope, followed by a filmed photograph of Eisenhower being embraced by Francisco Franco (fig. 67). The voice-over (here Debord's) explains:

> Official news is elsewhere. Society broadcasts to itself its own image of its own history, a history reduced to a superficial and static pageant of its rulers—the persons who embody the apparent inevitability of whatever happens. The world of the rulers is the world of the spectacle. The cinema suits them well. Regardless of its subject matter, the cinema presents heroes and exemplary conduct modeled on the same old pattern as the rulers.

In this work and those that follow Debord harnesses the power of communicative speech to repurpose photographic meaning toward alterative ends. Like the chiseling in Isou's *Traité*, Debord's voice-over challenges the idea that such footage should be understood as an image of reality. For both filmmakers the newsreel version of history constitutes both a material and an object of critique. But where Isou's chiseled marks redirect attention within the photographic image, so as to expose the performative dimensions of profilmic reality, his theorization of *montage discrépant* primarily upholds the independence of image and sound track. Debord, on the contrary, readily insists on the two tracks' relation: "The

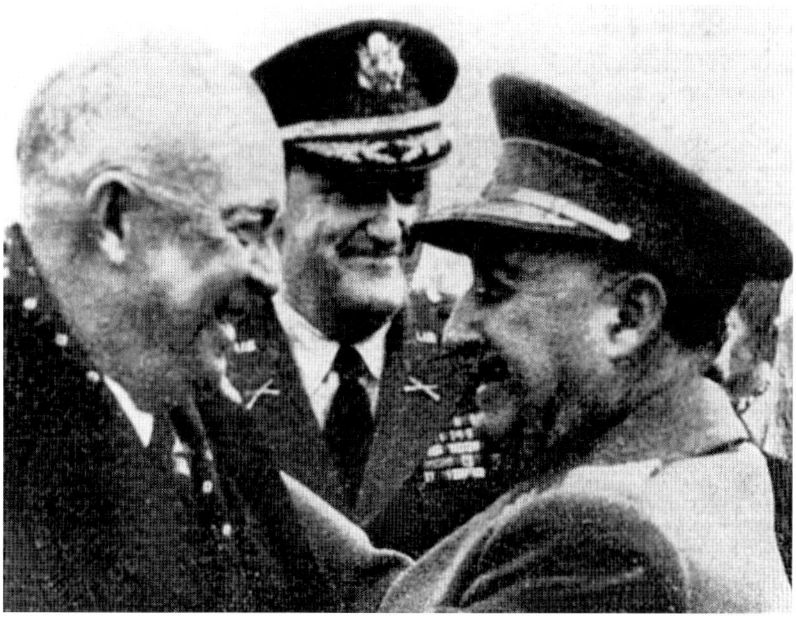

67. Guy Debord, *Critique de la séparation*, 1961. Frame enlargement.

relation between the images, the spoken commentary and the subtitles is neither complementary nor indifferent, but is intended to itself be critical."[47] What this statement points to, in no uncertain terms, is Debord's investment in language as a method by which to oppose the visuality of spectacle. Debord uses speech to disclose images' ideological meanings in a way that brings the lessons of Lemaître's cinematographic education to the specificity of film and the relation between its two tracks. Such a strategy, while it does not account for all of the relations between speech and image in Debord's films (e.g., *Critique* also places his authority in doubt through statements such as "we don't know what to say"[48]), is representative of his approach: Debord uses language to counter the purported truth of an image.

The work of the SI with the means of artistic production and representation gave way over the course of the late 1950s and 1960s to a more active political engagement that also included a trenchant critique of language and its alienating effects. Published in the eighth issue of *Internationale situationniste*, "Editorial Notes: All the King's Men" argues:

> [Power] creates nothing; it recuperates. If it created the meaning of words, there would be no poetry, but solely useful "information." We could never confront one another *within* language, and *every refusal would be outside it, would be purely lettrist.*[49]

For Debord and the SI, the Lettrists created nonmeaning as meaning, noncommunication as communication.[50] Their later politics of refusal, by contrast, was no longer to take place outside of language, a position articulated in 1952 (albeit in inchoate form) when Debord wrote that *Hurlements* was a "*dépassement du cri*" (surpassing of the scream).[51] Similarly, with regard to his actual film practice, Debord challenged the structure of representation and offered a sustained critique of capitalism, but he did so within the technical mechanisms and support of cinema. Within the functioning of the apparatus, Debord's films efface the conditions for absorption into an illusion in order to combat what the Situationists describe as the "reactionary force of the *spectacle* without participation."[52]

SPECTATORS ARE STILL NOT IN THE WORLD

At the time Debord was producing *Sur le passage* and *Critique*, not only was he working against the rise of French auteurism and its appreciation of Hollywood films, but also against cinema as an attraction in search of ever more perfected techniques to enthrall spectators. In 1958, Walt Disney featured its Circarama at the Brussels World's Fair (also known as Expo 58).

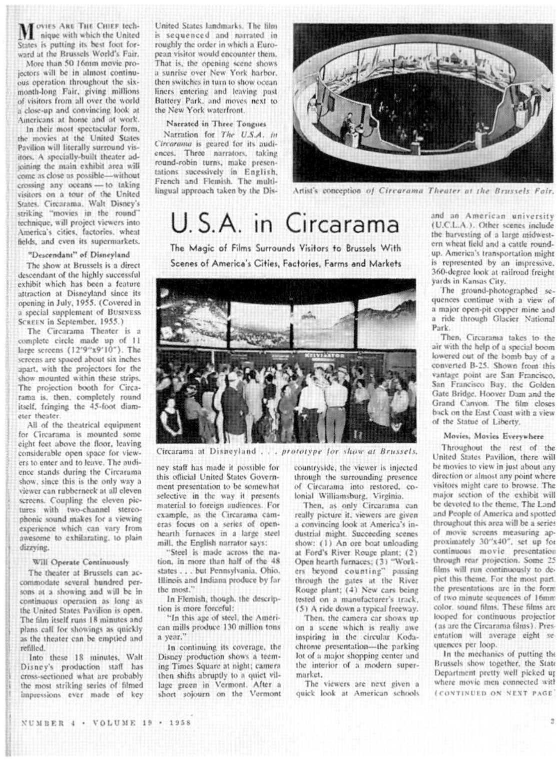

MOVIES ARE THE CHIEF technique with which the United States is putting its best foot forward at the Brussels World's Fair.

More than 50 16mm movie projectors will be in almost continuous operation throughout the six-month-long Fair, giving millions of visitors from all over the world a close-up and convincing look at Americans at home and at work.

In their most spectacular form, the movies at the United States Pavilion will literally surround visitors. A specially-built theater adjoining the main exhibit area will come as close as possible—without crossing any oceans—to taking visitors on a tour of the United States. Circarama, Walt Disney's striking "movies in the round" technique, will project viewers into America's cities, factories, wheat fields, and even its supermarkets.

"Descendant" of Disneyland

The show at Brussels is a direct descendant of the highly successful exhibit which has been a feature attraction at Disneyland since its opening in July, 1955. (Covered in a special supplement of BUSINESS SCREEN in September, 1955.)

The Circarama Theater is a complete circle made up of 11 large screens (12′9″x9′10″). The screens are spaced about six inches apart, with the projectors for the show mounted within these strips. The projection booth for Circarama is, then, completely round itself, fringing the 45-foot diameter theater.

All of the theatrical equipment for Circarama is mounted some eight feet above the floor, leaving considerable open space for viewers to enter and to leave. The audience stands during the Circarama show, since this is the only way a viewer can rubberneck at all eleven screens. Coupling the eleven pictures with two-channel stereophonic sound makes for a viewing experience which can vary from awesome to exhilarating, to plain dizzying.

Will Operate Continuously

The theater at Brussels can accommodate several hundred persons at a showing and will be in continuous operation as long as the United States Pavilion is open. The film itself runs 18 minutes and plans call for showings as quickly as the theater can be emptied and refilled.

Into these 18 minutes, Walt Disney's production staff has cross-sectioned what are probably the most striking series of filmed impressions ever made of key United States landmarks. The film is sequenced and narrated in roughly the order in which a European visitor would encounter them. That is, the opening scene shows a sunrise over New York harbor, then switches in turn to show ocean liners entering and leaving past Battery Park, and moves next to the New York waterfront.

Narrated in Three Tongues

Narration for *The U.S.A. in Circarama* is geared for its audiences. Three narrators, taking round-robin turns, make presentations sucessively in English, French and Flemish. The multilingual approach taken by the Disney staff has made it possible for this official United States Government presentation to be somewhat selective in the way it presents material to foreign audiences. For example, as the Circarama cameras focus on a series of open-hearth furnaces in a large steel mill, the English narrator says:

"Steel is made across the nation, in more than half of the 48 states . . . but Pennsylvania, Ohio, Illinois and Indiana produce by far the most."

In Flemish, though, the description is more forceful:

"In this age of steel, the American mills produce 130 million tons a year."

In continuing its coverage, the Disney production shows a teeming Times Square at night; camera then shifts abruptly to a quiet village green in Vermont. After a short sojourn on the Vermont countryside, the viewer is injected through the surrounding presence of Circarama into restored, colonial Williamsburg, Virginia.

Then, as only Circarama can really picture it, viewers are given a convincing look at America's industrial might. Succeeding scenes show: (1) An ore boat unloading at Ford's River Rouge plant; (2) Open hearth furnaces; (3) "Workers beyond counting" passing through the gates at the River Rouge plant; (4) New cars being tested on a manufacturer's track, (5) A ride down a typical freeway.

Then, the camera car shows up on a scene which is really awe inspiring in the circular Kodachrome presentation—the parking lot of a major shopping center and the interior of a modern supermarket.

The viewers are next given a quick look at American schools and an American university (U.C.L.A.). Other scenes include the harvesting of a large midwestern wheat field and a cattle round-up. America's transportation might is represented by an impressive, 360-degree look at railroad freight yards in Kansas City.

The ground-photographed sequences continue with a view of a major open-pit copper mine and a ride through Glacier National Park.

Then, Circarama takes to the air with the help of a special boom lowered out of the bomb bay of a converted B-25. Shown from this vantage point are San Francisco, San Francisco Bay, the Golden Gate Bridge, Hoover Dam and the Grand Canyon. The film closes back on the East Coast with a view of the Statue of Liberty.

Movies, Movies Everywhere

Throughout the rest of the United States Pavilion, there will be movies to view in just about any direction or almost any point where visitors might care to browse. The major section of the exhibit will be devoted to the theme, The Land and People of America and spotted throughout this area will be a series of movie screens measuring approximately 30″x40″, set up for continuous movie presentation through rear projection. Some 25 films will run continuously to depict this theme. For the most part, the presentations are in the form of two minute sequences of 16mm color, sound films. These films are looped for continuous projection (as are the Circarama films). Presentation will average eight sequences per loop.

In the mechanics of putting the Brussels show together, the State Department pretty well picked up where movie men connected with

(CONTINUED ON NEXT PAGE)

Artist's conception *of Circarama Theater at the Brussels Fair.*

U.S.A. in Circarama

The Magic of Films Surrounds Visitors to Brussels With Scenes of America's Cities, Factories, Farms and Markets

Circarama at Disneyland . . . *prototype for show at Brussels.*

NUMBER 4 • VOLUME 19 • 1958   3

68. Walt Disney's Circarama, featured in the article "Film at Brussels," *Business Screen Magazine* 19, no. 4 (1958).

The Circarama was a movies-in-the-round system comprising eleven synchronized 16-millimeter projectors and eleven screens, all situated within a rotunda-like architectural setting (fig. 68). At the fair, the Circarama presented day-long screenings of the film *America the Beautiful*, exposing audiences to a tour of what one *New York Times* columnist described as "'the face of America' on a room-circling screen."[53] With an eye to the film's reception in the anxious context of the Cold War, another reviewer noted, "And with the ending there is a loud applause . . . from persons of many countries . . . yes, even a few Russian visitors."[54] Other reports speak to the emotional and visceral impact of the film, with audience members covering their eyes on account of its intense realist effects.[55]

Such developments in film's technological (and ideological) presentation were not unknown to Debord. The SI's statement "Avec et contre le cinéma" (With and against Cinema, 1958), published in the first issue of *Internationale situationniste*, makes that awareness clear:

> After the wide screen, the beginnings of stereo sound, and various attempts at 3-D cinema, the United States presented a procedure called the "Circarama" at the Brussels exposition, within which—as *Le Monde* on April 17 [1958] reported—"we find ourselves at the center of the

spectacle and live it, since we are an integral part of it. When a car with a camera mounted on it charges through San Francisco's Chinatown, we experience the same reflexes and sensations as the car's passengers." Experiments have also been recently done with an aromatic cinema through the use of aerosols.[56]

Counter to the spectator's visually immersive interpellation in the Circarama, the unidentified SI writer avers that against that "no life, [in which] spectators are still not in the world," one needs to imagine otherwise "the interest and inherent value presented by new technical applications (stereo sound, smells)"[57] and how they might be used to create what the SI elsewhere describes as the "dialectical organization of partial and transitory realities."[58]

Such environmental techniques were explored the following year in the realm of Situationist exhibition practice. On May 13, 1959, Giuseppe "Pinot" Gallizio, then an SI member, opened his *Caverne de l'antimatière* (Cavern of Antimatter; fig. 69) at the Galerie René Drouin on the Rue Visonti in the Parisian neighborhood of Saint-Germain-des-Prés. For the exhibition, Gallizio lined the ceiling, walls, and floor of the space with his *pittura industriale* (industrial painting), nonexpressive and mechanically produced painting that he had exposed to the corrosive effects of gunpowder, sun, wind, and rain. Within the *Caverne*'s environment, visitors' movements triggered lights, colors, and sounds. They could also smell

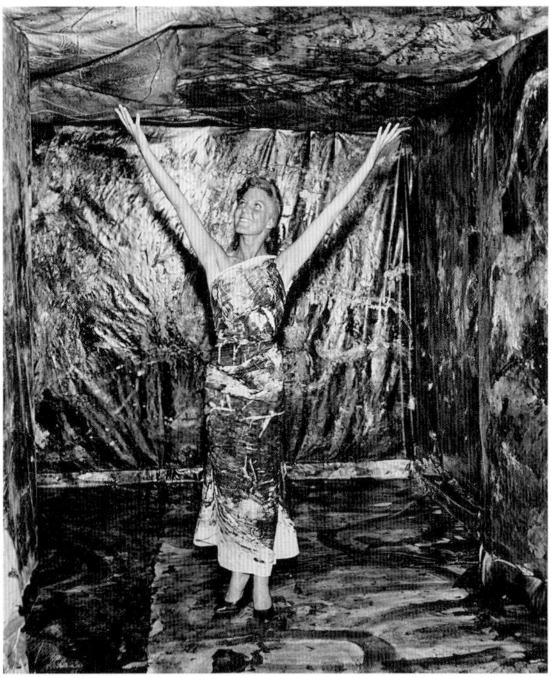

69. Giuseppe "Pinot" Gallizio, *Caverne de l'antimatière*, Galerie René Drouin, Paris, 1959. Installation view with model. Reproduced with the permission of the Fondazione Torino Musei.

herbal perfumes and incense.[59] Moreover, the artist arranged for a model to dress in his painting and walk around the space during the opening, thereby literalizing the work's bodily contact. In creating a space in dynamic relation with the spectator, Gallizio turned to corporeal reception as a way to resist contemplative viewing in art and to defy dominant modes of exhibition display.

Similar experiments with smell and an active environment within Situationist cinema existed only in theory, never in actuality. This might be explained in part by the growing prevalence of such sensorial tactics in the 1950s, part of the experimentation within the film industry provoked by changes in spectatorship due to the growth of television.[60] Developments in the realm of multimedia spectacle, from 3-D movies and the Circarama to Aroma-Rama and Smell-O-Vision (both systems to release odor during a film projection), aimed to produce sensorial immersion and the attendant "spectacle without participation" that the SI disavowed. Moreover, in the course of the 1960s, practitioners of what has come to be known as "expanded cinema" increasingly moved beyond the individual film projection, often revealing an uncomfortable proximity with capitalist media spectacle.[61] Against this emerging scene, Debord's work within the film apparatus reads as a strategic retreat into the medium and a preemptive refusal of the "synaesthetic mode" of participation that Gene Youngblood, in his account of expanded cinema, would eventually champion.[62]

The Situationist critique of nonparticipation under a spectacular regime brings me, by way of conclusion, to Jacques Rancière's discussion of Debord's film adaptation of *La société du spectacle* (The Society of the Spectacle, 1973). Debord's book and film open with the lines "The whole life of those societies in which modern conditions of production prevail presents itself as an immense accumulation of *spectacles*. All that once was directly lived has become mere representation."[63] As with Debord's two earlier films, *La société du spectacle* reveals spectacle as the inversion of life through the use of appropriated film sequences that include everything from political rulers to movie stars, from fashion models to ordinary commodities. With the exception of the opening still images of his partner Alice Becker-Ho, the remainder of the film bespeaks the same reality: "our existence separated from ourselves, transformed by the machine of the spectacle into dead images before us, against us."[64]

In *Le spectateur émancipé* (The Emancipated Spectator, 2008), Rancière situates Debord's diagnosis more generally within his own analysis of how the critique of spectacle has stifled critical thought by maintaining oppositions such as the binary of active and passive spectatorship. The persistence of this binary informs Rancière's assessment of what he calls the "intolerable image regime." In an eponymous chapter, Rancière asks us to consider the production of images that aim to expose real suffering—that is, images of "reality" counterposed to the realm of "appearance." He situates political montage within this dialectic, whereby "one [image] must play the role of the reality that denounces the other's mirage." "By the same token," he continues, "it denounces the mirage as the reality of our existence in which the image is included."[65] What Rancière thus identifies is a historical impasse in which the intolerable *in* the image has become the intolerable *of* the image, and the complicity of all images in the system they denounce. In accounting for this condition, he indentifies how Debord's critique of spectacle maintains that "the mere fact of viewing images . . . is a bad thing" and presents action "as the only answer to the evil of the image."[66]

Accordingly, Rancière analyzes the strategic game between images, action, and speech played out in *La société du spectacle*:

> Thus, it now seemed impossible to confer on any image whatsoever the power of exhibiting the intolerable and prompting us to struggle against it. The only thing to do seemed to be to counter-pose the passivity of the image, to its alienated existence, *living action*.[67]

Rancière points to how *La société du spectacle*'s actual images—with sources from Hollywood westerns to war films—allegorize a call to action with which the spectator is supposed to identify in order "to adopt the heroism of the battle for our own purposes" (fig. 70).[68] Fittingly, given the privileging of the sound track in all of Debord's films, Rancière hones in on the voice-over's speech. Here, Debord's voice is imbued with personal reflection but also theoretical reflexivity, revealing to the spectator the state of passivity with which he or she consumes images.[69] Consequently, Rancière charges the film with having preserved the "virtue of activity . . . [which is here] absorbed by the authority of the sovereign voice," one that explains the truth of social relations in an act of unidirectional communication.[70]

But, as noted above, Debord's earlier films such as *Critique* also insist on the limits of communication. In each film he uses *détournement* as a consistent linguistic strategy, often through subtitles and intertitles that refer to the authors of other historical and political works.[71] Thus, contrary to Rancière's assessment of *La société du spectacle*'s voice-over, Debord's work does not represent a single authorial voice, nor is its voice necessarily sovereign—even when, at times, it hews close to didacticism. Rather than secure his position as the sovereign subject of speech, Debord actively situates his voice within collective history and a specifically Marxist genealogy. In this way, he resists making his voice an instrument

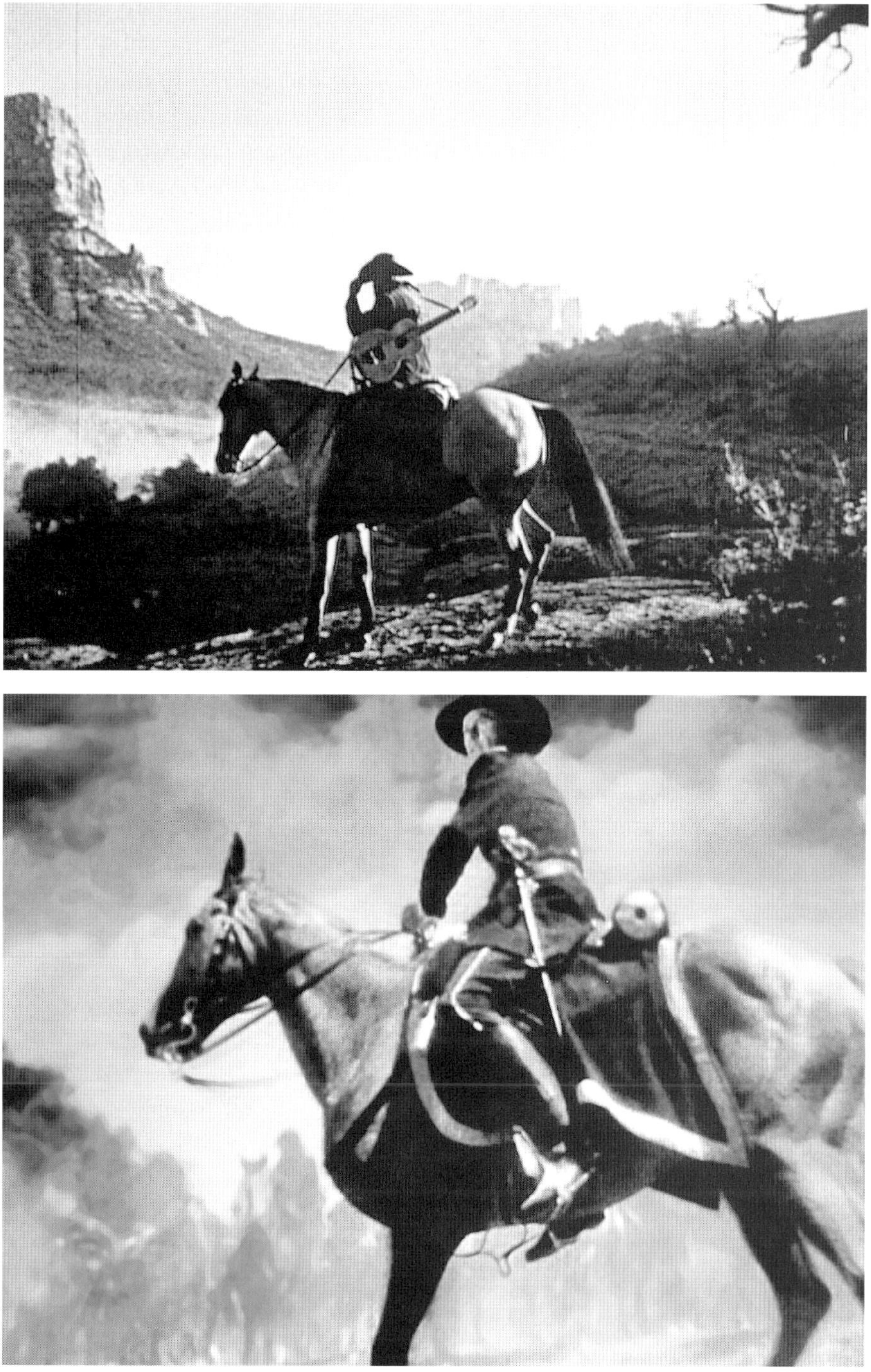

70. Guy Debord, *La société du spectacle*, 1973. Frame enlargements.

of the self or the positive sign of presence, even as he keeps language's conceptual content intact.[72] That is, we hear no cries, whistles, or screams.

Beyond his critique of the sovereign voice in *La société du spectacle*, Rancière engages Debord's work more specifically in order to develop an alternative to his critique of spectacle, whereby images are a priori understood as an inversion of reality. The philosopher wants "to rescue the analysis of images from [such a] trial-like atmosphere" and to thereby displace the structure that opposes the "anaesthetizing power of the image" to the ability to act.[73] Rancière's challenge to oppositions such as passivity/activity, image/living reality, and viewing/knowing is key to his reimagination of aesthetics and politics, whereby to claim images' capacity to "sketch new configurations of what can be seen, what can be said and what can be thought" is also to assert the spectator's capacity to view and understand.[74] (He has thus opened new ways to discuss and analyze spectatorship in the present.[75]) Yet *Le spectateur émancipé* never illustrates its call for an art that points to "a different politics of the sensible" through abstraction nor, hence, through the alternating black-and-white rhythm that characterizes Debord's first film.[76]

Keeping in mind Rancière's analysis, I would like to return to *Hurlements* and its undeniable difference from Debord's other work in film, a difference that does not rest solely on the absence of iconic images. Inveighing against the purely allegorical call to action in *La société du spectacle*, Rancière writes, "But for that [i.e., living action], was it not necessary to abolish images, to plunge the screen into darkness so as to summon people to the action that was alone capable of opposing the lie of the spectacle? In the event, *Guy Debord did not install darkness on the screen*."[77] Rancière does not dwell on or invoke *Hurlements*, other than in a cursory footnote in which he acknowledges, "On the other hand, we might recall that he had done so [i.e., installed darkness on the screen] in a previous film, *Hurlements en faveur de Sade*."[78] As a result of the film's repression within the structure of his text (Rancière confesses knowledge of *Hurlements* only in a footnote), the philosopher does not engage how and when Debord installed darkness on the screen, thereby failing to address the film's potential purchase on a reconsideration of aesthetics and politics in the present, just as he holds at bay the institutional context and communicative practices of the ciné-clubs in which *Hurlements* was originally shown by focusing on the sovereign effect of Debord's voice-over in the later film.[79]

Within Debord's cinematic production, *Hurlements* remains singular: it continues to engender an active reception, even when the terms are reversed as suggested at the outset of this chapter. In contrast to *L'anticoncept*, which asks the viewer to recognize a subject produced through resistance to articulate language, *Hurlements*' appropriated language demonstrates an early instance of *détournement*. But the black sequences' refusal of iconic images presents neither Rancière's intolerable image regime nor the communicative conceit of spoken language. In the absence of a voice-over and when darkness takes over the screen, the public acts and speaks.

WE'RE SO DE-BORED

About six weeks after the screening of *Hurlements* at the Walter Reade Theater, the film was presented as part of the series "VØID for FILM: *imageless cinema*." Curated by Bradley Eros in the context of the first Migrating Forms Film Festival at Anthology Film Archives in New York, "VØID for FILM" presented a seven-hour marathon of imageless cinema on April 17, 2009 (fig. 71). In Eros's words: "A range of works beyond abstraction, from the filmless to the projectorless, all without images. Zero degree cinema, past and present."[80] Unlike the screening at the Walter Reade, Eros's presentation of *Hurlements* took some creative license, exemplified by the following: (1) No print of *Hurlements* was used. Rather, the projector was turned on and off, while on occasion a loop of clear leader was projected. (2) The sound track was read by members of the audience, and

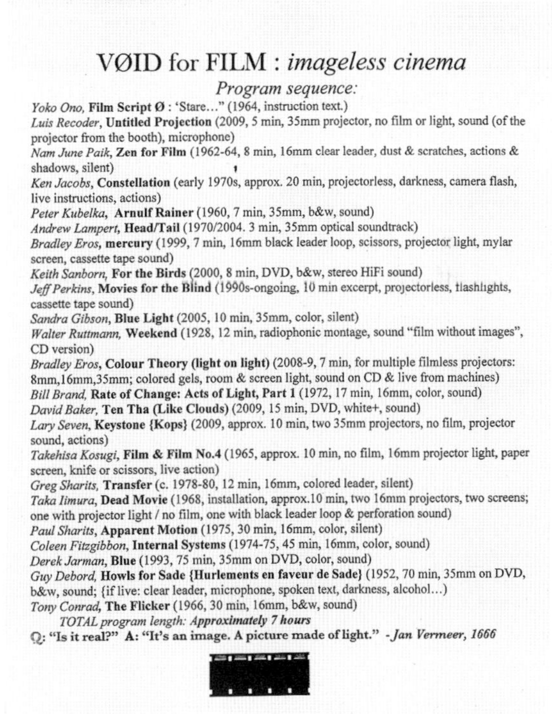

VØID for FILM : *imageless cinema*

Program sequence:

Yoko Ono, **Film Script Ø** : 'Stare..." (1964, instruction text.)
Luis Recoder, **Untitled Projection** (2009, 5 min, 35mm projector, no film or light, sound (of the projector from the booth), microphone)
Nam June Paik, **Zen for Film** (1962-64, 8 min, 16mm clear leader, dust & scratches, actions & shadows, silent)
Ken Jacobs, **Constellation** (early 1970s, approx. 20 min, projectorless, darkness, camera flash, live instructions, actions)
Peter Kubelka, **Arnulf Rainer** (1960, 7 min, 35mm, b&w, sound)
Andrew Lampert, **Head/Tail** (1970/2004. 3 min, 35mm optical soundtrack)
Bradley Eros, **mercury** (1999, 7 min, 16mm black leader loop, scissors, projector light, mylar screen, cassette tape sound)
Keith Sanborn, **For the Birds** (2000, 8 min, DVD, b&w, stereo HiFi sound)
Jeff Perkins, **Movies for the Blind** (1990s-ongoing, 10 min excerpt, projectorless, flashlights, cassette tape sound)
Sandra Gibson, **Blue Light** (2005, 10 min, 35mm, color, silent)
Walter Ruttmann, **Weekend** (1928, 12 min, radiophonic montage, sound "film without images", CD version)
Bradley Eros, **Colour Theory (light on light)** (2008-9, 7 min, for multiple filmless projectors: 8mm,16mm,35mm; colored gels, room & screen light, sound on CD & live from machines)
Bill Brand, **Rate of Change: Acts of Light, Part 1** (1972, 17 min, 16mm, color, sound)
David Baker, **Ten Tha (Like Clouds)** (2009, 15 min, DVD, white+, sound)
Lary Seven, **Keystone {Kops}** (2009, approx. 10 min, two 35mm projectors, no film, projector sound, actions)
Takehisa Kosugi, **Film & Film No.4** (1965, approx. 10 min, no film, 16mm projector light, paper screen, knife or scissors, live action)
Greg Sharits, **Transfer** (c. 1978-80, 12 min, 16mm, colored leader, silent)
Taka Iimura, **Dead Movie** (1968, installation, approx.10 min, two 16mm projectors, two screens; one with projector light / no film, one with black leader loop & perforation sound)
Paul Sharits, **Apparent Motion** (1975, 30 min, 16mm, color, silent)
Coleen Fitzgibbon, **Internal Systems** (1974-75, 45 min, 16mm, color, sound)
Derek Jarman, **Blue** (1993, 75 min, 35mm on DVD, color, sound)
Guy Debord, **Howls for Sade {Hurlements en faveur de Sade}** (1952, 70 min, 35mm on DVD, b&w, sound; {if live: clear leader, microphone, spoken text, darkness, alcohol...)
Tony Conrad, **The Flicker** (1966, 30 min, 16mm, b&w, sound)

*TOTAL program length: **Approximately 7 hours***

Q: "Is it real?" A: "It's an image. A picture made of light." -*Jan Vermeer, 1666*

71. Program for "VØID for FILM: *imageless cinema*," April 17, 2009. Curated by Bradley Eros for the first Migrating Forms Film Festival, Anthology Film Archives, New York.

certain lines were uttered simultaneously by multiple individuals. (3) The timing of the light and dark sequences was decidedly off. (4) The sound track's delivery continued during the dark sequences. And (5) the entire "screening" lasted only twenty-nine minutes. As the performed version of the film increasingly unraveled in the final five minutes, the remaining lines of the script were interspersed with verbal interventions from other members of the audience: "Play the Sharits film"; "This is a real human moment"; "We're so De-bored."

The screening at Anthology demonstrates the extent to which the meaning of the film does not reside primarily within either the final script or the technological mechanisms of the film's support. Just as Wolman's improvised *mégapneumie* remain outside their purview, so too do the myriad responses to *Hurlements*'s black-and-white sequences, which enable moments whose precise meaning and effects cannot be wholly anticipated. Insofar as visual and verbal images are negated, spectators answer the darkness in different ways, voicing multiple subject positions: from the literary to the sentimental, the revolutionary to the banal. At times, contrary to Debord's intentions, audience members even revel in the aesthetic contemplation of darkness. Rather than legislate what and how one must see, *Hurlements* engenders a different public with each new instance of its projection. Rather than a top-down model of communication in which we see our alienation put on display while at the same time being told about it, *Hurlements*' darkness alters the relations between seeing, speaking, and doing in the cinema and for its spectators. In short, *Hurlements* implicates the spectator's actual participation in a way that Debord's other films fail to do. Perhaps this is what Debord was suggesting when he wrote, "What has caused most displeasure in the long term is what I did in 1952."[81]

EPILOGUE

THE FACT THAT CINEMA, like theater, cannot be reduced to a single technical support pushes any account of Lettrist cinema beyond the formal boundaries of film and toward a consideration of what I call heterodox modernism. With their films the Lettrists enlisted various artistic practices, consciously framing their work in relation to multiple histories: from the modern novel (Marcel Proust, James Joyce) and sound poetry, to theater and painting. Lettrist work on cinematic speech also forced the issue of the experimental possibilities of film sound at a time when critics such as André Bazin were almost exclusively attuned to the ontology of the photographic image and privileged the shot. Accordingly, within film studies we could identify possible afterlives of Isidore Isou's theory and practice of *montage discrépant* (discrepant editing) among directors of the Nouvelle Vague and Left Bank groups, each of which broke with traditional narrative and continuity editing.[1] What emerges as crucial in the context of *Off-Screen Cinema* is how the Lettrists' commitment to ciné-club debate inscribes within their films cinema's social network, counting spectators' responses among the actual materials for their film practice. In what follows, I turn to the effects of Lettrist experimentation as it relates to visual art's entwinement with avant-garde film in postwar Europe. Lettrist cinema not only provides the discursive ground for painting's expansion beyond its conventional frame; it also offers, I argue, another possible prehistory for the practices associated with institutional critique.

Casting a retrospective glance on his film production in 1985, Guy Debord wrote the following:

> The painter Yves Klein, whom I knew at the time of *Hurlements* and who attended the first, very tumultuous showing of this film, was dazzled by a convincing 24-minute sequence of darkness, and must have derived from that, some years later, his "monochrome" paintings which—enveloped in a bit of zen mysticism during his famous "blue period"—made many an expert cry genius.[2]

Klein did indeed attend the first screening of *Hurlements en faveur de Sade* (Howls for Sade) at the Ciné-Club Avant-Garde 52 on June 30, 1952, but he would not have seen the final sequence. As noted in chapter 4, the film was not shown in its entirety that day. Thus Debord's assertion that *Hurlements*' final sequence served as Klein's inspiration is misleading, even if he does not go so far as to take sole credit for the development of Klein's work: "When it comes to painting," he continued, "it is not I who could possibly obscure the glory of Yves Klein. That is, rather, what Malévitch had done 40 years before."[3] Debord, as he had done almost thirty years earlier in the pages of the *Internationale situationniste*, suggests that Klein's work constitutes an instance of neo-avant-garde repetition vitiated of critical force. Yet by insisting on Klein's presence at the screening of *Hurlements* (even though Klein was never officially part of Lettrism), Debord tellingly locates the painter in the heady mix of Lettrist cinematic experimentation.[4]

Prior to *Hurlements*, Klein had attended the screening of Isou's *Traité de bave et d'éternité* (On Venom and Eternity, 1951) at the Studio de l'Etoile in Paris on January 25, 1952, after it had already achieved notoriety at the Cannes Film Festival. Some three months later, on May 4, he attended the premiere of François Dufrêne's *Tambours du jugement premier* (Drums of the First Judgment) in Cannes. Known today primarily for his work in phonetic poetry and for showing the backs of urban posters, Dufrêne went even further than Isou in his assertion of sound's independence from the photographic image, and beyond Maurice Lemaître and Gil J Wolman in his rethinking of film's support.[5] In the darkened theater on the day of the film's premiere, an individual (whom Dufrêne calls "*diseur*," or pronouncer/sayer) was stationed in each corner, armed only with a flashlight and a script. Wolman and Marc'O (Marc-Guilbert Guillaumin) read and sang "aphorisms," respectively, while Debord spoke the image track and Dufrêne recited phonetic poetry. At the same time, someone repeatedly opened and closed the curtain in front of the screen.[6] Performed in a cinema, the film enacted a displacement of attention from image to sound and from screen to space to the extent that cinema's effects were no longer tethered to its technological mechanisms and material supports. (The film was recorded once, more than twenty years later; see fig. 72). In the film script, published in the pages of *Ion*, Dufrêne explicitly framed

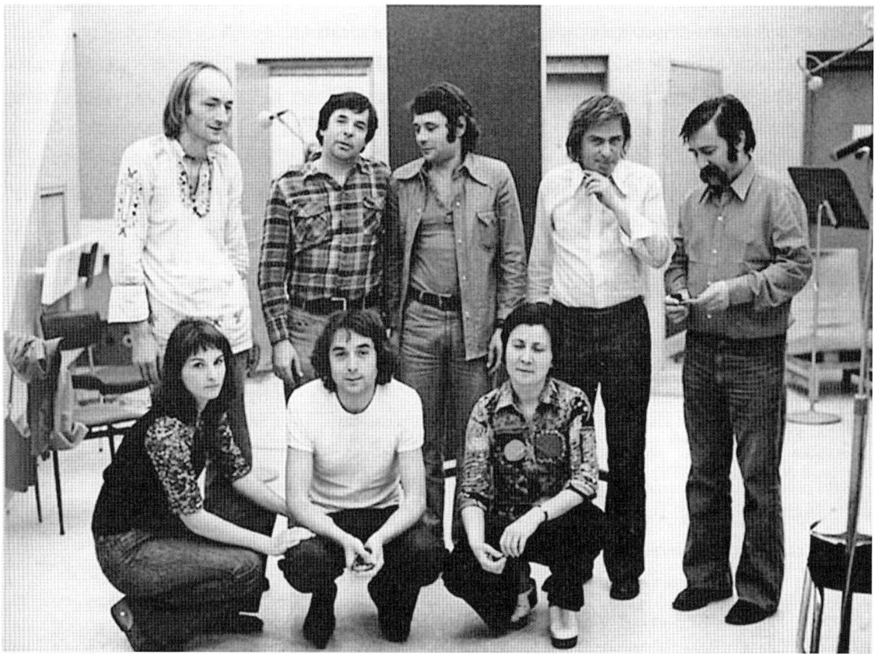

72. Meeting at the Maison de la Radio in 1973 to record for France Culture the live sound of the film *Tambours du jugement premier* (1952), by François Dufrêne. From left to right: Ralph Rumney, François Dufrêne, M. Grenier (technician), Jacques Spacagna, and Gil J Wolman. Below: M. F. Lafosse, Bordet, and Ginette Dufrêne.

Tambours in relation to Antonin Artaud, claiming that the *diseur* should have "a voice that varies in intensity from the natural tone to the most irritating artifice."[7]

Dufrêne asserts that no one talked about this "imaginary film" in the wake of its performance, except, that is, the Lettrists and Klein.[8] "From that moment and until his passing away," he recalls, "when speaking with me, [Klein] rarely failed to greet me with '*Salut O toi l'Auteur du Film sans Ecran ni Pellicule*' [Hello to you, author of the film with no screen nor filmstrip]."[9] In the years 1953–1962, Klein produced approximately sixteen films, which vary in both production and effects. They range from scripts that were never realized to completed films employing professional cameramen, such as Albert Weil (who recorded Klein's work for Gaumont). Some show Klein in the various roles he assumed: from that of a judoka, in 1953, to that of an orchestra conductor for his *Symphonie Monoton-Silence* (Monotone-Silence Symphony), the performance of which accompanied *Anthropométrie de l'époque bleue* (Anthropometry of the Blue Epoch; fig. 73) in 1960. These films, alongside his multiple photographic self-representations, demonstrate the role of media in his process and in the production of his multifaceted artistic identity.[10]

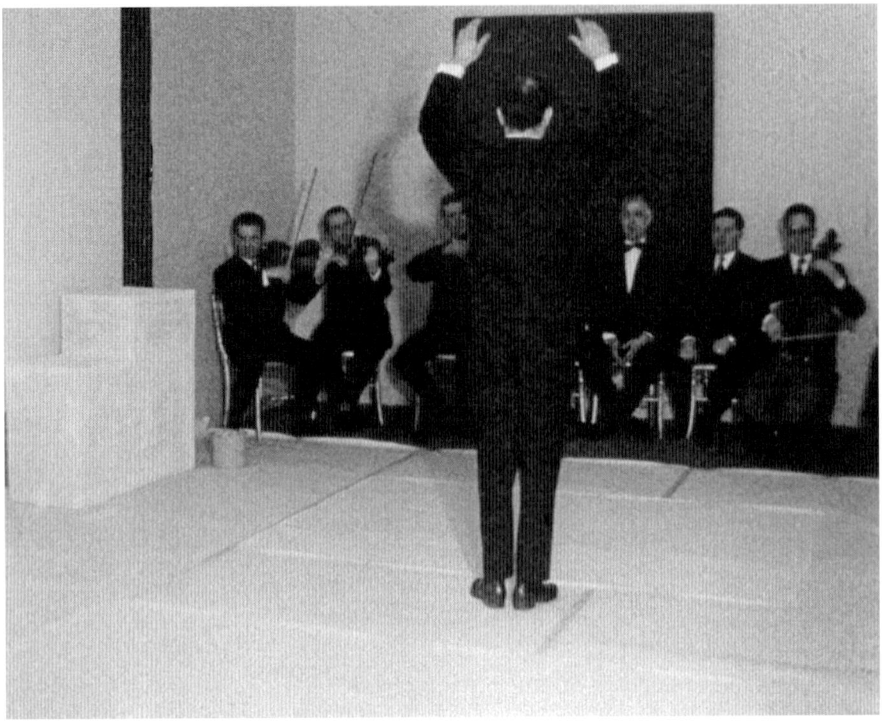

73. Yves Klein, *Anthropométrie de l'époque bleue*, March 1960. Frame enlargement.

If Dufrêne and his fellow Lettrists waged an attack on the traditional terms of spectatorship—the frontal subject-object relation that defines the primary axis of conventional theater and cinema—Klein claimed to have similarly reworked the dominant model of spectatorship in relation to painting, a model he believed lingered on in abstract art. Beginning in 1957, Klein attempted to cleave painting from any of the possible effects it might achieve in his application of paint. It follows that Klein's indebtedness to Lettrist cinema is not to be located in his films as film per se, but rather in his staging of "immaterial pictorial sensibility," perhaps nowhere more notoriously than in his production of the exhibition known as *Le vide* (The Void).

On April 28, 1958, Klein presented *La spécialisation de la sensibilité à l'état de matière première en sensibilité picturale stabilisée* (Specialization of Sensibility in the Raw Material State of Stabilized Pictorial Sensibility; fig. 74), popularly referred to as *Le vide*, at the Galerie Iris Clert. For the exhibition, Klein painted the façade as well as the gallery windows in his signature International Klein Blue. The gallery's street entrance was closed, so the twenty-five hundred visitors (according to Klein) had to enter through an adjacent passageway, walking through the blue curtains that framed the entrance, where two private guards checked invitations

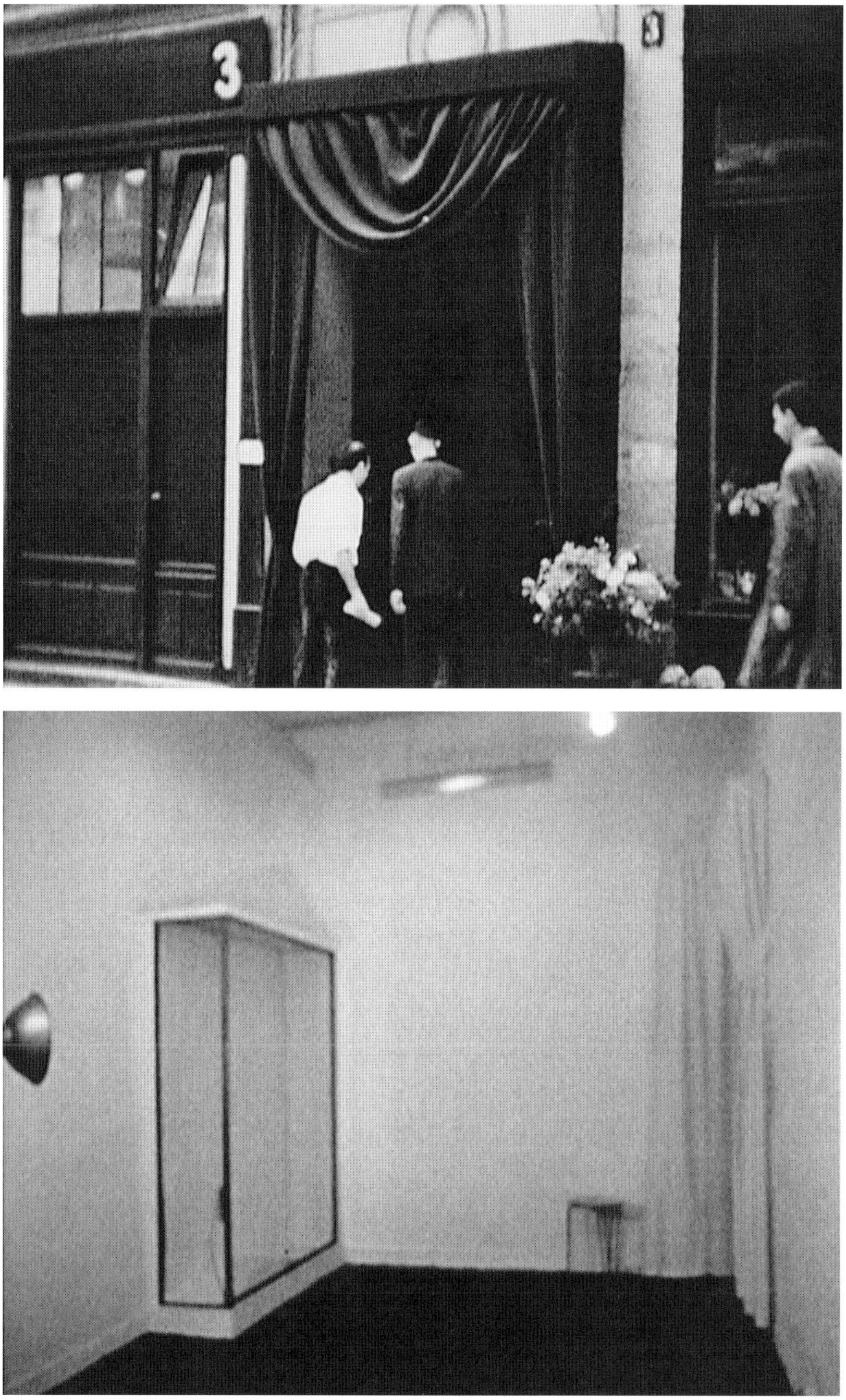

74. Yves Klein, *La spécialisation de la sensibilité à l'état de matière première en sensibilité picturale stabilisée* (also known as *Le vide*), Galerie Iris Clert, Paris, 1958. View from the street and inside the gallery.

and two Republican Guards dressed in full regalia were stationed. (The guards were there to provide security for a minister of state who never showed up, but their presence added to Klein's penchant for ceremonial pomp.) The passageway also served as a reception area, where visitors were offered cocktails of Cointreau, gin, and methylene blue. At the back of the passage, where two more guards restricted admittance to ten at a time, the visitors entered the gallery, which Klein had repainted white.[11] The empty interior, Klein's space of pictorial sensibility, was to be perceived as the immaterialization of the blue exterior.

As I have elsewhere argued (at length), with *Le vide* Klein may have abandoned the materials of painting, but he did so only to entrench the medium more firmly in a discursive "apparatus" beyond its material support—from the commercial transactions for visitors' "impregnation" in the space to the presence of Republican Guards—an apparatus that regulated the experience of space and the subjects it produced.[12] Hence, when developing his invisible painting, Klein animated rather than dissolved his work's institutional frame, continuing to signify painting but doing so through the absence of a material referent. If, in the American context, one legacy of the environmental character of Jackson Pollock's all-over paintings was the multisensory happenings that prompted artists like Allan Kaprow to move beyond painting's frame, in Paris it was cinema (and more specifically Dufrêne's imaginary cinema) that provided the conditions of possibility for Klein's abandonment of painting's conventional support. But where the Lettrists employed dissociative strategies to resist representation, Klein's performances of "immaterial pictorial sensibility" do not resist representation but rather are explicitly and knowingly *performative*; their efficacy depends on precisely the facts and practices that govern the appearance of a message and is bound to both social convention and public ritual.

If Klein preserved painting by performatively activating art's institutional frame, a subsequent generation of artists would turn to such performative conventions in order to critique the institution of art, and in so doing, I argue, draw upon the legacy of Lettrist film in competing ways. Here it is worthwhile to invoke Marcel Broodthaers's well-known founding of the Musée d'Art Moderne, Département des Aigles, Section XIXième siècle (Museum of Modern Art, Department of Eagles, Nineteenth-Century Section), a four-year project that began in the artist's studio in Brussels in 1968. As a fictive institution, Broodthaers's Musée nevertheless engaged in the discursive activities of a real one: as museum director he circulated *lettres ouvertes* stamped with the official name and address of the Musée and organized inaugural speeches, exhibitions of its various sections, and publicity campaigns.

Broodthaers's object labels in his museum's "Section des Figures" flagrantly declare, "This is not a work of art," in three languages. Broodthaers complicates Marcel Duchamp's nominalist gesture (namely, the statement "This is a work of art," in reference to his 1917 readymade *Fountain*) by offering an alternative proposition, mediated by René Magritte's 1929 painting *Le trahison des images* (The Treachery of Images), which plays on the incongruity of visual and verbal signification with the statement "*Ceci n'est pas une pipe*" (This is not a pipe) painted just beneath an image of a pipe. Broodthaers shifts the stakes from the question of what object can or cannot legitimately be called art to that of the institutional authority that underwrites museum classification and display, as instantiated in his museum labels and their relationship to his rather absurd presentation of eagles from all media and genres, both high and low.[13] With his shift from art producer to administrator and his cultivation of a series of museum fictions, Broodthaers sought to draw attention to the language and institutions within which art and its discourse are framed.

Broodthaers's simultaneous turn to Duchamp and Magritte in the development of his practice of institutional critique is well established in the critical literature on his work.[14] In contrast, I would like to ask what it might mean for the historiography of institutional critique to consider how Lettrist film served as an early object lesson for Broodthaers. After all, Broodthaers in all likelihood saw Lettrist films in Brussels, an important center for experimental film, in the early 1950s. On October 31, 1952, the association L'Écran du Séminaire des Arts screened Isou's *Traité* at the Palais des Beaux-Arts and printed an excerpt of Maurice Schérer's *Cahiers du cinéma* review on the back of the program.[15] This was followed by a screening of *Le film est déjà commencé?* (Has the Film Already Started), presented by Lemaître himself, on February 10, 1954 (fig. 75).[16] Did Broodthaers attend these screenings? Did he listen as Lemaître listed the new developments in cinema introduced by his and Isou's films: from the chiseled image to the creation of a new screen, from discrepant montage to the proposal for professional spectators? Crucial here is the fact that the seventh installment of Broodthaers's fictional museum was a "Section cinéma," which exhibited editing equipment and props and also featured a film program, including newsreels and his own *Une discussion inaugurale* (An Inaugural Discussion, 1968), thereby placing cinema at the heart of his fictional museum.

Echoing Daniel in the sound track to Isou's *Traité*, Broodthaers maintains, "At the origin of my intentions was the idea of cinema that moves away from the notion of movement."[17] Referring to the visual and textual heterogeneity at the core of a film like *Le corbeau et le renard* (The Crow and the Fox, 1967), which evokes the eponymous fable by Jean de La Fontaine (1668)—Broodthaers writes, with regard to its production, "On a special

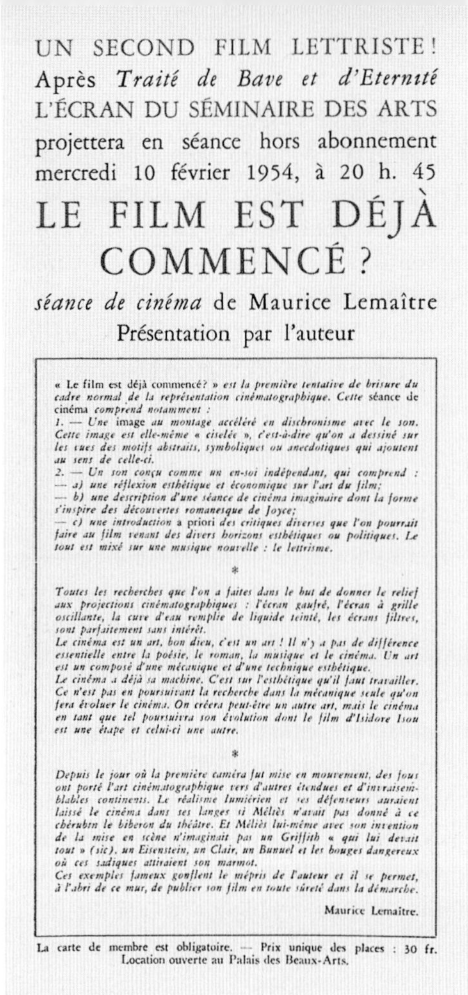

UN SECOND FILM LETTRISTE !
Après *Traité de Bave et d'Eternité*
L'ÉCRAN DU SÉMINAIRE DES ARTS
projettera en séance hors abonnement
mercredi 10 février 1954, à 20 h. 45

LE FILM EST DÉJÀ COMMENCÉ ?

séance de cinéma de Maurice Lemaître
Présentation par l'auteur

« Le film est déjà commencé? » *est la première tentative de brisure du cadre normal de la représentation cinématographique.* Cette séance de cinéma *comprend notamment :*
1. — Une image *au montage accéléré en dischronisme avec le son. Cette image est elle-même « ciselée », c'est-à-dire qu'on a dessiné sur les vues des motifs abstraits, symboliques ou anecdotiques qui ajoutent au sens de celle-ci.*
2. — Un son conçu comme un en-soi indépendant, qui comprend :
— a) une réflexion esthétique et économique sur l'art du film;
— b) une description d'une séance de cinéma imaginaire dont la forme s'inspire des découvertes romanesque de Joyce;
— c) une introduction a priori *des critiques diverses que l'on pourrait faire au film venant des divers horizons esthétiques ou politiques. Le tout est mixé sur une musique nouvelle : le lettrisme.*

*

Toutes les recherches que l'on a faites dans le but de donner le relief aux projections cinématographiques : l'écran gaufré, l'écran à grille oscillante, la cuve d'eau remplie de liquide teinté, les écrans filtres, sont parfaitement sans intérêt.
Le cinéma est un art, bon dieu, c'est un art ! Il n'y a pas de différence essentielle entre la poésie, le roman, la musique et le cinéma. Un art est un composé d'une mécanique et d'une technique esthétique.
Le cinéma a déjà sa machine. C'est sur l'esthétique qu'il faut travailler. Ce n'est pas en poursuivant la recherche dans la mécanique seule qu'on fera évoluer le cinéma. On créera peut-être un autre art, mais le cinéma en tant que tel poursuivra son évolution dont le film d'Isidore Isou est une étape et celui-ci une autre.

*

Depuis le jour où la première caméra fut mise en mouvement, des fous ont porté l'art cinématographique vers d'autres étendues et d'invraisemblables continents. Le réalisme lumiérien et ses défenseurs auraient laissé le cinéma dans ses langes si Méliès n'avait pas donné à ce chérubin le biberon du théâtre. Et Méliès lui-même avec son invention de la mise en scène n'imaginait pas un Griffith « qui lui devait tout » (sic), un Eisenstein, un Clair, un Bunuel et les bouges dangereux où ces sadiques attiraient son marmot.
Ces exemples fameux gonflent le mépris de l'auteur et il se permet, à l'abri de ce mur, de publier son film en toute sûreté dans la démarche.

Maurice Lemaître.

La carte de membre est obligatoire. — Prix unique des places : 30 fr.
Location ouverte au Palais des Beaux-Arts.

75. Maurice Lemaître, *Le film est déjà commencé?*, 1951. Program for the February 10, 1954, screening of the film by the association L'Écran du Séminaire des Arts, Palais des Beaux-Arts, Brussels, Belgium.

screen—in photographic canvas—the book becomes a film, the film becomes a painting (the screen). It is on an image (which summarizes the film) that all the film's images are projected. This is not a film" (figs. 76–77).[18] Through the repeated use of intertitles and subtitles, which explore how visible language affects visual meaning, as well as his development of a new screen that includes textual elements, Broodthaers challenges the voice in cinema as it is traditionally conceived, just as he uses one medium (book) to elaborate the parameters of another (film). Broodthaers's use of cinema refuses narrative absorption and, by extension, the naturalized discourses of the institution of art; he turns not only to the devices of early cinema but perhaps also aspects of the Lettrist films he may have seen in these years.[19]

Even my admittedly cursory review of Broodthaers's practice puts in relief how various Lettrist aesthetic strategies are critically reflected in his work. Lettrist cinema, then, emerges as a crucial site for establishing an alternative genealogy for the intersections between art and film in the postwar moment as well as the critique of the institution of art. Lettrist

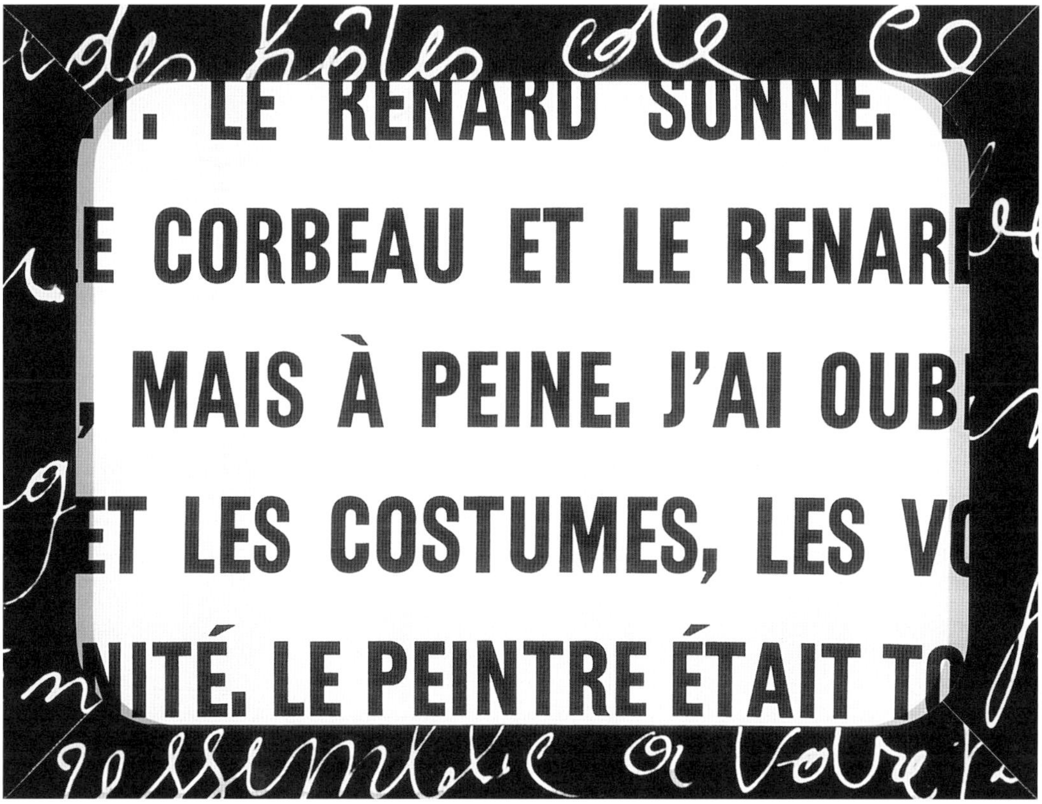

76. Marcel Broodthaers, *Le corbeau et le renard*, 1967. Projection screen. Photo: Rocco Ricci. Collecció MACBA. Consorci MACBA. Dipòsit Herbig.

work with film is critical of formal categories, testing the conventional limits of the medium through the chiseling of the image and attention to sound. In subsequent years they extended such experimentation through the production of imaginary, infinitesimal, and supertemporal films.[20] Second-generation Lettrist Roland Sabatier, for example, exhibited *Les preuves* (The Proof, 1966), a sealed 35-millimeter film canister meant to provoke the experience of an immaterial film exceeding all concrete beauty.

Beyond their initial experiments with sound-image relations in film and with the space of the theater, the Lettrists insistently hoped to fashion another modality for experiencing and administering cinema as an institution. That is, they imagined other ways in which cinema might "conduct" a public: from Lemaitre's call for a new production company to the designation of the ciné-club debate as a constitutive material of film. Lettrism thus contributes to a history of avant-garde film practices that challenge film-as-film (the formalist tradition) and at once attempt to transform the institution of cinema.[21] To understand Lettrism in this

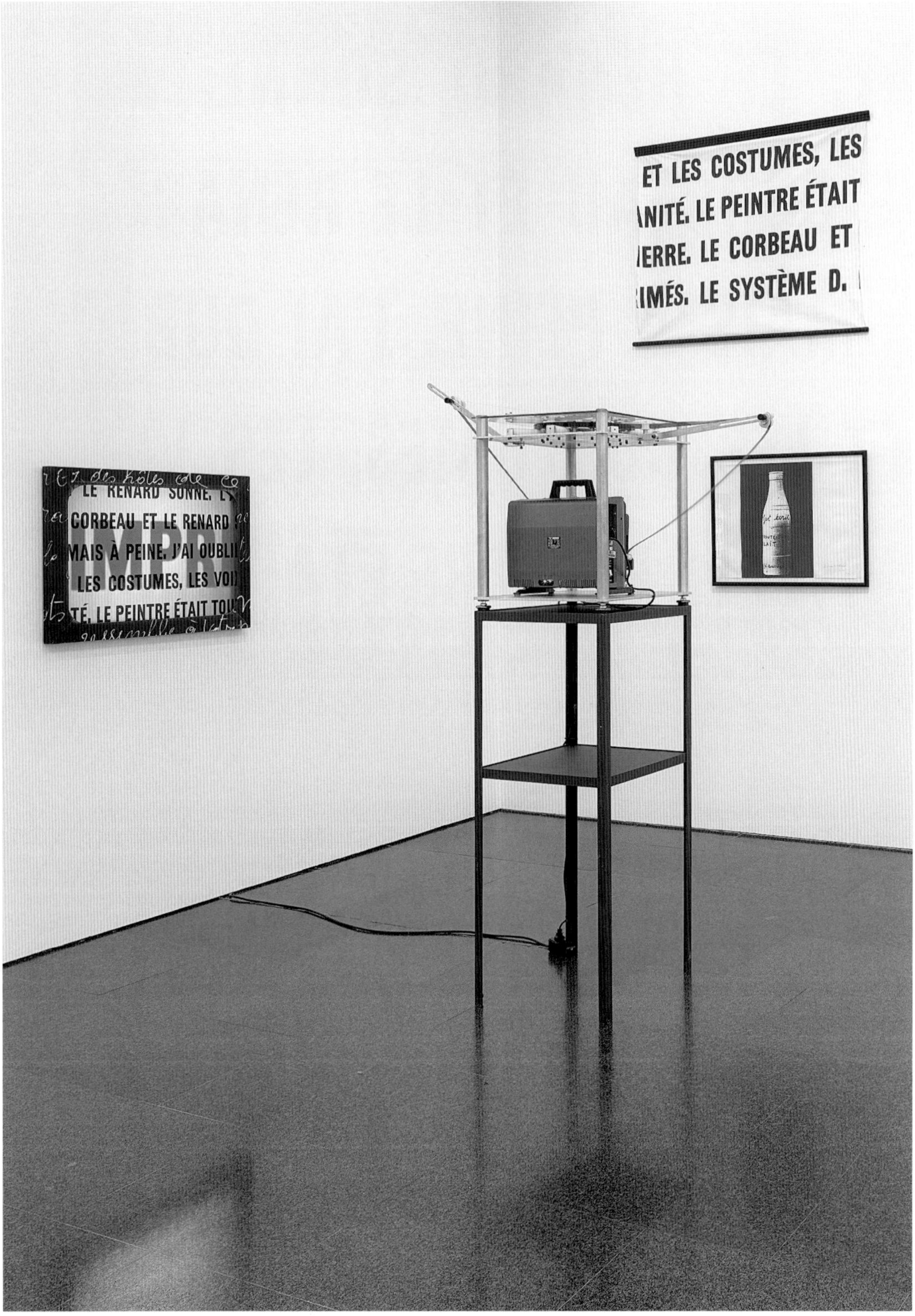

77. Marcel Broodthaers, *Le corbeau et le renard*, 1967. Diverse materials, various dimensions. Installation view. Photo: Gasull Fotografia. Col·lecció MACBA. Consorci MACBA. Dipòsit Herbig.

way is to understand both parts of its challenge—to form and to the institution—which together contribute to its heterodox modernism.

Engaging Lettrism today demands creatively imagining what it might have meant to be a spectator who, denied the comfortable passive viewership of spectacle, participated in a contentious and nonconsensual discussion about developments in film, while experiencing competing images and sounds both on and off the screen. Last but not least, the Lettrists' work obliges one to conjure the specter of what could have happened had Lettrist experimentation in actuality led to the absence of film.

APPENDIX

LETTERS FROM STAN BRAKHAGE TO LETTRIST FILMMAKERS

Stan Brakhage
650 Shotwell St.
San Francisco 10, Calif.
U.S.A.

November 5, 1962

Dear Isidore Isou,

This is a long overdue letter to express grateful thanks for all you have given me. Some, almost, 10 years ago I saw what is here titled "Venom and Eternity." It immediately worked one of the most profound and lasting changes upon all my development as a film-maker. It still continues to inspire (if you'll pardon these big, usually phoney, words) me and to re-direct thoughts (break up past cinematic ideology) whenever they start to crowd out my own filmic development. It is, and always has been, particularly marvelous to me that "Venom and Eternity" does actually free me without, as so many other sources of so-called freedom, imposing its own new forms upon that freedom. That is why it is, to my mind, an absolutely unique touchstone for anyone with sensitivity enough, filmwise, to see it. In that sense, it remains a film-maker's film at the present deplorable state of lack-of-vision generally—that is, that only film-maker's (and very few of them) have, at this blind time, enough vision to put themselves under your cine-magic, and altogether unharmful, spell. Later, hopefully, it will be recognized, even generally, as the land-sea-air-mark in film history which it is.

When I was at Brussels (World's Fair Exposition of Experimental Film) in 1958, I named you as not only a major influence in my own cinematic development but as one of the most important film-makers in this 20th-century world. Much to my surprise, your name was not recognized. Well, this is to let you know that it is recognized here in San Francisco and, generally, in the U.S. and very specifically among my closest friends, including poets, composers, painters, etc., and most gratefully within myself. I have gone out of my way to view "Venom and Eternity" some 15 to 20 times; and I would, as always I'm sure, go out of my way to see it again. Have you made any further films, or are there any earlier—i.e. any other films at all? Well, I do very much hope so; and I also wish your writing were available here in the U.S. If I can be of any help in that respect, and/or especially regarding films and film-distribution (where I do have some authority), let me know.

Best,
Stan Brakhage

[*Typed letter, signed by hand. Archives Isou-Goldstein, Paris. Reproduced with the permission of the Estate of Stan Brakhage.*]

Stan Brakhage
c/o Collom
Silver Spruce
Nederland Star Route
Boulder, Colorado
U.S.A.

March 20, 1963

Dear Isidore Isou,

I was very pleased to receive a letter from you, and especially glad to know that you are still working, considering making a new film, and that there still is a group of lettristes—so much that I have loved, so many friends, groups, even entire "movements," have vanished, been vanquished by the difficulties and pressures of the forces-of-destruction in the world of this time . . . many individuals of The American Film Movement haven't made a film in 6 or 7 years; but then there seems to be new incentive, springing from heaven-only-knows-where, for suddenly, this last year, a number of people have begun to work again . . . and this is a joy.

Unfortunately, however, we have no real recognition from the society in which we live, therefore no where-with-all, money or other power to extend to each other either in this country or abroad—we have not even enough to properly extend our own works to the ignorant public around us . . . so each film-maker works alone, supporting himself, his family, his films, as best he can, with commercial jobs, etc., often (as I now am) separated from his comrades by 1000 miles of wasteland, a cultural (as well as actual) desert, continuing his own work with no thought of having it really seen, perceived, in his life-time, often editing film material (as I now am) which he has no money to print when the work is finished. So, you see, you cannot really say there *is* an American Film Movement; but there are at least 30 individuals known to me, and friends of mine, whose films I very much respect, each one of whom is currently making, or has just made, a film, all working and living in various parts of this large country. Now, the situation is somewhat different in New York City: there are a number of film-makers (and some of the best) who work together (even, occasionally, collaborate on films) and meet quite often, and are involved in publicity and public recognition. (Please understand that when I say "public" I mean "the very small segment of the people interested in the arts"—recognition of "the public-at-large" is unthinkable.) But New York City is, after all, just a large Market Place; and the NY film-makers are always running the risk of being led very much astray from their actual works by the commercial considerations they are constantly surrounded by and prey to. But they have, this last year, formed THE FILM-MAKERS' COOPERATIVE, 414 PARK AVE. SOUTH, N.Y. 16, N.Y. and are distributing their own films, as well as mine and many other film-makers in this country, and are very interested in trying to get films from abroad. I suggest you write to them. It is a non-profit organization (and, indeed, so far has made no profit for the film-makers.)

The New York people also produce the very finest film magazine in the country: FILM CULTURE: and it is unquestionably the efforts of these people which has made my work in film as widely known as it is and my films as distributed as they are . . . altho' I should add that this public recognition has probably cost me as much money as it has brought in. I have also devoted a lot of time to helping the N.Y. group by getting them films for distribution from film-makers all over the country, by writing articles (and they probably would very much like to print an article by you—tho' again, they cannot afford to pay) etc.

Now—you asked about the U.S. Distribution of "Venom and Eternity." The man who says he owns the prints is RAYMOND ROHAUER, 7165 BEVERLY BLVD., LOS ANGELES 36, CALIFORNIA. He distributes the film thru a regular distribution company (write MR. WILLARD MORRISON, C/O AUDIO FILM CENTER, 406 CLEMENT, SAN

FRANCISCO, CALIFORNIA). It is only fair to warn you that any number of American Film-Makers have considered, and even tried, to sue Mr. Rohauer and have failed. Mr. Rohauer is a very clever, and many would say "ruthless," businessman with "good" (i.e. *bad*) lawyers, and has generally proved very successful in court. The major trouble, however, is that (considering the expenses of a trial) it simply is not worth the cost of suing anyone over a breach of contract in the area of the "art films," or "experimental film," etc. While "Venom and Eternity" *has* had some good distribution by American "art-film" standards and has been *comparatively* widely seen, I would guess that it probably hasn't yet made enough money to pay Mr. Rohauer's cost of putting titles on it . . . but that's my guess, based on my own experiences. Naturally this lack of profit has discouraged Mr. Rohauer with the whole field of "the art film" (thank heavens); and he recently *gave* me back the ownership of a film I had been cheated (in my opinion) out of some six years ago . . . to him, you see, it (business: i.e. "cheating people legally") is all a game. Your best bet is *not* to attack him (as he loves to defend himself) but simply to ask him for your rights (giving him the chance to be magnanimous.)

We had to leave San Francisco, due to lack of money, and are now living (as before) in the mountains. We just had a baby boy, our first boy in 4 children, and are finding life difficult, as always, but very exciting and beautiful. I would like to hear more of your life and, especially, your (to me) wondrous ideas on film, and (of course) to see more of your work—Best Stan

[*Handwritten letter; italicized words underlined in original. Archives Isou-Goldstein, Paris. Reproduced with the permission of the Estate of Stan Brakhage.*]

Stan Brakhage
2142 Canyon Blvd.
#203
Boulder, Colorado U.S.A.
80302

December 5, 1992

Dear Maurice Lemaitre

Your works are wondrous to me. I was immediately amazed when Jean-Michel showed me part of the video during my trip to Paris. From just that brief, partial, viewing I was prepared to say to the audience later that afternoon (during my lecture) that if one considered Melies and Lumiere Bros. the two wings of cinema, then (along a line of that same metaphor) Isou would have to be considered the body of cinema (in the sense one knows mitosis of cells thru the retch of growth prior to splitting) and that you, then, would be something more kin to the electrical synapsing of the nervous system. I went on to praise the biological rhythms, the catalyst of your cuts and cathexis-like balance and counter balance of the progression of your editing. I remember flailing with my arms and some, perhaps, rather frantic finger motions as words failed me . . . as they do now. It is really just a kind of feeling that I picked up on immediately I was exposed to your work. And now I am happy to report that the material you have sent, especially the video-tape, has more than confirmed my original impression. I am very grateful for what you have sent.

[Jonas] Mekas has his limits, yes; and I quarrel with him about once a season: but it is the whole wretched refusal of Art Institutes (all over the world) to fairly exhibit and otherwise promote anything which has to do with moving visual imagery—it is deliberate ignorance, thus—which I hold responsible for the fact that I only came to know your work a couple months ago . . . (I say "deliberate" ignorance because I know full well that Film has been carefully ignored by the bureaucracies of aesthetics simply because it is a medium which cannot ever be owned in that exclusive sense a painting or sculpture can be owned, thus can never be worth very much as an investment). The American Independent Film Movement, as it has been called, has been essentially killed by this ignorance. Of my generation of film makers, and the generations on either side of me, only 7 or 8 people are left who have been enabled to make a film in the last decade. I myself can no longer afford to print my new films, though I do continue to make them. The young in this country shoot (mostly 8mm) and run their originals, not even dreaming they'll be enabled ever to print their films. Jonas has managed to salvage a few names and films from this slaughter. *I don't always agree with what he chooses to help; and the fact that I (who am always searching for the visions and new, and older, makers of film) should come to my 59th year before hearing of you shall certainly be yelled in his direction as loudly and firmly as I'm able.*

And (more optimistically) in every other way I'm enabled, I shall sing your praises and recommend your genius to all those I know.

Sincerely,
Stan Brakhage

[*Typed letter, signed by hand; italicized sentence underlined by hand in original. Bismuth-Lemaître Papers, Beinecke Rare Book and Manuscript Library, Yale University. Reproduced with the permission of the Estate of Stan Brakhage.*]

NOTES

Unless otherwise noted, all translations from non-English editions are my own. I would like to thank Frédéric Acquaviva for his assistance on aspects of the translations from French. Original emphases are maintained, with any alterations noted. With an eye to consistency, I have opted for the consistent application of American spelling for words such as *theater*.

INTRODUCTION

1 Isidore Isou, "Préambule à un film," *Le film français (Cinémonde)*, no. 9–11 (April 1951) (my italics).

2 Antonin Artaud, as cited in Stephen Barber, *The Screaming Body/Antonin Artaud: Film Projects, Drawings, and Sound Recordings* (London: Creation Books, 1999), 16.

3 In Artaud's film scenarios, of which only *La coquille et le clergyman* (The Seashell and the Clergyman, 1926) was produced, noises and screams were to lacerate the flow of visual images, opening onto a cinematic experience that, like the experience described in his subsequent writing on theater, aimed to resist representation. Denis Hollier analyzes Artaud's discussion of "pure cinema" and his attendant claim that the medium would "always be visual." Artaud resisted audiovisual suture through his proposals for what Hollier aptly terms "negative synchronization." Hollier highlights instances in which Artaud continues to write of silent films even when they were to have recourse to sound. The result was Artaud's paradoxical designation of a "cinéma muet non muet" (nonsilent silent cinema). See Hollier, "The Artaud Case: The Prompter," in *Specters of Artaud: Language and the Arts in the 1950s*, ed. Kaira M. Cabañas with Frédéric Acquaviva (Madrid: Museo Nacional Centro de Arte Reina Sofía, 2012), 51–61. See also Hollier, "The Death of Paper, Part Two: Artaud's Sound System," *October*, no. 80 (Spring 1997), 27–37. Artaud would not live to experience Lettrist experiments in cinema. However, prior to his death he was familiar with at least some of the work of the Lettrists, who are cited in Antonin Artaud, "Chiotte à l'esprit" (March 1947), *Tel quel* 3 (Fall 1960): 3–8.

4 See Foucault, "The Subject and Power," afterword in *Michel Foucault: Beyond Structuralism and Hermeneutics*, ed. Hubert L. Dreyfus and Paul Rabinow, 2nd ed. (Chicago:

University of Chicago Press, 1983), 208–26, esp. 220–21. "Conduct of conduct" is my translation of the phrase "conduire des conduites" from the original French version of the essay. See Foucault, *Dits et écrits*, vol. 4, *1980–1988* (Paris: Gallimard, 1994), 237.

5 Among the practices that defined the cinema as governance in occupied France were the following: (1) German newsreels were shown in every theater, with a mandate that the houselights be half on to allow identification of any troublemakers in the cinema; (2) German film policy, primarily instantiated through the German-owned film company Continental Films, promoted French film as a way of demonstrating Germany's liberalism, expanding the international market for European film, and thereby overcoming US dominance; (3) German-produced French films treated historical and fantastic subjects as a way of providing "reassurance" and "entertainment" to the French population and of tapping into French nationalism; (4) Jews were barred from involvement in any aspect of the film industry, as actors or producers or distributors, thereby securing the Aryanization of the industry. See Evelyn Ehrlich, "The Film Industry and the Jews," chap. 4 in *Cinema of Paradox: French Filmmaking under the German Occupation* (New York: Columbia University Press, 1985), 57–70.

6 For an incisive account of the affinity between the French and American film industries in these years, see Vanessa R. Schwarz, *It's So French! Hollywood, Paris, and the Making of Cosmopolitan Film Culture* (Chicago: University of Chicago Press, 2007).

7 Exhibitions dedicated to the projected image in modern and contemporary art include *Into the Light: The Projected Image in American Art, 1964–1977* (Whitney Museum of American Art, 2001); *X-Screen: Film Installations and Actions in the 1960s and 1970s* (Vienna: Mumok, 2004); *Slide Show: Projected Images in Contemporary Art* (Tate Modern/Baltimore Museum, 2005); and *Le mouvement des images* (Centre Pompidou, 2006–2007). In addition, anthologies such as *Screen/Space: The Projected Image in Contemporary Art*, ed. Tamara Trodd (Manchester: Manchester University Press, 2011); *Expanded Cinema: Art, Performance, Film*, ed. A. L. Rees, Duncan White, Steven Ball, and David Curtis (London: Tate Publishing, 2011); and *Art and the Moving Image: A Critical Reader*, ed. Tanya Leighton (London: Tate Publishing, 2008), also cover historical and contemporary work but do not mention Lettrist film. The front matter in *Expanded Cinema* includes, over two spreads, a chart that tracks various expanded cinema practices and includes a box on "Lettrist and Situationist Cinema," but the volume contains no essay that covers this work.

8 While I was writing this book, the papers of Gil J Wolman and Maurice Lemaître were acquired by the Beinecke Rare Book and Manuscript Library at Yale University. Around the same time, Guy Debord's papers entered the Bibliothèque Nationale de France, although the collection contains only scant material related to his Lettrist years.

9 The following articles are among the few that discuss Lettrist film: Andrew Uroskie, "Beyond the Black Box: The Lettrist Cinema of Disjunction," *October*, no. 135 (Winter 2011), 21–48; Rochelle Fack, "Bazin's Chaplin Myth and the Corrosive Lettrists," in *Opening Bazin: Postwar Film Theory and Its Afterlife*, ed. Dudley Andrew with Hervé Joubert-Laurencin (New York: Oxford University Press, 2011); Nicole Brenez, "Improvised Notes on French Expanded Cinema," *Millennium Film Journal*, nos. 43/44 (Summer 2005), 112–29; and Thomas Y. Levin, "Dismantling the Spectacle: The Cinema of Guy Debord," in *Guy Debord and the Situationist International*, ed. Tom McDonough (Cambridge, MA: MIT Press, 2002), 321–453, originally published in *On the Passage of a Few People through a Rather Brief Moment in Time: The Situationist International, 1957–1972* (Cambridge, MA: MIT Press; Boston: Institute of Contemporary Art, 1989), 72–123. Greil Marcus touches on the Lettrists' film production in *Lipstick Traces: A Secret History of the Twentieth Century* (Cambridge, MA: Harvard University Press, 1990), 323–43. Isou, Lemaître, and Dufrêne receive small mention in an entry on sound in Hans Scheugl and Ernst Schmidt Jr., *Eine Subgeschichte des Films: Lexikon des Avantgarde-, Experimental- und Undergroundfilms*, 2 vols. (Frankfurt: Suhrkamp Verlag, 1974), 2:931, 942, and in A. L. Rees, *A History of Experimental Film and Video* (London: BFI Publishing, 1999). Lettrism is not, however, included within general histories of avant-garde

and experimental film, such as David Curtis, *Experimental Cinema* (New York: Universe Books, 1971), or Malcolm Le Grice, *Abstract Film and Beyond* (London: Studio Vista, 1977). More recently, Hannah Feldman and Pavle Levi have each included analysis of Lettrist cinema in their books. See Feldman, *From a Nation Torn: Decolonizing Art and Representation in France, 1945–1962* (Durham, NC: Duke University Press, 2014), chap. 3; and Levi, *Cinema by Other Means* (New York: Oxford University Press, 2012), chap. 4.

10 In French, only Frédérique Devaux's *Le cinéma lettriste: 1951–1991* (Paris: Éditions Paris Expérimental, 1992) offers a comprehensive overview of Lettrist cinema. While her book is rich with descriptive and factual details, Devaux (also a practicing Lettrist filmmaker) does not offer an external analytic perspective through which to assess the historical specificity of Lettrist film. Other French books offer brief analyses of Lettrist film in the context of broader studies on experimental film. See Dominique Noguez, *Eloge du cinéma expérimental: Définitions, jalons, perspectives* (Paris: Musée national d'art moderne, Centre Georges Pompidou, 1979; rev. ed., Paris: Éditions Paris Expérimental, 2010); *Jeune, dure et pure! Une histoire du cinéma d'avant-garde et expérimental en France*, ed. Nicole Brenez and Christian Lebrat (Paris: Cinémathèque Française; Milan: Mazzotta, 2001); and Jean-Michel Bouhours, *Quel cinéma*, vol. 5 of *Documents—Documents sur l'art*, ed. Lionel Bovier and Xavier Douroux (Zurich: JRP Ringier; Dijon: Les Presses du réel, 2010), esp. 156–203.

11 Dufrêne's *Tambours du jugement premier* premiered in Cannes on May 4, 1952. In the darkened theater, an individual—whom Dufrêne calls "diseur" (pronouncer/sayer)—stood in each corner, carrying only a flashlight and a script. Wolman and Marc'O read and sang "aphorisms," while Debord spoke the image track and Dufrêne recited Lettrist poetry. Performed in a theater, the film displaced attention from image to sound, a subject I take up again in this volume's epilogue. The film as originally performed at Cannes was recorded only once, over twenty years later. In 1973, Ralph Rumney directed a recording for the program *Atelier de création radiophonique* for France Culture, with the voices of François Dufrêne, Ginette Dufrêne, Gil J Wolman, Jacques Spacagna, and Claude Torey. In 1981, Dufrêne recorded the "Prodrome" and the film's opening section up until the second image (a female voice, not included in the 1973 version). The version of the film in the Centre Pompidou collection includes the 1973 and 1981 recordings, together with other recordings made after Dufrêne's death. For its 2012 installation at the Reina Sofia, in order to move beyond the single-channel recording and capture the spatiality of the original performance, the individual voices were separated onto four separate tracks and emitted from loudspeakers placed in the four corners of the gallery. The voices were distributed among the four speakers as follows: front left, Ginette Dufrêne and Torey; front right, François Dufrêne; back left, Spacagna; back right, Wolman. Thanks are due to Frédéric Acquaviva for investigating the differences between the 1973 and 1981 recordings and for his meticulous work toward the film's quadraphonic installation.

12 Thanks are due to Catherine Goldstein for granting me access to Isou's archive and for her patience as I went through the material in search of Brakhage's original letters to Isou, dated November 5, 1962, and March 20, 1963. Archives Isou-Goldstein, Paris. These letters are transcribed in the appendix to this volume. See also Brakhage's comments in "Inspirations," in *The Essential Brakhage*, ed. Bruce McPherson (New York: McPherson, 2001), 208–9, and the interview with Scott MacDonald in *A Critical Cinema: Interviews with Independent Filmmakers*, no. 4 (Berkeley: University of California Press, 2005), 48. Isou's *Traité* was also the subject of a 1993 letter from Brakhage to Frédérique Devaux on the occasion of her research for *Traité de bave et d'éternité de Isidore Isou* (Paris: Éditions Yellow Now, 1994).

13 The flyer announcing *Traité* does not list a specific date for the screening, and Tim Lanza, curator of the Raymond Rohauer archive, was unable to specify a date based on existing records. Lanza, e-mail correspondence with author, June 10, 2013.

14 Leon Vickman, Alfred Stern, and Reinaldo V. Gutierrez, "Lettrisme, A New Philosophy from Paris: (Avant-Garde Cinema)," trans. Leon Vickman, *Pendulum* (Autumn 1954),

12–25. Archives Isou-Goldstein, Paris. I would like to thank Fabrice Flahutez for bringing this publication to my attention. Isou's archive also contains a clipping from the Cal Tech newspaper: "Pendulum Features French Philosophy," *California Tech* 54, no. 9 (December 4, 1952).

15 Richard Foreman, interview with author, June 20, 2013.

16 A few other notable exceptions: Isou's and Lemaître's films were screened at the First International Symposium on Letterism, Lewis and Clark College, Portland, Oregon, May 24–29, 1976. Wolman's *L'anticoncept* was shown in the context of *Film Modernism and Its Discontents: A Perspective from Paris*, organized by Keith Sanborn at Exit Art in New York, November 7–10, 1990. Two versions of Debord's *Hurlements en faveur de Sade* screened in New York in the spring of 2009, one on March 1 at Lincoln Center's Walter Reade Theater, the other as part of the series "VØID for FILM: *imageless cinema*," curated by Bradley Eros at Anthology Film Archives, on April 17.

17 *Ion* also includes the essay by Serge Berna, "Jusqu'à l'os" (To the Bone), and texts by Poucette, Yolande de Luart, and Monique Geoffroy. For a facsimile of the original magazine, published in 1952 by the Centre de Création, see *Ion* (Paris: Jean-Paul Rocher, 1999).

18 Isou, "Esthétique du cinéma," in *Ion*, 67.

19 Ibid., 59.

20 Ibid., 60 (original in boldface).

21 Ibid., 55 (in original, "cinématographe" and "cinéma" are boldface).

22 See S. M. Eisenstein, "Montage 1938," in *S. M. Eisentein Selected Works: Towards a Theory of Montage*, ed. Michael Glenny and Richard Taylor, trans. Michael Glenny (London: BFI Publishing, 1991), 2:296. Isou's discussion of sound and image relations in cinema shares with the Soviet avant-garde a rejection of the naturalist use of either sound or speech. In their 1929 manifesto, V. I. Pudovkin, Eisentein, and G. V. Alexandrov claim that it was precisely the use of sound as illustration for visual images that would "destroy the culture of montage." Eisenstein, Pudovkin, and Alexandrov, "A Statement," in Sergei Eisenstein, *Film Form: Essays in Film Theory*, ed. and trans. Jay Leyda (1949; San Diego: Harcourt Brace and Company, 1977), 258. Nevertheless, they advanced an audiovisual counterpoint wherein sound would remain independent but metaphorically function within a "single, generalizing audiovisual image." For Eisenstein, "the change from silent-film montage to audiovisual montage change[d] nothing *in principle*." See S. M. Eisentein, "Vertical Montage," in *S. M. Eisenstein Selected Works*, 2:329, 327. That nothing changed "in principle" with the introduction of sound in Soviet montage was an issue for Isou: "If Poudovkin and Eisenstein enriched the *montage* or the *narrative movement* (to the subject) of Griffith, Ruttman enriched the *suggestive movement* (the theme without theme) of Dulac. Neither has anything to do with *the destruction of the heart of the relation* [between image and sound]." Isou, "Esthétique du cinéma," 68n3 (original emphasis: boldface).

23 Isou, "Esthétique du cinéma," 61.

24 See *Amos ou Introduction à la métagraphologie* (Paris: Arcanes, 1953); published in facsimile, with a short conclusion contextualizing the work, as *Amos ou Introduction à la métagraphologie* (Marseille: La Termitière, 2000).

25 For examples of Lettrist notation systems, see Isidore Isou, *Introduction à une nouvelle poésie et à une nouvelle musique* (Paris: Gallimard, 1947), 314; and Maurice Lemaître, *Sistème de notasion pour les lètries* (Paris: Éditions Richard-Masse, 1952), 44–46.

26 Antonin Artaud, *The Theater and Its Double*, trans. M. C. Richards (New York: Grove, 1958), 46.

27 Wolman, Dufrêne, and Jean-Louis Brau responded more explicitly to Artaud by externalizing sounds whose enunciation begins *within* the body and thus is anterior to the modulation provided for by the organs of speech. Conceived in 1950, Wolman's *mégapneumie* are based on breath (rather than on the letter, as with Isou) and probe the use of "all human sounds." Two years earlier, in 1949, Dufrêne had created a Lettrist poem that was to be shouted, "in memory of Antonin Artaud," and that subsequently

was featured on the sound track to Isou's *Traité*. His 1953 manifesto for a "cri automatique" (automatic cry) or *crirythme* (rhythm cry) continues the Artaudian alliance in the manifesto's epigraph: "Toute l'écriture est de la cochonnerie" (All writing is pig shit). I discuss Wolman's *mégapneumie* in chapter 3.

28 Artaud, *Theater and Its Double*, 46.

29 Isou, "Esthétique du cinéma," 46 (original emphasis: boldface).

30 See P. Adams Sitney, *Visionary Film: The American Avant-Garde 1943–2000* (1974; New York: Oxford University Press, 2002), 348.

31 The emphasis on cinematic speech also differentiates Lettrist work from American avant-garde cinema produced in the years 1935–1955. With the exception of a few films that include music on the sound track, the notion of the silent film is kept alive in the American experimental tradition, while it had largely disappeared during these years in France. I would like to thank P. Adams Sitney for drawing my attention to this distinction.

32 Isou, "Esthétique du cinéma," 148.

33 See Vincent Pinel, *Introduction au ciné-club: Histoire, théorie, pratique du ciné-club en France* (Paris: Éditions Ouvrières, 1964). I take up the legacy of the ciné-club in chapter 2.

34 See Gene Youngblood, *Expanded Cinema* (New York: E. P. Dutton, 1970). See also note 7 for more recent publications on expanded cinema.

35 Readings that usefully address the specificity of critical practices of expanded cinema include Pamela M. Lee, "Bare Lives," in *X-Screen*, 70–86, and Branden W. Joseph's discussion in "Plastic Empathy: The Ghost of Robert Whitman," *Grey Room*, no. 25 (Fall 2006), 64–91.

36 Liz Kotz offers an excellent account of the uncomfortable proximity that often exists between expanded cinema's seemingly countercultural endeavors and the display of modern mass media in "Disciplining Expanded Cinema," in *X-Screen*, 51. In the 1960s, new image technologies such as television were also championed as a return to self-presence through a subjective extension achieved by technological advance. See, for example, Marshall McLuhan, *Understanding Media: The Extensions of Man* (New York: McGraw Hill, 1964).

37 See Jonathan Walley's discussion of paracinema in "The Material of Film and the Idea of Cinema: Contrasting Practices in Sixties and Seventies Avant-Garde Film," *October*, no. 103 (Winter 2003), 15–30.

38 Isou's work provides an early instance of an investigation into how phonation and sound-and-speech recordings signify and have determinate effects in film. Recent studies have increasingly turned to the nonvisual and auditory presence of the voice and its signifying possibilities in cinema. Michel Chion offers an incisive study of the voice in relation to film narrative, giving the designation *acousmêtre* to the power of a voice whose body remains outside the frame. He focuses his analysis on the shifting relations between a visualized situation and an acousmatic situation, and thus the various combinations between filmed image and filmed voice. See Chion, *The Voice in Cinema*, trans. Claudia Gorbman (1982; New York: Columbia University Press, 1999). Chion's study is limited to a discussion of film qua film (the possibilities of voice related to the presence of a "source" in the film), and thus does not extend to a discussion of physical space or real sounds in the theater, which are central to Lettrist cinematic practice.

39 Clement Greenberg, "Modernist Painting" (1960), in *Clement Greenberg: The Collected Essays and Criticism*, vol. 4, *Modernism with a Vengeance, 1957–1969*, ed. John O'Brian (Chicago: University of Chicago Press, 1986), 86.

40 Isou, "Esthétique du cinéma," 69.

41 Barber, *Screaming Body*, 27.

42 Antonin Artaud, *Oeuvres complètes*, vol. 4, ed. Paule Thévenin (Paris: Gallimard, 1970), 297. The citation is located in the appendix, "Dossier du Théâtre et son double," in the section for notes concerning the essay "Sur le théâtre balinais."

43 Artaud, as cited in Hollier, "Death of Paper," 34.

44 Artaud, *Theater and Its Double*, 12. Asked whether the theater possesses its own language, Artaud affirms, "One finds in any case that this language, if it exists, is necessarily identified with the *mise-en-scène* considered: 1. as the visual and plastic materialization of speech, 2. as the language of everything that can be said and signified upon a stage independently of speech, everything that finds its expression in space, or that can be affected or disintegrated by it." Ibid., 69.

45 See Rosalind E. Krauss, *"A Voyage on the North Sea": Art in the Age of the Post-Medium Condition* (London: Thames and Hudson, 2000); and Krauss, *Under Blue Cup* (Cambridge, MA: MIT Press, 2011). My discussion of heterodox modernism differs, however, from Krauss's account of a post-medium condition, which implies a *coming after* a historical moment when notions of a medium were based on its purported purity and self-identity. To insist on a heterodox modernism, via Artaud, is to foreground how such pure and impure conceptions and practices temporally coincide. In the context of this study, the Lettrists' heterodox modernism also responds to their attention to film as a social (not autonomous) practice.

46 For an insightful discussion of what he calls Artaud's "modernism without organs" and its importance to conceptualizing an alternative genealogy for postwar artistic practices, see Branden W. Joseph, "Modernism without Organs," *Artforum* 51, no. 1 (September 2012) 494–501, 538. Joseph also uses the adjective *heterodox* to designate the specificity of Artaud's modernism, 496.

47 See Antoine de Baecque, *La cinéphilie: Invention d'un regard, histoire d'une culture, 1944–1968* (Paris: Fayard, 2003).

48 Lemaître references these filmmakers' attendance of early Lettrist film screenings in *First International Symposium on Letterism (Lewis and Clark College, Portland, Oregon, May 24–29, 1976)*, ed. Pietro Ferrua (Portland, OR: Avant-Garde Publishers, 1978), 123–25. Moreover, the DVD version of his *Le film est déjà commencé?* includes a short "Annonce" (1979) that introduces the film, claiming it as a precursor to the work of Resnais, Marker, Godard, and Marguerite Duras. See Maurice Lemaître, *Le film est déjà commencé?* (Has the Film Already Started?), 1951, Fondation Bismuth-Lemaître (color, 65 minutes).

49 The publications are available in the Bismuth-Lemaître Papers, Beinecke Rare Book and Manuscript Library, Yale University.

50 For a recent study of Lettrism as a movement, see the informative volume Fabrice Flahutez, *Le lettrisme historique était une avant-garde* (Dijon, France: Les presses du réel, 2011). For a history of Lettrist poetry, see Jean-Paul Curtay, *La poésie lettriste* (Paris: Éditions Seghers, 1974). In English, see "Lettrisme: Into the Present," special issue, *Visible Language* 17, no. 3 (Summer 1983), as well as the exhibition catalogue *Letterism and Hypergraphics: The Unknown Avant-Garde 1945–1985* (New York: Franklin Furnace, 1985).

51 According to the Lettrist collector François Letailleur, *La barque de la vie courante* was produced in the years 1951–1952. In the context of his lecture at the Centre Pompidou on 19 February 2011, Letailleur plays a long sequence from the film's sound track, which consists of the sounds and rhythms for which Lettrist sound tracks are known. Given the unrealized image track, he describes how one could imagine an alternating dark and lit screen, or a purely transparent film. He describes how the film's objective was in large measure to affect the spectator's brain through its sound waves. (See http://www.centrepompidou.fr/cpv/ressource.action;jsessionid=6CDE77D665AF3C30F17C49AF3F49E3B?param.id=FR_R-f8b02be61daf1e99f1a4e126e32e590&param.idSource=FR_P-c92aafd90ffaa393bb214b5662783d4, accessed January 26, 2013). Such an effect on the spectator is ultimately achieved with Wolman's completed film *L'anticoncept* (1951), the subject of chapter 3.

CHAPTER ONE

1 Marc'O confirms that the photograph shows the group walking in the street after having picked up Isou at the train station. Marc'O, interview with author, June 15, 2010. This contradicts the previously published caption—"Cannes Film Festival, April 20, 1951, after the screening of Isidore Isou's film *Traité de bave et d'éternité*"—which appears alongside the photograph in Vincent Kaufman, *Guy Debord: La révolution au service de la poésie* (Paris: Librairie Arthème Fayard, 2001). Kaufman's study was translated as *Guy Debord: Revolution in the Service of Poetry*, trans. Robert Bononno (Minneapolis: University of Minnesota Press, 2006).

2 *Combat*, 1951. As cited in Frédérique Devaux, *Le cinéma lettriste* (Paris: Éditions Paris Expérimental, 1992), 56. A journalist from *Nice-Matin* further revealed, "At the last minute, we learn that the famous film of the Lettrists, Isidore Isou's *Traité de bave et d'éternité*, composed of nineteen reels, representing 5,200 meters of film or more than four hours of projection, which should revolutionize the art of cinema, yet which has not been selected by the festival, will be screened Friday morning at the Vox movie theater in Cannes. The nineteen reels of film are already on site." *Nice-Matin*, April 18, 1951. See the overview of press response to the film in Devaux, *Le cinéma lettriste*, 55–61.

3 Isidore Isou, "Préambule à un film," *Le film français (Cinémonde)*, nos. 9–11 (April 1951) (my italics).

4 All times are based on the authorized DVD edition of the 35-millimeter print restored by the French National Film Archives. Isidore Isou, *Traité de bave et d'éternité* (1951), DVD (Paris: Re:Voir Video, 2008). The film was originally shot in 16-millimeter and then transferred to 35-millimeter. For the script, see Isidore Isou, *Traité de bave et d'éternité* (Paris: D'ARTS, 2000); originally published in Isidore Isou, *Oeuvres de spectacle* (Paris: Gallimard, 1964), 7–86.

5 The complete sound track ran for four hours and thirty minutes, reduced to two hours for the final cut. Based on my conversations with Frédéric Acquaviva and his extensive knowledge of the subject, it is unlikely that the entire sound track was played at the first screening at Cannes.

6 Jean Cocteau, cited by Isidore Isou in "Rectification à propos d'un film," *Combat*, April 26, 1951.

7 Regarding the effects that result when the continuity provided for by projection breaks down, Jean-Louis Baudry describes how "the spectator is brought abruptly back to discontinuity—that is, to the body, to the technical apparatus which he had *forgotten*." Jean-Louis Baudry, "Ideological Effects of the Basic Cinematographic Apparatus," in *Narrative, Apparatus, Ideology: A Film Theory Reader*, ed. Philip Rosen (New York: Columbia University Press, 1986), 291.

8 Isidore Isou, "Esthétique du cinéma," in *Ion* (1952; Paris: Jean-Paul Rocher, 1999), 69.

9 Ibid., 100 (original emphasis: boldface).

10 Ibid., 102 (original emphasis: boldface).

11 Isou describes how rhetoric became prose through the elimination of the sonorous aspects of language and affirms, "*The pathos* of Aristotelian discourse, basic belief, the living part of eloquence, withdrew before the laws of writing." For Isou, language in literature from Stendhal to James Joyce developed novelistic conventions rather than expanding language's eloquence—its spoken qualities destined for a public. As a result, the body's implication in speech was held at bay and the printed page became a site for the representation of language independent of phonation. Ibid., 102 (original emphasis: boldface).

12 Ibid.

13 See Michel Chion, *The Voice in Cinema*, trans. Claudia Gorbman (1982; New York: Columbia University Press, 1999).

14 For transcriptions of the poems, see François Dufrêne, "J'interroge et j'invective: Poème a hurler / À la mémoire d'Antonin Artaud" (1949) and "Marche" (1950), *Ur: Cahiers pour*

un dictat culturel, no. 1 (1950), 27–30. The poems are also reproduced in *Archi-made*, ed. Marie-Anne Sichère and Didier Semin (Paris: École Nationale Supérieure des Beaux-Arts, 2005), 29–30, 33–34.

15 My discussion of /k/ is indebted to Allen S. Weiss, "K," in *Antonin Artaud: A Critical Reader*, ed. Edward Scheer (London: Routledge, 2004), 151–58.

16 *Bave* can signify the dribble or drool of saliva. When shown in the early 1950s at the San Francisco Film Society and Cinema 16, "Treatise" was omitted from the English translation of the title and it was billed as "Venom and Eternity." In *Lipstick Traces*, Greil Marcus uses "slime" without offering any rationale for this choice.

17 Marc Beigbeder, "*Traité de bave et d'éternité*: Saliver n'est pas parler (Français)," n.d., press clipping in Gil J Wolman Papers, Beinecke Rare Book and Manuscript Library, Yale University.

18 See Alan Williams's excellent discussion in "Is Sound Recording Like a Language?," *Yale French Studies*, no. 60, "Cinema/Sound" (1980), 51–66. See also Chion, *Voice in Cinema*.

19 Jean-Louis Baudry, "Le Dispositif," *Communications*, no. 23 (1975), 61; trans. Bertrand Augst, "The Apparatus," *Camera Obscura*, no. 1 (Fall 1976), 110 (my italics).

20 Ibid.

21 Jay David Bolter and Richard Grusin, *Remediation: Understanding New Media* (Cambridge, MA: MIT Press, 2000), 98 (my italics).

22 Pavle Levi, "Cinema by Other Means," *October*, no. 131 (Winter 2010), 65. See also Levi, *Cinema by Other Means* (New York: Oxford University Press, 2012), esp. 42–45.

23 One of Levi's primary examples is the assemblage work *The Frenzied Marble* (1930) by Yugoslav artists Aleksandar Vučo and Dušan Matić. The work's tripartite vertical distribution evokes a filmstrip, thereby invoking film through nonfilmic media. Isou, by contrast, transfers a vinyl recording onto a more advanced sound recording technology. In each instance, however, one might say, following Levi, that remediation is premised on *inadequacy*: on the one hand, a static object refers to a sequence of images; on the other hand, the crackling of vinyl maintains imperfections with regard to optical sound. While the former case emphasizes the properties of film form as it relates to film's technical apparatus, the latter emphasizes the materiality of a specific technology, in this case sound recording. Devaux also discusses how Isou endows mechanical recording with aesthetic value. See Devaux, *Le cinéma lettriste*, 49.

24 Williams, "Is Sound Recording Like a Language?," 63.

25 In the early 1920s, László Moholy-Nagy advocated the transformation of the instruments of reproduction—in his case, the gramophone, photography, and film—for productive purposes. For Moholy-Nagy, as later for Isou, mere reproduction was a question of virtuosity, the virtuosity of a mechanical recording: "We must turn to media which have up to now been used only for reproductive purposes, and try to open them up to productive ends." See László Moholy-Nagy, "Production-Reproduction" (1922), in *Photography in the Modern Era: European Documents and Critical Writings, 1913–1940*, ed. Christopher Phillips (New York: Metropolitan Museum of Art; Aperture, 1989), 80. This assessment of mechanical reproduction is echoed by Isou when he writes, "Reproduction [is] the opposite of the truth of cinema." Isou, "Esthétique du cinéma," 86–87 (original in boldface).

26 See Henri Chopin's sound poetry magazine *Revue OU*, 1963–1974. Alga Marghen published a new edition (four CDs plus book and complete inserts) in 2007.

27 *Traité* was not listed in *Cinéma 51*, no. 4 (April 1951), but the following issue devoted a box to Isou, in which *Traité* was billed as "the most important experimental film ever made." See Devaux, *Le cinéma lettriste*, 61. The film was projected again at the Alexandra Theater in Paris on June 5.

28 For an account of Godard's early exposure to Lettrist cinema, see the biography by Richard Brody, *Everything Is Cinema: The Working Life of Jean-Luc Godard* (New York: Metropolitan Books/Henry Holt and Company, 2008), esp. 20, 30–31. Yves Klein published his essay "Des bases (fausses), principes, etc. et condamnation de l'évolution" in the first issue of the Lettrist newspaper *Soulèvement de la jeunesse* in June 1952.

29 See the section on "L'éco-cinématographie" in Isou, "Esthétique du cinéma," 143.
30 "Applaudissements, injures et sifflets accueillent le film d'Isidore Isou," *Le Figaro*, January 26–27, 1952.
31 Jean-Jacques Gautier, "Au Studio de l'Etoile: 'Traité de bave et d'éternité," *Le Figaro*, January 28, 1952.
32 Beigbeder, "*Traité de bave et d'éternité*: Saliver n'est pas parler (Français)."
33 Gautier, "Au Studio de l'Etoile."
34 François Brigneau, *Rivarol*, n.d. Clipping in Gil J Wolman Papers.
35 J.N., "Traité de bave et d'éternité," *Franc-tireur*, January 29, 1952. Clipping in Gil J Wolman Papers.
36 Maurice Schérer, "Isou ou les choses telles qu'elles sont," *Cahiers du cinéma*, no. 10 (March 1952), 30 (my italics).
37 Ibid., 31.
38 With his emphasis on the realist ontology of the filmed image, André Bazin, for example, establishes the visuality of the image as primary for understanding film. Also at this time, Parisian cinephile culture worked to establish a canon of classical cinema, displayed an obsession with para-scholarly erudition, and often emphasized taste as the ultimate criterion for judging a film. See Antoine de Baecque, *La cinéphilie: Invention d'un regard, histoire d'une culture, 1944–1968* (Paris: Fayard, 2003).
39 Schérer, "Isou ou les choses telles qu'elles sont," 28.
40 Ibid., 32.
41 See Jay Leyda, *Films Beget Films* (New York: Hill and Wang, 1964).
42 My account of the film is based on its English adaptation. Nicole Védrès, *Paris 1900* (1947), DVD (Phoenix: Grapevine Video, 2012).
43 André Bazin, "Nicole Védrès," in *Le cinéma français de la Libération à la Nouvelle vague (1945–1958)*, ed. Jean Narboni (Paris: Éditions de l'Étoile, 1983), 168. Originally published in *L'écran français*, September 30, 1947.
44 William C. Wees's distinction between found footage films that "do not challenge the representational nature of images" (as in most compilation films) and those that "criticize, challenge, and possibly subvert the power of images produced by, and distributed through, the corporate media" (as in most collage films) is key. For Wees the critical effect of what he designates as "collage film" is premised on the formal structure of montage and its metaphoric effects. Within the framework Wees proposes, Isou's film presents a curious, hybrid exception to the use of montage in found footage film. Wees, *Recycled Images: The Art and Politics of Found Footage Films* (New York: Anthology Film Archives, 1993), 36, 33.
45 In Catherine Russell's estimation, "the key years [for the use of found footage] are perhaps more correctly pegged as the period between 1955 and 1965." See Russell, *Experimental Ethnography: The World of Film in the Age of Video* (Durham, NC: Duke University Press, 1999), 242.
46 Conner arrived in San Francisco in late 1957. In the Bay Area, he and Lawrence Jordan founded the Camera Obscura Film Society, which showed avant-garde classics. Conner would have undoubtedly known of or seen Isou's *Traité*, which was shown on October 23, 1953, at the San Francisco Museum of Modern Art (programed by Frank Stauffacher). As noted in the introduction, Stan Brakhage was among those in attendance.
47 Kevin Hatch, *Looking for Bruce Conner* (Cambridge: MIT Press, 2012), 121.
48 See Wees, *Recycled Images*, 39. For a more recent, and more nuanced, alternative reading of the film's montage, see Hatch, *Looking for Bruce Conner*, esp. 113–31.
49 *A MOVIE*'s shots of militarized movement are accentuated by the film's brisk montage rhythm, engendered by the relatively short shot length. For some, such quick editing conjures the contemporary experience of switching television channels. Like the television viewer, Hatch explains, the viewer of *A MOVIE* is required "to intuit conceptual links between shots rather than receive them via conventional cinematic cues." Hatch, *Looking for Bruce Conner*, 129. That television viewing serves as an appropriate analogue for the experience of watching *A MOVIE* also puts into relief the extent to which the

development and reception of new media in the United States differed from that on the European continent and in France in particular. While television may have formed part of a larger international imaginary regarding the production of images and their effects on the human sensorium, avant-garde filmmakers in Europe, and the Lettrists in particular, were primarily looking to newsreels and the institutional role of cinema. In France, the state broadcasting organization Radiodiffusion-Télévision Française (RTF; later the Office de Radiodiffusion-Télévision Française, ORTF) offered the sole television channel until 1964; commercial advertising was first introduced in 1968. For a useful analysis and statistics regarding television in France, see "Television under de Gaulle," chap. 4 in Raymond Kuhn, *The Media in France* (London: Routledge, 1995), esp. 109–13, 128–30.

50 Frédérique Devaux writes, "Although these lines [*traits*] are frequently applied to human faces, in this way de-figured and de-faced, these deletions are not comparable, despite appearances, to bands to hide their faces. They temporarily unite two inert elements in the image—for example, two poles, as a banner would function. . . . The texture of these lines varies as much as their other attributes and [shows] that *there exists no rule for chiseling*, not even between the frames." Devaux, *Traité de bave et d'éternité d'Isidore Isou* (Crisnée, Belgium: Éditions Yellow Now, 1994), 53, 55 (my italics).

51 See Ivone Margulies's excellent discussion of Bazinian contingencies in "Bodies Too Much," her editor's introduction to *Rites of Realism: Essays on Corporeal Cinema* (Durham, NC: Duke University Press, 2003), 4. See also, in the same volume, Philip Rosen, "History of Image, Image of History: Subject and Ontology in Bazin," 42–79, and Mary Ann Doane, "The Object of Theory," 80–89.

52 In 1951, the year Isou produced his film, the "Henri Martin affair" began. Martin, a French sailor, had enlisted in the French navy to fight the Japanese who had occupied Vietnam during World War II. He ended up fighting Vietnamese nationalists, and soon thereafter began distributing tracts denouncing French imperialism. Martin was ultimately arrested for demoralizing French troops and sentenced to five years in prison. See the discussion in Philip Watts, "Sartre's Republic, 1953," *Nottingham French Studies* 45, no. 2 (Summer 2006): 27–38. I would like to thank the late Philip Watts for his generosity in bringing this article and the stakes of the Henri Martin affair to my attention.

53 P. Adams Sitney suggests that Isou may have acted out of "legal timidity" when deciding to totally obscure the faces of state officials. P. Adams Sitney, conversation with author, March 1, 2013.

54 "Indochine: L'arrivée du Général de Lattre," *Journal Actualité (Journal Gaumont)*, sound film, black and white, 13 seconds. Gaumont-Pathé Archives, Paris. REF 5051GJ 000004.

55 Maurice Lemaître, *Sur quelques erreurs commises à propos du film d'Isidore Isou, Traité de bave et d'éternité* (Paris: Centre de Créativité/Maurice Lemaître, 1995), 9 (original emphasis: underline).

56 Ibid. (my italics). Some readers may question how Lemaître, in characteristic credit-seeking fashion, claims responsibility for the chiseling effects of Isou's *Traité*. Nevertheless, a careful viewing of the film reveals that the chiseled marks on the filmstrip correspond to Lemaître's description. Moreover, his 1995 testimony was published as a corrective to assertions regarding Isou's chiseled images published three years earlier in Devaux's *Le cinéma lettriste*.

57 See the discussion of the use of sound to satirize visual images in Wees, *Recycled Images*, 21.

58 Gautier, "Au Studio de l'Etoile."

59 See *Bulletin mensuel de l'Union française des Offices du Cinéma éducateur Laïque (UFOCEL informations)*, no. 44 (1951), as cited in Devaux, *Le cinéma lettriste*, 61. The original French reads, "L'ensemble n'inspire que de l'ennui."

60 Michel Foucault, *The Archaeology of Knowledge and the Discourse on Language*, trans. A. M. Sheridan Smith (1969; New York: Pantheon, 1972), 129. Given the contemporaneity of Isou's found footage, Foucault's assertion that "it is not possible for us to describe our own archive, since it is from within these rules that we speak" (130) would seem

to disqualify an understanding of Isou's chiseled shots as archival in the Foucaultian sense. I suggest that Isou's practice does not so much "describe" the archive as put pressure on the regime of visibility upheld by newsreel footage through his chiseling of these official shots. Consequently, these shots lose their self-evidence as documents of historical truth.

61 Lettrist metagraphic novels also display an attention to the everyday context of war. I am thinking here of Maurice Lemaître's *Canailles I* (1950) published in *Ur: Cahiers pour un dictat culturel*, no. 1 (December 1950), and in expanding series subsequently; as well as Gabriel Pomerand, *Saint Ghetto des prêts, grimoire*, with preface by Jacques Baratier (Paris: O. L. B., 1950). For an insightful discussion of these novels in relation to World War II, see Hannah Feldman, "New Writing Systems/Writing New Systems," in *Specters of Artaud: Language and the Arts in the 1950s*, ed. Kaira M. Cabañas with Frédéric Acquaviva (Madrid: Museo Nacional Centro de Arte Reina Sofía, 2012), 117–28.

62 The streets of Paris remain largely untouched by scratches on the celluloid emulsion. However, Isou does include shots of Paris projected in reverse and inverted, suggesting 180-degree camera rotation.

63 Isou, "Esthétique du cinéma," 86–87 (my italics; in the original, entire phrase is boldface).

64 The original French reads, "Le montage discrépant foule les certitudes de 'positif' et les transforme en mensonges." Ibid., 87 (original in boldface).

CHAPTER TWO

1 Maurice Lemaître, *Le film est déjà commencé?* (Has the Film Already Started), 1951. Fondation Bismuth-Lemaître. Color, 65 minutes. All times provided for the film in this chapter are based on the DVD, which includes a short "Annonce" (1979).

2 Maurice Lemaître, *Le film est déjà commencé?* (Paris: Éditions André Bonne, 1952), 170–74.

3 Ibid., 168 (my italics).

4 See Frédérique Devaux, *Le cinéma lettriste: 1951–1991* (Paris: Éditions Paris Expérimental, 1992), 89.

5 For announcements of the film's presentation on December 7, 1952, see *Cinéma 51*, no. 6 (1951), and J.P., "'Que les salles de cinéma deviennent des Luna-Park' déclare Maurice LEMAITRE," n.d., Bismuth-Lemaître Papers, Beinecke Rare Book and Manuscript Library, Yale University. See also "La première du 'cinéma tridimensionnel' aura lieu sous la protection de la police," *France-soir*, December 8, 1951.

6 Lemaître writes that at the time of the film's avant-première he had not yet obtained the visa for projection. Thus, he and his friends reduced to a minimum the interventions by the public and the form of the new screen. See Lemaître, *Le film est déjà commencé?*, 86, 93. See also comments by Lemaître in *First International Symposium on Letterism (Lewis and Clark College, Portland, Oregon, May 24–29, 1976)*, ed. Pietro Ferrua (Portland, OR: Avant-Garde Publishers, 1978), 123–25. For an overview of Lemaître's production, projection instructions, and scripts, see the essays and documents in *Maurice Lemaître: Oeuvres de cinéma, 1951–2007* (Paris: Éditions Paris Expérimental, 2007).

7 Lemaître, *First International Symposium on Letterism*, 101. See also the discussion in Lemaître, *Le film est déjà commencé?*, 82–83.

8 Lemaître, *Le film est déjà commencé?*, 164.

9 The ciné-club as a social forum for the presentation and discussion of film emerged from the broader discursive network of the late 1910s and early 1920s that worked to establish cinema as an art. Opposing the dominant film industry in France, which largely considered cinema as entertainment, the emergence of film criticism, specialized journals, and cinemas (e.g., Théâtre du Vieux-Colombier, Studio des Ursulines) acted in concert with film exhibitions and ciné-clubs in order to establish an "alternate cinema network." The purpose of the ciné-club movement was to encourage an informed audi-

ence and to seek official recognition of cinema as an art. See Richard Abel, "The Alternate Cinema Network," chap. 3 in *French Cinema: The First Wave, 1915–1929* (Princeton, NJ: Princeton University Press, 1984), 241–75; Malte Hagener, *Moving Forward, Looking Back: The European Avant-Garde and the Invention of Film Culture, 1919–1939* (Amsterdam: Amsterdam University Press, 2007), esp. 77–120, for an overview of film clubs in a broader European context. In French, refer to Christophe Gauthier's formidable study *La passion du cinéma: Cinéphiles, ciné-clubs et salles spécialisées à Paris de 1920 à 1929* (Paris: Association Française de recherche sur l'histoire du cinéma; École des Chartes, 1999); and Vincent Pinel, *Introduction au ciné-club: Histoire, théorie, pratique du ciné-club en France* (Paris: Éditions Ouvrières, 1964).

10 In the years 1924–1925, several ciné-clubs merged. At this time, the Ciné-Club de France embarked on a schedule of monthly film screenings and lecture-presentations. Subsequently, the Tribune Libre du Cinéma was organized by Charles Léger, who—in the wake of Louis Delluc's pioneering work—consolidated the ciné-club format. See Abel, *French Cinema*, 251–52 and, for a discussion of Léger's presentation format, 257. See also Pinel, *Introduction au ciné-club*, 29. Léger's tripartite format subsequently dominated most ciné-clubs, and similarly informed, as we have seen, Isou's sound track.

11 The alternative history that I propose is neither driven by the ontology of the image, as in the contemporary work of André Bazin (evoked in chapter 1), nor limited to the parameters of 1970s theorizations of the film apparatus, in which the analytical emphasis on visuality and spectatorial identification were central concerns. The work of Jean-Louis Baudry is exemplary of apparatus theory, which focuses on the visuality of cinema in order to analyze the specific ways in which spectatorial identification and narrative absorption are achieved in film. See Baudry, "Ideological Effects of the Basic Cinematographic Apparatus," in *Narrative, Apparatus, Ideology: A Film Theory Reader*, ed. Philip Rosen (New York: Columbia University Press, 1986), 286–98. More recently, Pavle Levi also aims to craft what he calls an "alternative cine-history" by looking to those avant-garde artists whose work materializes the discrepancy between cinema as an idea and cinema as the technological realization of the idea. Within this gap or non-coincidence of concept and specific technology, he situates the works he describes as achieving "cinema by other means." To be sure, Levi's model is largely circumscribed by the material support and technology of the apparatus itself (e.g., the filmstrip and its frames), even as he upholds the difference between the idea of cinema and its practical realization. For my purposes, Levi includes as part of his larger trajectory of an alternative "cine-history" Lettrist hypergraphics and performative "syncinema," and claims that in the 1950s the Lettrists were programmatic in their response to technology and "re-define[d] the existing media by re-materializing them." Yet Levi's analysis separates cinema from what one might call its attendant living reality. As I argue, what Lettrist film resuscitates in no uncertain terms are the live elements that accompanied film screenings in the context of the Parisian film clubs. See Pavle Levi, "Cinema by Other Means," *October*, no. 131 (Winter 2010), 68, as well as the discussion of Lettrist film in Levi, *Cinema by Other Means* (New York: Oxford University Press, 2012), 86–93.

12 Isidore Isou, "Préface," in Lemaître, *Le film est déjà commencé?*, 26.

13 Lemaître, *Le Film est déjà commencé?*, 97.

14 Ibid., 116, 118.

15 Ibid., 120.

16 Ibid., 128.

17 Ibid., 164.

18 Maurice Lemaître, "Base d'une éducation cinématographique du public par la critique permanente," *Ur: La dictature lettriste*, no. 2 (1952): 19–20. Also published in Lemaître, *Le film est déjà commencé?*, 42–47.

19 Ibid., 19.

20 Ibid.

21 "Spectateurs professionnels," *Ciné-coulisses*, March 27, 1952 (my italics). Bismuth-Lemaître Papers, Beinecke Rare Book and Manuscript Library, Yale University.

22 See Lemaître, *Le film est déjà commencé?*, 76–77.

23 See Lev Kuleshov, "In Maloi Gnezdnikovsky Lane," in *Kuleshov on Film: Writings of Lev Kuleshov*, ed. and trans. Ronald Levaco (Berkeley: University of California Press, 1974), 200. Levaco maintains that Kuleshov forgot the exact content of the shots to which he juxtaposed Mozhukhin's neutral face. He notes that Vsevolod Pudovkin remembered the experiment including a shot of steaming soup, a shot of a woman in a coffin, and a shot of a child playing with a toy bear. See his introduction to ibid., 8.

24 Lemaître, "Base d'une éducation cinématographique," 19–20.

25 See the discussion of the film lecturer in André Gaudreault, *Film and Attraction: From Kinematography to Cinema*, trans. Timothy Barnard (2008; Urbana: University of Illinois Press, 2011), 27–31.

26 Tom Gunning, "An Aesthetic of Astonishment: Early Film and the (In)Credulous Spectator," *Art and Text* 34 (Spring 1989): 36. See also the discussion of the "voice of attraction" in Germain Lacasse, "The Lecturer and the Attraction," in *The Cinema of Attractions Reloaded*, ed. Wanda Strauven (Amsterdam: Amsterdam University Press, 2006), 181–91.

27 Although legally forbidden, clandestine film club screenings were organized by Jacques Marel, Jean Pleury, and Henri Langlois during the occupation. See Crisp, *The Classic French Cinema*, 229. During the same period, André Bazin organized a film group at the Maison des Lettres. See the discussion in Dudley Andrew, *André Bazin* (New York: Columbia University Press), esp. 52–60.

28 See the statistics provided in Crisp, *Classic French Cinema*, 229.

29 Cited in ibid., 229.

30 Pinel, *Introduction au ciné-club*, 41.

31 André Bazin, "Comment présenter et discuter un film!," *Ciné-club*, April 1954, 10.

32 Ibid. Philip Watts offers an alternative reading of Bazin's text, relating it to the classical rhetorical tradition; the function of rhetoric, he claims, was central to Bazin's understanding of cinema as a social activity. Watts frames Bazin's model for the ciné-club debate as counter to that of critics who feel compelled to demystify film for audiences. Bazin's notion of "directed freedom," by contrast, allows for and depends on the spectators' interpretive aptitude. See Watts, "The Eloquent Image: The Postwar Mission of Film and Criticism," in *Opening Bazin: Postwar Film Theory and Its Afterlife*, ed. Dudley Andrew with Hervé Joubert-Laurencin (New York: Oxford University Press, 2011), esp. 220–21.

33 Pinel, *Introduction au ciné-club*, 41.

34 Jacques Rancière aims to move beyond the dichotomy between active and passive spectatorship in order to consider the knowledge that one might also gain through contemplative modes of viewing. See Rancière, *The Emancipated Spectator*, trans. Gregory Elliott (London: Verso, 2009). For the original French version, see Rancière, *Le spectateur émancipé* (Paris: Éditions La Fabrique, 2008). Claire Bishop draws upon Rancière's discussion of spectatorship in *Artificial Hells: Participatory Art and the Politics of Spectatorship* (London: Verso, 2012). In chapter 4, I discuss Rancière's study in relation to Guy Debord's first film, *Hurlements en faveur de Sade* (Howls for Sade, 1952).

35 Serge Daney, "From Movies to Moving" (1989), trans. Brian Holmes, reprinted in *Art and the Moving Image: A Critical Reader*, ed. Tanya Leighton (London: Tate/Afterall, 2008), 334.

36 Tom McDonough, *"The Beautiful Language of My Century": Reinventing the Language of Contestation in Postwar France, 1945–1968* (Cambridge, MA: MIT Press, 2007), 44.

37 Isou, "Esthétique du cinéma,"152 (original in boldface).

38 Marc'O, "Première Manifestation d'un cinéma nucléaire," reproduced in *Ion*, 242–43 (original emphases removed).

39 "Langlois, although he usually made a brief presentation of the film, was dead against the didactic *ciné-club* tradition." His programs for his Cercle du Cinéma included the proclamation: *Sans Débats* (Without debates). Richard Rod, *A Passion for Films: Henri*

Langlois and the Cinémathèque Française (1983; Baltimore: Johns Hopkins University Press, 1999), 27.

40 Jacques Rancière, *Dis-agreement: Politics and Philosophy*, trans. Julie Rose (Minneapolis: University of Minnesota Press, 1999), 25.

41 Lemaître, "Base d'une éducation cinématographique," 20.

42 Michel Foucault, "The Subject and Power," afterword in *Michel Foucault: Beyond Structuralism and Hermeneutics*, ed. Hubert L. Dreyfus and Paul Rabinow, 2nd ed. (Chicago: University of Chicago Press, 1983), 222.

43 Lemaître's practice also recalls that other short-lived history of the film club in France: Léon Moussinac's Amis de Spartacus, which, rather than exclusively uphold film as art, saw it as a means of combat and social liberation. In the French context, only Moussinac and René Clair (albeit to a lesser extent) argued for an alternative cinema that would be conceived politically and economically. Moussinac was inspired by the desire to create a popular cinematographic movement; his Amis de Spartacus screened Soviet films otherwise banned by the censors, including *Battleship Potemkin* (1925) by Eisenstein and *The End of St. Petersburg* (1927) by Pudovkin. After only five months of activity, its membership had reached eighty thousand. On account of its success, the police had it shut down, ostensibly to maintain public order. See Pinel, *Introduction au ciné-club*, 30–31, and Abel, *French Cinema*, 274.

44 Maurice Lemaître, "Les vrais et les faux pionniers du cinéma," in *Cahiers du cinéma*, no. 40 (November 1954), 54–55.

45 Ibid., 55

46 See Maurice Lemaître, "1967–1969: Le Café-Cinéma Lemaître," followed by "Huit Films Lettristes," in *Les cahiers de Paris Expérimental*, no. 13 (Paris: Éditions Paris Expérimental, 2003), 15–16.

47 See de Baecque, *La cinéphilie*.

CHAPTER THREE

1 *L'anticoncept* was shown in the context of "Film Modernism and Its Discontents: A Perspective from Paris," organized by Keith Sanborn at Exit Art in New York City, November 7–10, 1990. *L'anticoncept à New York* is a very dark film; my calculation of the screening's initial attendance is approximate, as is my timing of individual departures. Gil J Wolman, *L'anticoncept à New York*, color, approx. 65 minutes.

2 Jean-Michel Bouhours explains that Wolman used found ("readymade") 35-millimeter footage with holes, covered the filmstrip's remaining images with opaque black paint, and printed *L'anticoncept* from this material. Jean-Michel Bouhours to author, November 16, 2009.

3 All quotations from *L'anticoncept* are taken from *Ion* (1952; Paris: Jean-Paul Rocher, 1999), 167–86.

4 Frédéric Acquaviva, interview with author, November 3, 2009. Wolman likely recorded separate optical sound tracks and then edited and mixed them down to one channel for the final sound track, thereby creating the effect of superimposed voices in "TRITS" and the concluding *mégapneumie*.

5 Although Wolman apparently wrote this text, certain phrases (such as a list of food items and attendant prices) seem to be appropriated from preexisting material. The content includes descriptions of sensorial excess, sexual innuendos and encounters, bodily excretions, and seemingly biographical snippets.

6 See Gil J Wolman, "Autour de la mégapneumie," in *Défense de mourir* (Paris: Éditions Allia, 2001), 23. This volume includes important primary sources and, among other notable secondary texts, Jean-Michel Bouhours's indispensable "De l'anticoncept à L'anticoncept." See also *Wolman résumé: Des chapitres précédents* (Paris: Éditions Spiess, 1981).

7 A.P., "Quand l'avant garde abolit l'écran," *Le Figaro*, February 13, 1952, reproduced in Gil

J Wolman, *L'anticoncept* (Paris: Éditions Allia, 1994), 53. This slim and informative volume was produced in conjunction with a VHS tape of *L'anticoncept*. All times provided for the film in this chapter are based on this VHS tape. Gil J Wolman, *L'anticoncept* (1952; Paris: Éditions Allia, 1994), black and white, 60 minutes.

8 A.P., "A propos 'd'Anticoncept,'" *Le Figaro*, February 18, 1952, reproduced in Wolman, *L'anticoncept*, 53.

9 Ibid., 53.

10 Dr. Philm, "Films expérimentaux," *Cinéma* 52, no. 4 (Paris, April 1952), Gil J Wolman Papers, Beinecke Rare Book and Manuscript Library, Yale University; also reproduced in Wolman, *L'anticoncept*, 55. Wolman also emphasizes spectators' mutable reactions in his text "Pourquoi les spectateurs hurleront pendant la projection de *L'anticoncept*," in *Cinéma* 52, 1952; reproduced in *Défense de mourir*, 28.

11 Dr. Philm, "Films expérimentaux."

12 The priority given to speech in *L'anticoncept* further differentiates Wolman's work from the subsequent work of structural filmmakers, like Peter Kubelka's *Arnulf Rainer* (1958/1960) and Tony Conrad's *The Flicker* (1966), each of which experiment with stroboscopic alternation but not with cinematic speech. Conrad's film extends the harmonic principles of music to his experiments with flicker. See Branden W. Joseph, *Beyond the Dream Syndicate: Tony Conrad and the Arts after Cage* (New York: Zone Books, 2008), chap. 6.

13 Gil J Wolman, "Le Cinématochrone—Nouvelle amplitude," *Ur: La dictature lettriste*, no. 2 (Paris, 1952), 10; also reproduced in *Défense de mourir*, 30–31.

14 Noël Burch, "Primitivism and the Avant-Gardes: A Dialectical Approach," in *Narrative, Apparatus, Ideology: A Film Theory Reader*, ed. Philip Rosen (New York: Columbia University Press, 1986), 499.

15 Noël Burch, *Life to Those Shadows* (Berkeley: University of California Press, 1990), 214.

16 See Burch, "Primitivism and the Avant-Gardes," 498–500. See also Tom Gunning's discussion of the characteristics of early cinema, which do not disappear with the dominance of narrative "but [go] underground, both into certain avant-garde practices and as a component of narrative films." Gunning, "The Cinema of Attractions: Early Film, Its Spectator and the Avant-Garde," in *Early Cinema: Space, Frame, Narrative*, ed. Thomas Elsaesser with Adam Barker (London: British Film Institute, 1990), 57.

17 As discussed in chapter 1, Cocteau was crucial to the reception of Isou's *Traité de bave et d'éternité* at Cannes in 1951, and he designed the poster for its official release at the Studio de l'Etoile in Paris in 1952. Cocteau even made an appearance in the film's completed version, which references *Le sang d'un poète*.

18 Paul Virilio, *War and Cinema: The Logistics of Perception*, trans. Patrick Camiller (1984; London: Verso, 1989), 3. See also Friedrich Kittler's claim that "the history of the movie camera thus coincides with the history of automatic weapons." Kittler, *Gramphone, Film, Typewriter*, trans. Geoffrey Winthrop-Young and Michael Wutz (Stanford, CA: Stanford University Press, 1999), 124, and, for a broader discussion, 124–33.

19 Virilio, *War and Cinema*, 3.

20 First used by French meteorologist Léon Teisserenc de Bort in 1896, the weather balloon carries instruments to record information regarding atmospheric conditions, including pressure, temperature, humidity, and wind. Aerial observation balloons were used in the Boer War and Russo-Japanese War. The French military observation balloon *L'Intrépide* of 1795 is the oldest preserved aircraft in Europe.

21 See Merton E. Davies and William R. Harris, *RAND's Role in the Evolution of Balloon and Satellite Observation Systems and Related U.S. Space Technology* (Santa Monica, CA: RAND Corporation, 1988), 19–20.

22 According to a RAND report, the development objective for Project Gopher was "unmanned, high-altitude, altitude-stabilized, recoverable photoreconnaissance platforms. The altitude has to be so high as to exceed the air defense capabilities of target nations. And the balloons should be, insofar as possible, invisible to the naked eye and to radar sensors." Ibid., 21. According to another study, "516 camera-laden balloons

were launched, mainly from Turkey and other sites in Western Europe, with 40 recovered and producing photographs covering a significant section of the Soviet Union." Bruno W. Augenstein and Bruce Murray, *Mert Davies: A RAND Pioneer in Earth Reconnaissance and Planetary Mapping from Spacecraft* (Santa Monica, CA: RAND Corporation, 2004), 7.

23 Virilio explains, "As sight lost its direct quality . . . the soldier had the feeling of being not so much destroyed as derealized or dematerialized, any sensory point of reference suddenly vanishing in a surfeit of optical targets." See Virilio, *War and Cinema*, 19.

24 Thanks are due to Jérôme Saint-Loubert Bié for directing me to this potential reading. Conversation with author, July 30, 2009.

25 Although beyond the scope of this study, two early precedents for an alternatively shaped screen are Marcel Duchamp's experiments in *Anémic Cinema* (1926) and László Moholy-Nagy's *Lichtspiel: Schwarz-Weiss-Grau* (Lightplay: Black-White-Gray, 1930), whose opening credits appear on a transparent rotating sphere.

26 Wolman, "Le Cinématochrone," 31.

27 Noam Elcott raised the question of whether the rhythm of the blinking eye could be related to Georges Bataille's *Histoire de l'oeil* (Story of the Eye, 1928), which creates a verbal image of an eye that is at times both an egg and a testicle (response to author's lecture, February 11, 2010). Some of the phrases in *L'anticoncept*'s sound track may disturb through what they signify, but the weather balloon remains largely independent of the sound track's verbal images. Consequently, I align the film's "blinking eye" more precisely with the "eyeless vision" described above through its use of the weather balloon as a support.

28 Wolman's work with tape should be held apart from the subsequent manipulations of Henri Chopin, for example. See the discussion of Wolman's sound manipulation in Frédéric Acquaviva, "Le tank musical d'Isou," in *Figures de la négation: Avant-gardes du dépassement de l'art*, ed. Yan Ciret (Paris: Paris-Musées; Saint-Étienne, France: Musée d'Art Moderne de Saint-Étienne Métropole, 2004), 174–75. It is important to note that while Wolman may have initially recorded the sound on magnetic tape, the material was eventually translated into an optical signal and printed at the edge of the 35-millimeter filmstrip.

29 See the discussion of microphone distance in Alan Williams, "Is Sound Recording Like a Language?" *Yale French Studies*, no. 60, "Cinema/Sound" (1980), 59.

30 Gil J Wolman, "Introduction à Wolman," *Ur*, no. 1 (Paris, 1950), 19; reproduced in *Défense de mourir*, 13.

31 See Hannah Feldman, *From a Nation Torn: Decolonizing Art and Representation in France, 1945–1962* (Durham, NC: Duke University Press, 2014), 80–85, 99–107 (in relation to being Jewish in Paris after the war).

32 See Isidore Isou, "Le manifeste de la poésie lettriste," in *Introduction à une nouvelle poésie et à une nouvelle musique* (Paris: Gallimard, 1947), 12.

33 Wolman, "Introduction à Wolman," 19.

34 Gil J Wolman, "Autor de la mégapneumie," unpublished manuscript reproduced in *Défense de mourir*, 22.

35 Wolman, "Introduction à Wolman," 21.

36 As noted in chapter 1, the letter *k*, infrequent in French, frequently appears also in Artaud's glossolio/glossographia. See also Allen S. Weiss, "K," in *Antonin Artaud: A Critical Reader*, ed. Edward Scheer (London: Routledge, 2004), 151–58.

37 Gil J Wolman, "La mégapneumie," *OU*, no. 32 (1967); reproduced in *Défense de mourir*, 21.

38 As a model of speech based on breath, the *mégapneumie* radically diverge from Jean-Jacques Rousseau's search for the origin of language and the existence of a speech before words, a pneumatic speech at once interior and homogeneous that exists prior to and independent of its actual expression. Fulfilling a desire for a utopia of pure presence, Rousseau's model of language was, as Jacques Derrida explains, "not grammatological but pneumatological"; Rousseau's was a reflection on the possibility of "pure

vocalization" independent of the body and the contingencies of context. See Derrida, *Of Grammatology*, trans. Gayatri Chakravorty Spivak (Baltimore: Johns Hopkins University Press, 1974), 17. Wolman's discussion of breath could be profitably read in relation to Artaud's discussion of "affective athleticism." Artaud's theater was in part to be based on breath: "The actor's body is supported by his breath. . . . This question of breath is in fact primary; it is in inverse proportion to the strength of the external expression." Artaud also details different temporalities of breathing and ways in which the actor's breathing was to affect the spectator. See Artaud, *The Theater and Its Double*, trans. M. C. Richards (New York: Grove, 1958), 133–34. I take up Wolman's relation to Artaud later in this chapter.

39 In the early 1950s, Wolman consulted a series of works on musicology, phonetics, and physiology from the late nineteenth and early twentieth centuries. These include Albert Lavignac, *La musique et les musiciens*, 1895; Paul Passy, *Petite phonétique comparée des principales langues européennes*, 1912; Pierre Blaserna, *Le son et la musique*, followed by *Causes physiologiques de l'harmonie musical* by H. Helmoltz, 1892; and Henri Piéron, *Psychologie éxperimentale*, 1927. Together they form a set of historical references from which Wolman develops his work. Piéron's study, for example, speaks to the rigidity of limiting thought to language and discusses how conceptual schemas do not account for sensorial contingencies or affective influences. See also Vincent Barras, "Wolman! Poésie? Physique!," in *Défense de mourir*, 369–71.

40 The *mégapneumie* are improvised and recorded without a score. In this, they differ from the sound track recordings of Lettrist poetry used for Isou's *Traité*. The Lettrist chorus includes an improvised voice, but this voice is still structured by the chorus for which there is a score. Wolman's conscious manipulation of the recording tape provides a further instance of improvisation in this context. Conversation with Frédéric Aquaviva, January 13, 2013.

41 Wolman's rejection of writing may recall the phonological orientation that structures the science of linguistics, which brackets writing in order to privilege speech, as in the work of Ferdinand de Saussure and his *Course in General Linguistics* (1916). But contrary to Wolman's work, Saussure's emphasis on language and system held at bay the materiality of language in order to maintain the proximity of speech to thought and thus to the mind. Wolman instead pursued a direct and unrepeatable poetry along the lines desired by Artaud. In his essay "No More Masterpieces," Artaud affirmed, "Let us do away with this foolish adherence to texts, to written poetry. Written poetry is valid [only] once and then ought to be torn up." See Artaud, *Theater and Its Double*, 59.

42 Wolman, "Autour de la mégapneumie," in 22–23. For a discussion of Wolman's earlier compositions and his *mégapneumie*, see Yves Botz, "Tu vas la taire ta gueule," in *Défense de mourir*, 361–68.

43 For examples of Lettrist notation systems, see Isou, *Introduction à une nouvelle poésie*, 314, and Maurice Lemaître, *Sistème de notasion pour les lètres* (Paris: Éditions Richard-Masse, 1952), 44–46.

44 Isidore Isou,"Les grandes poètes lettristes," *bizarre*, no. 32–33 (1964); reproduced in *Wolman résumé*, 11.

45 Isidore Isou, as cited in Botz, "Tu vas la taire ta gueule," 361.

46 Maurice Lemaître, "Du lettrisme à la mégapneumie" (1952), in *Wolman résumé*, 14.

47 François Dufrêne, "Pragmatique du crirythme," in *OU*, no. 28–29 (1965) (translation modified).

48 In mid-January 1947, Jean-Louis Brau, François Dufrêne, and Gabriel Pomerand met Artaud at the Bar Vert, rue Jacob, in Paris. The meeting more or less coincided with Artaud's last public appearance at the Théâtre du Vieux-Colombier.

49 In 1946, Artaud's *Les malades et les médecins* (The Patients and the Doctors, June 8) and *Aliénation et magie noire* (Madness and Black Magic, July 16) were recorded and broadcast in the context of the Parisian radio program *Club d'Essai*. Until 1995, they could only be consulted in the archives of Radio France. *Pour en finir avec le jugement de Dieu* existed only in a handful of clandestine copies and was published as a cassette tape

and LP by Alain and Odette Virmaux with Éditions La Manufacture in 1986. See Helga Finter, excerpt from "Antonin Artaud and the Impossible Theater: The Legacy of the Theater of Cruelty," in *100 Years of Cruelty: Essays on Artaud*, ed. Edward Scheer (Sydney: Power Publications and Artspace, 2000), 187n3. See also Stephen Barber, *The Screaming Body/Antonin Artaud: Film Projects, Drawings, and Sound Recordings* (London: Creation Books, 1999), 93–106.

50 As cited in Stephen Barber, *Blows and Bombs: Antonin Artaud: The Biography* (1992; London: Creation Books, 2003), 209.

51 Antonin Artaud, *The Theatre and Its Double*, trans. Victor Corti (London: Calder and Boyars, 1970), 59 (my italics). In this one instance I use Corti's British translation on account of the cited phrase's specific translation.

52 In the 1950s, the notion that verbal meaning and action might coincide was a problematic also taken up in the philosophy of language, including in the work of J. L. Austin. For Austin, language and its effects derive from convention: saying something equals doing something so long as one speaks within the established rules that govern speech and performs as a subject "authorized" to do so. The crux of Austin's theory of performative language is to challenge the regime of descriptive language in order to analyze language's *force*. For Austin, explicit performatives include statements such as "I apologize," "I criticize," and "I approve," utterances coincident with the performance of an action. See Austin, *How to Do Things with Words* (Cambridge, MA: Harvard University Press, 1962).

53 Artaud speaks of a "visual and plastic materialization of speech." See Artaud, *Theater and Its Double*, 69. As Derrida suggests, Artaud is committed to a language in which "gesture and speech have not yet been separated by the logic of representation." See Derrida, "The Theater of Cruelty," in *Writing and Difference*, trans. Alan Bass (Chicago: University of Chicago Press, 1978), 240.

54 Jean Desternes, "Dernière visite à Antonin Artaud," *Le Figaro littéraire* (Paris), March 13, 1948, 3.

55 Gil J Wolman, unpublished note reproduced in *Défense de mourir*, 23.

56 Allen S. Weiss, "Radio, Death, and the Devil: Artaud's *Pour en finir avec le jugement de Dieu*," in *Wireless Imagination: Sound, Radio, and the Avant-Garde*, ed. Douglas Kahn and Gregory Whitehead (Cambridge, MA: MIT Press, 1992), 300.

57 With *poésie physique*, writing as a graphic trace is replaced by magnetic tape as a new site of inscription that opens new productive possibilities. At the same time, tape results in a new codification: a representation of a physical poetry that contrarily aims to resist representation.

58 Around 1994, Jean-Michel Bouhours, together with Wolman and Gérard Berréby, went to the commission's archives to search for the minutes of the debate about *L'anticoncept*. They found no such documentation. See Bouhours, "De l'anticoncept à L'anticoncept," 351n3. For a list of screenings of *L'anticoncept* after its censoring, see *Défense de mourir*, 389–90. More recent presentations include Frédéric Acquaviva's program at the Cinémathèque Française (2004); a screening at the Museu d'Art Contemporani de Barcelona (MACBA, 2005); Acquaviva's program at the Centre Internationale de Poésie Marseille (2008); the Centre Georges Pompidou screening in conjunction with the *Vides* exhibition (2009); the installation included in the exhibition *Gil J Wolman I am immortal and alive* (MACBA, 2010–2011); screenings for students enrolled in my seminar at Capacete's Summer University in Rio de Janeiro, February 7, 2012, and January 7, 2013; and the installation included in the exhibition *Specters of Artaud: Language and the Arts in the 1950s* (Museo Nacional Centro de Arte Reina Sofía, 2012).

59 Guy-Ernest Debord, "Totem and Taboo," in *Internationale lettriste*, no. 3 (August 1953); reproduced in *Documents relatifs à la fondation de l'Internationale situationniste* (Paris: Éditions Allia, 1985), 156.

60 Ibid.

61 Gil J Wolman, *Le sens perdu de l'interruption* (Paris: Éditions inconnues, 1987), as cited in *Défense de mourir*, 361.

62 The "speaking body" refers to Shoshana Felman's study, which offers an incisive meditation on the relation between language and the body and how the *speaking body* disturbs metaphysical dichotomies. More specifically, she explores the relation between speech and the erotic through a consideration of Molière's Don Juan in light of Austin's inaugural work on the performative. In this context, her study is crucial insofar as it engages with the question of how the performance of language requires a body that is the condition of speech. See Felman, *The Scandal of the Speaking Body: Don Juan with J. L. Austin, or Seduction in Two Languages* (Stanford, CA: Stanford University Press, 2003).

63 See the discussion in Judith Butler, *Excitable Speech: A Politics of the Performative* (New York: Routledge, 1997), 133.

64 For a study of the parameters of the voice in cinema, see Michel Chion, *The Voice in Cinema*, trans. Claudia Gorbman (1982; New York: Columbia University Press, 1999).

65 See the discussion in Mary Ann Doane, "The Voice in Cinema: The Articulation of Body and Space," *Yale French Studies*, no. 60, "Cinema/Sound" (1980), 46.

66 Butler, *Excitable Speech*, 133.

67 Jacques Villeglé, "Le dire Wolmanien" (1999), in *Défense de mourir*, 335. One might ask, following Villeglé, if Wolman's poetry becomes a potential site for reenacting the sounds of suffering in war—of World War II, the Holocaust, its victims, their screams.

68 My discussion of a common corporeality is indebted to Judith Butler. For Butler, common corporeality is premised on vulnerability, which is a precondition for humanization. If "humanization takes place differently through variable norms of recognition," she writes, "then it follows that vulnerability is fundamentally dependent on existing norms of recognition if it is to be attributed to any human subject." See Butler, *Precarious Life: The Powers of Mourning and Violence* (London: Verso, 2004), 42–43.

69 "*L'anticoncept* renders the concept subjective and variable through the spectators' reactions; a physical phase [*phase physique*] begins." With this statement in 1952, Wolman implies how the body's speechless speech takes effect: it is not due to "concepts" or conceptual understanding, but on account of the film's subjective reception through the spectators' physical, nonconceptual, response. Wolman, "Le Cinématochrone," 31.

70 I allude here to Austin, *How to Do Things with Words*.

CHAPTER FOUR

1 At the Walter Reade Theater, the film's institutional implementation was dubious: the blank screen was disrupted by subtitles, making the sound track a visual-typographic element of the film. Even during the dark sequences, a lighter gray field (the space of the subtitles' projection) remained on the bottom half of the screen, thereby creating a composition on the screen's surface.

2 As cited in Zack Winestine, "Howls for Guy Debord," *Film Quarterly* 62, no. 4 (Summer 2009) 14.

3 Guy Debord, *Considerations on the Assassination of Gérard Lebovici*, trans. Robert Greene (Los Angeles: Tam Tam Books, 2001), 30.

4 Winestine, "Howls for Guy Debord," 14.

5 Scott Foundas, "Reflections of a Darkened Screen," *LA Weekly*, March 2, 2009, http://blogs.laweekly.com/foundas/uncategorized/reflections-on-a-darkened-scre/ (accessed May 19, 2010).

6 That the extrafilmic actions seemed contrived is substantiated by one reviewer's claim that he was "feeling a lot of adrenaline and really *working hard to figure out* how to spark some kind of participation." Winestine, "Howls for Guy Debord," 15 (my italics).

7 Ibid.

8 Guy Debord, "Prolégomènes à tout cinéma futur," in *Ion* (1952; Paris: Jean-Paul Rocher, 1999), 217. Debord's text continues by announcing a shift from a concern with "création" to the "conditionnement du spectateur" (conditioning of the spectator) and ends by asserting, "The arts of the future can be nothing less than disruptions of situations,"

thereby suggesting what he and the Situationists will later develop as "situations" over the course of the 1950s.

9 See the discussion in Isidore Isou, "Esthétique du cinéma," in *Ion*, 7–153.

10 Guy Debord, script for *Hurlements en faveur de Sade*, in *Ion*, 230.

11 Isidore Isou, description, on a martini napkin, of a scene from *Traité de bave et d'éternité*, 1951, Fonds Guy Debord, Département des Manuscrits, Bibliothèque Nationale de France, Paris. Many thanks to Catherine Goldstein (Isou's daughter) and Frédéric Acquaviva for assisting me in identifying the handwriting. Goldstein, e-mail correspondence with author, August 11, 2013; Acquaviva, e-mail correspondece with author, August 11, 2013. Our attribution of the handwriting to Isou is also based on the fact that Isou signs one of the napkins. This conclusion differs from the identification of the handwriting as Debord's in the recent BNF publication dedicated to the exhibiton of his archive. See *Guy Debord: Un art de la guerre*, ed. Emmanuel Guy and Laurence Le Bras (Paris: Bibliothèque nationale de France; and Gallimard, 2013), 63.

12 Isou, "Esthétique du cinéma," 41.

13 Debord apparently used magnetic tape (used at the time for sound editing) for the opaque leader. When magnetic tape passes through the gate of a film projector, it is utterly opaque and erases the borders of the film frame, creating, according to Keith Sanborn, a "palpable, eerie void." Moreover, when passing through the optical sound head of a film projector, it is silent (in contrast to the optical sound track on the clear leader). See the technical specifications described by Sanborn in "Return of the Supressed," *Artforum* 44, no. 6 (February 2006), esp. 188–89.

14 The inclusion in the sound track of "diverse articles from the Civil Code" was announced as a possibility in the original script but regularly punctuates the realized version. Also, two phrases from the "Prolégomènes" make their way to the sound track. These include the twice-repeated "L'amour n'est valable que dans une période prérévolutionnaire" (Love is valid only in a prerevolutionary period) and "Les arts futurs seront des bouleversements de situations, ou rien" (The arts of the future can be nothing less than disruptions of situations). For an excellent account of the changes in the sound track, see Guy Claude Marie, *Guy Debord: De son cinéma en son art et en son temps* (Paris: Éditions Vrin, 2009), chap. 1.

15 See Guy Debord, "Grande fête de nuit" (preface) and "Hurlements en faveur de Sade" (script), in *Les lèvres nues*, no. 7 (December 1955), 18–23.

16 Guy Debord and Gil J Wolman, "Methods of Détournement," in *Situationist International Anthology*, ed. and trans. Ken Knabb (Berkeley, CA: Bureau of Public Secrets, 1981), 9.

17 All voice-over citations from Debord's films are taken from the English translations in *Guy Debord: Complete Cinematic Works*, ed. and trans. Ken Knabb (1978; Edinburgh: AK Press, 2003) (translation modified).

18 Thomas Levin's work remains an exception. In a 1989 essay he notes, "*Hurlements* remains a decidedly Lettrist work." In this context, Levin speaks to Debord's reduction of cinema to the apparatus: the filmstrip, projector, light, and screen, upon which the actual mechanics of a screening depend. Levin was also among the first scholars to note Debord's debt to Isou's conception of *montage discrépant*. Nevertheless, he ultimately dissociates the film from the live elements that were so crucial to Lettrist cinema in these years, instead granting *Hurlements* the honor of being the "first truly dada film." Levin, "Dismantling the Spectacle: The Cinema of Guy Debord," in *Guy Debord and the Situationist International*, ed. Tom McDonough (Cambridge, MA: MIT Press, 2002), 344, 347–48. See also Allyson Field, "*Hurlements en faveur de Sade*: The Negation and Surpassing of 'Discrepant Cinema,'" *Substance* 28, no. 3 (1999): 55–70.

19 See "Les lettristes désavouent les insulteurs de Chaplin," *Combat*, November 1, 1952.

20 Originally refused by *Combat*, "Position de l'international lettriste," was published in the first issue of *Internationale lettriste*, which publically announced the dissident group. See Serge Berna, Jean-L. Brau, Guy-Ernst Debord, and Gil J Wolman, "Position de l'international lettriste," in *International lettriste*, no. 1 (1952), reprinted in *Documents*

relatifs à la fondation de l'Internationale situationniste, ed. Gérard Berréby (Paris: Éditions Allia, 1985), 151.

21 "La retraite," *Potlatch*, no. 28 (May 1957), n.p.; reproduced in *Potlatch: 1954–1957* (Paris: Éditions Allia, 1996), 141.

22 Ibid.

23 Ibid. "La retraite" makes no mention of Wolman's collaboration on the theories (and practices) of *détournement* and *dérive*, published in *Les lèvres nues* the previous year. While the text limits Wolman's aesthetic practice to his *mégapneumie* and *cinématochrone*, both *détournement* and *dérive* continued to be elaborated in theory and in practice by the SI, and the original essays were later republished in the pages of the *Internationale situationniste*. The slight shifts in content and title of the essays are less significant than a telling absence: Wolman's name is nowhere to be found. "Mode d'emploi du détournement" and "Théorie de la dérive" were published in *Les lèvres nues* in, respectively, May (no. 8) and November (no. 9) 1956, and each was signed by both Wolman and Debord. After the founding of the SI, they were republished without Wolman's name as Guy Debord, "Théorie de la dérive," *Internationale situationniste*, no. 2 (December 1958), 19–23; and Guy Debord, "Le détournement comme négation et comme prélude," *Internationale situationniste*, no. 3 (December 1959), 10–11.

24 Letter from Guy Debord to Gil J Wolman, n.d., Gil J Wolman Papers, Beinecke Rare Book and Manuscript Library, Yale University. The excerpt cited is also reproduced in *Défense de mourir* (Paris: Éditions Allia, 2001), 24; in this publication, the letter is dated "vers avril 1957" (around April 1957).

25 See Jean-Michel Bouhours, "De l'anticoncept à L'anticoncept," in *Défense de mourir*, 356 and note 19.

26 See Guy Debord, "Technical Notes on the First Three Films," in *Guy Debord: Complete Cinematic Works*, 211 (translation modified). Originally published as Guy Debord, "Fiches techniques," in *Contre le cinéma* (Aarhus, Denmark: Scandinavian Institute of Comparative Vandalism, 1964).

27 See Guy Debord, "Technical Notes on the First Three Films," 211.

28 Letter from Isidore Isou to Guy Debord, July 3, 1952 (original emphasis: underline). Fonds Guy Debord, Département des Manuscrits, Bibliothèque Nationale de France, Paris.

29 Ibid.

30 See the accounts by Mension and Rajsfus in Jean-Michel Mension, *The Tribe*, trans. Donald Nicholson-Smith (San Francisco: City Lights Books, 2001), 86-91. For the original French see *La tribu* (Paris: Éditions Allia, 1998). For other accounts of the second screening, see Greil Marcus, *Lipstick Traces: A Secret History of the Twentieth Century* (Cambridge, MA: Harvard University Press, 1989), 323–43, and Christophe Bourseiller, *Vie et mort de Guy Debord: 1931–1994* (Paris: Plon, 1999), 56–57. In the 1950s, in addition to the two screenings in Paris, the film was shown in 1957 at the Institute for Contemporary Arts (ICA) in London, where its reception was equally contentious. See the review "Contemporary Arts: Anti-Art," *Spectator*, July 12, 1957, clipping in ICA archive, Research Centre for the Tate Library and Archive. Debord reports, "Last June, we obtained the scandal which we expected upon presenting in London a film which I had made in 1952, a film which is not a mystification and even less a Situationist work. Rather this film is based on a number of complex Lettrist motivations from that period (the work on the cinema by Isou, Marco [*sic*] Wolman) and thus participated fully in the phase of decomposition, indeed, to be precise, in its most extreme form, yet, with the exception of a few programmatic allusions, devoid of the desire to make positive developments which is characteristic of the works to which I just alluded." G.-E. Debord, "Encore un effort si vous voulez être situationnistes," *Potlatch*, no. 29 (November 1957); reproduced in *Potlatch: 1954–1957*, 146. For the English translation, see Guy Debord, "One More Try If You Want to Be Situationists (The SI *in* and *against* Decomposition)," trans. John Shepley, in *Guy Debord and the Situationist International*, ed. Tom McDonough (Cambridge, MA: MIT Press, 2002), 58.

31 Mension, *The Tribe*, 87.
32 Rasjfus, cited in ibid., 88. The original account is published in Maurice Rajsfus, *Une enfance laïque et républicaine* (Paris: Manya, 1992), esp. 299–300.
33 Maurice Rasjfus, interview with author, June 14, 2010.
34 Mension, *The Tribe*, 88. Rasjfus also remembers, "Nobody could believe that the director would leave his audience—there was an admission fee, after all—without offering them a single image: in the end, no doubt, one would probably get a little something, some kind of provocation, at least. With the uproar gradually gaining ground in the orchestra, the Lettrists and their allies in the balcony bombarded the public below with stink bombs and sneezing powder. The better equipped had water-filled condoms." Rasjfus, cited in ibid., 88.
35 Michèle Bernstein, conversation with author, June 18, 2010.
36 Ibid.
37 Rasjfus, cited in Mension, *The Tribe*, 88, 91.
38 Maurice Rasjfus, interview with author, June 14, 2010.
39 Isou, "Esthétique du cinéma," in *Ion*, 147–48.
40 See Frédérique Devaux, *Le cinéma lettriste: 1951–1991* (Paris: Éditions Paris Expérimental, 1992), 132.
41 "Panorama intelligent de l'avant-garde à la fin de 1955," *Potlatch*, no. 24 (November 1955).
42 See the dicussion in Guy Debord and Gil J Wolman, "Mode d'emploi du détournement," *Les lèvres nues*, no. 8 (May 1956).
43 See, for example, *Guy Debord: Complete Cinematic Works*; Guy Claude Marie, *Guy Debord: De son cinéma en son art et en son temps*; *Guy Debord (contro) il cinema*, ed. Enrico Ghezzi and Roberto Turigliatto (Milan: Editrice Il Castoro/Biennale di Venezia, 2001); *Consumato dal fuoco: Il cinema di Guy Debord*, ed. Monica Dall'Asta and Marco Grosoli (Pisa: Edizioni ETS, 2011); and *Grey Room*, special edition on Guy Debord, ed. Jason E. Smith, no. 52 (Summer 2013), which includes an excerpt from this chapter.
44 All times provided for the films in this chapter are based on the DVD box set, Guy Debord, *Oeuvres cinématographiques complètes* (Gaumont Vidéo, 2005).
45 See Debord, "Technical Notes on the First Three Films," 212.
46 As the notes to the film suggest, "In order to adopt a position opposed to that of documentary films in terms of the construction of spectacle, every time there was a danger of encountering a monument we avoided filming it by shooting instead from the point of view of the monument." As a result the social organization of the space represented in the film responds to the Situationists' desire for "psychogeography," a means by which to navigate the built environment and experience its subject effects in a manner at odds with a city's dominant pattern of development and circulation. Debord, "Technical Notes on the First Three Films," 212 (translation modified).
47 Ibid., 213.
48 Tom McDonough offers an insightful analysis of *Critique de la séparation* in relation to the near contemporaneous *cinéma-vérité* film *Chronique d'un été* (Chronicle of a Summer, 1960), a collaboration between Jean Rouch and Edgar Morin. He draws attention to Debord's avowals of confusion and how the communicative function of language breaks down at moments in the voice-over. See McDonough, "Calling from the Inside: Filmic Topologies of the Everyday," *Grey Room*, no. 26 (Winter 2007), 6–29, esp. 16–17. McDonough's analysis differs from Thomas Y. Levin's earlier assessment of Debord's films. For Levin, Debord's refusal of narrative coherence in his films matches the incoherence of a contemporary reified life, thereby producing a film whose deliberate heterogeneity amounts to an aesthetic strategy, which Levin designates as a "mimesis of incoherence." Levin, "Dismantling the Spectacle," 360.
49 "Editorial Notes: All the King's Men," trans. Tom McDonough, in *Guy Debord and the Situationist International*, ed. McDonough (Cambridge, MA: MIT Press, 2002), 154 (my italics).
50 As early as 1958 Debord establishes "communication" as counter to "information,"

insisting that "all forms of pseudocommunication must be consigned to utter destruction, so that one day we may achieve real, direct communication." See Guy Debord, "Theses on Cultural Revolution," trans. John Shepley, in *Guy Debord and the Situationist International*, 65.

51 Debord, "Prolégomènes à tout cinéma futur," 230.

52 "With and against Cinema," trans. Jason E. Smith, *Grey Room*, no. 52 (Summer 2013), 19. Originally published as "Avec et contre le cinéma," *Internationale situationniste* 1 (1958) 8–9.

53 Walter H. Waggoner, "U.S. to Be Candid at Brussels Fair," *New York Times*, March 5, 1958.

54 Jerry Hulse, "Miniature World Unfolds at the Fair," *Los Angeles Times*, April 23, 1958.

55 See the audience reactions discussed in Sara Nilsen, *Projecting America, 1958: Film and Cultural Diplomacy at the Brussels World's Fair* (Jefferson, NC: McFarland and Company, 2011), esp. 77–79.

56 "With and against Cinema," 19.

57 Ibid.

58 "Editorial Notes: The Meaning of Decay in Art," trans. John Shepley, in *Guy Debord and the Situationist International*, 91.

59 See Frances Stracey, "The Caves of Gallizio and Hirschhorn: Excavations of the Present," *October*, no. 116 (Spring 2006), 87–100. See also Nicola Pezolet, "The Cavern of Antimatter: Giuseppe 'Pinot' Gallizio and the Technological Imaginary of the Early Situationist International," *Grey Room*, no. 38 (Winter 2010), 62–89.

60 The absence of such cinematic experimentation within Situationist practice may also be due to the fact that such practice remained external to the conventions of cinema as it was consolidated as an institution in the course of the 1950s. After all, the column further explains that some "destructive works . . . are still rejected even in ciné-clubs." "With and against Cinema," 19.

61 For an account of the frequent proximity between expanded cinema and modern mass media display, see Liz Kotz, "Disciplining Expanded Cinema," in *X-Screen: Film Installations and Actions in the 1960s and 1970s* (Vienna: Mumok, 2004), 44–57. As Branden W. Joseph has noted, a confusion between image and reality often characterized expanded cinema's techniques and consequently haunted its critical reception. See his nuanced reading of Whitman's work in Joseph, "Plastic Empathy: The Ghost of Robert Whitman," *Grey Room*, no. 25 (Fall 2006), 64–91.

62 See Gene Youngblood, *Expanded Cinema* (New York: E. P. Dutton, 1970), 76.

63 Guy Debord, *The Society of the Spectacle*, trans. Donald Nicholson-Smith (New York: Zone Books, 1995), 12. For the original French, see Guy Debord, *La société du spectacle* (Paris: Buchet-Chastel, 1967), 9.

64 Jacques Rancière, *The Emancipated Spectator*, trans. Gregory Elliott (London: Verso, 2009), 86. For the original French version, see Jacques Rancière, *Le spectateur émancipé* (Paris: Éditions La Fabrique, 2008).

65 Rancière. *Emancipated Spectator*, 85.

66 Ibid., 87.

67 Ibid., 86 (my italics).

68 Ibid.

69 Debord's use of voice-over in part aligns his work with the conventions of the essay film: from the use of verbal language to draw attention to an issue through film, to the fact that the language is persuasive and well written. For a discussion of the genre's investment in expository prose, see Philip Lopate, "In Search of the Centaur: The Essay Film," in *Beyond Document: Essays on Non-Fiction Film*, ed. Charles Warren (Middletown, CT: Wesleyan University Press, 1996), 243–70. For a detailed account of the essay film's origins and primary characteristics, see Timothy Corrigan, *The Essay Film: From Montaigne, after Marker* (New York: Oxford University Press, 2011), esp. 50–75.

70 Rancière, *Emancipated Spectator*, 88.

71 These include references to Mikhail Bakunin, Carl von Clausewitz, Karl Marx, Alexis

de Tocqueville, and the Sorbonne Occupation Committee. Over the course of the 1960s, Situationist film theory was increasingly aligned with the political stakes of writing. In 1967 René Viénet recommended that SI members be equally capable of writing an article and making a film, given the medium's accessibility and the way film could "intensify" the written articulation of the same problems. See Viénet, "The Situations and the New Forms of Action against Politics and Art," trans. Tom McDonough, in *Guy Debord and the Situationist International*, 184–85. For the French original, see Viénet, "Les situationnistes et les nouvelles formes d'action contre la politique et l'art," *Internationale situationniste*, no. 11 (October 1967), 35.

72 On the one hand, language in Debord's films serves as a means of dialectical *negation*, as when the voice-over unveils an image's ideological meaning (recall the newsreel sequence that concludes with Eisenhower embraced by Franco). On the other hand, quoted speech, rather than serving exclusively as a means by which to negate the negation, is dialectically *intensified* in relation to images of recent history, thereby extending Marx's analysis of capitalism, for example, to have critical purchase in the present. To affirm that Debord situates his voice within collective history and a specifically Marxist genealogy is not, however, to imply that his use of language is polyvocal. Rather, he draws upon fragments from Marxist works so as to redeem and thus remotivate their meaning in relation to the present, an operation that could more properly be considered allegorical. As Walter Benjamin notes, the allegorist is motivated by "an appreciation of the transience of things, and the concern to rescue them for eternity." Benjamin, *The Origin of German Tragic Drama*, trans. John Osborne (1928; London: Verso, 1998), 223. That said, the cumulative *effect* of the particular genealogy Debord mines reveals, contrary to his intention, Marxism's discursive (and gendered) constraints: the majority of the verbal citations come from men and serve to reveal the truth of commodified images that largely include women.

73 Rancière, *Emancipated Spectator*, 95, 103. Rancière challenges not only dicourse of the spectacle, but also the critique of the image in the name of the unrepresentable. See also ibid., 88–94.

74 Ibid.

75 See Claire Bishop, *Artificial Hells: Participatory Art and the Politics of Spectatorship* (London: Verso, 2012).

76 Rancière, *Emancipated Spectator*, 105. Among the works Rancière discusses are Alfredo Jaar's installations and Sophie Ristelhueber's photographs. As Claire Bishop observes, the "'distribution of the sensible' is never demonstrated through abstract forms unrelated to a political theme." Bishop, *Artificial Hells*, 29.

77 Rancière, *Emancipated Spectator*, 86 (my italics).

78 Ibid., 86n1.

79 Rancière also refers to *Hurlements* in his essay "Quand nous étions sur le Shenandoah," *Cahiers du cinéma*, no. 605 (October 2005), 92–93. Here he takes issue with the fact that Debord did not "stop the projection and declare the end of cinema," as suggested by Voice 5 (Isou) in the sound track to *Hurlements*. A translation of the text appears in Rancière, "When We Were on the Shenandoah," trans. Jason E. Smith, *Grey Room*, no. 52 (Summer 2013), 129–34. As noted above, it was ultimately Isou who proclaimed that cinema was dead and that the debate itself constituted the film.

80 Bradley Eros, as cited in "Migrating Forms—Friday, April 17—VOID for FILM: Imageless Cinema," *Invisible Cinema*, April 16, 2009, http://invisiblecinema.typepad.com/invisible_cinema/2009/04/migrating-forms-friday-april-18-void-for-film-imageless-cinema.html (accessed June 18, 2014).

81 Guy Debord, *Panégyrique tome premier* (Paris: Éditions Gérard Lebovici, 1989), 35.

EPILOGUE

1 As I note in the introduction, these connections remain to be explored. The Lettrists form an unacknowledged bridge not only to the films of the Nouvelle Vague directors, who explored the use of jump cuts and chronological dislocations, but also to those of the Left Bank directors—including Alain Resnais, Marguerite Duras, and Chris Marker—who, more literary in inflection, often turned to the voice-over as a way to problematize the visual image and narrative closure (e.g., Resnais's *Hiroshima mon amour*, 1959). For a detailed account of Left Bank filmmakers, see Robert Farmer, "Marker, Resnais, Varda: Remembering the Left Bank Group," *Senses of Cinema*, no. 52 (September 2009), http://sensesofcinema.com/2009/52/marker-resnais-varda-remembering-the-left-bank-group/ (accessed August 12, 2013).

2 Guy Debord, *Considerations on the Assassination of Gérard Lebovici*, trans. Robert Greene (Los Angeles: Tam Tam Books, 2001), 30.

3 Ibid., 30–31.

4 While speculation about how Debord's film might have "influenced" Klein's work peppers the increasingly expansive literature on the Situationists, in this context the specificity of Klein's work and its relation to Lettrist cinema, as well as his work with film, is left unexamined. See, for example, Thomas Y. Levin, "Dismantling the Spectacle: The Cinema of Guy Debord," in *Guy Debord and the Situationist International*, ed. Tom McDonough (Cambridge, MA: MIT Press, 2002), 342, and Jean-Marie Apostolidès, "Du Surréalisme à l'Internationale situationniste: la question de l'image," *MLN* 105, no. 4, "French Issue" (September 1990), 749.

5 *Tambours du jugement premier* was originally meant to have an image track, but it was ultimately abandoned, more than likely due to lack of funds. See Frédérique Devaux, *Le cinéma lettriste: 1951–1991* (Paris: Éditions Paris Expérimental, 1992), 276n83.

6 Marc'O, interview with author, June 15, 2010.

7 François Dufrêne, "Prodrome," in *Ion* (1952; Paris: Jean-Paul Rocher, 1999), 196.

8 Klein's work could also be read, albeit more literally, in relation to Dufrêne's assertion that the work of cinema was ultimately to "doubt the very essence of cinema through the existence of 'IMAGINARY CINEMA.'" Ibid. The creation of imaginary art was further explored by Isidore Isou in his "Introduction à l'esthétique imaginaire," *Front de la jeunesse*, no. 7 (May 1956). I thank Christian Lebrat for referring me to this work.

9 François Dufrêne, "Une action en marge du Festival de Cannes 1952," in *Archi-made*, ed. Marie-Anne Sichère and Didier Semin (Paris: École Nationale Supérieure des Beaux-Arts, 2005), 39.

10 See the filmography in *Yves Klein: Corps, couleur, immatériel* (Paris: Centre Pompidou, 2006), 310. I base my number on the films for which Klein exercised oversight.

11 I follow Klein's description as presented in his book *Le dépassement de la problématique de l'art* (La Louvière, Belgium: Éditions Montbliart, 1959). Klein's account of *Le vide* differs in some details from Iris Clert's recollections in Clert, *Iris-time (L'artventure)* (Paris: Éditions Denoël, 2003).

12 For an account of *Le vide* in relation to Lettrist cinema, see Kaira M. Cabañas, "Ghostly Presence," in *Yves Klein: With the Void, Full Powers* (Minneapolis: Walker Art Center; Washington, DC: Hirshhorn Museum and Sculpture Garden, 2010), 174–91. Here I describe how Klein developed a "painting séance," taking my cue from Maurice Lemaître's designation of his Lettrist work in film as a "*séance de cinéma*" (*séance* translated as "session" by Lemaître). To the best of my knowledge, there is no record of Klein's having attended Lemaitre's *Le film est déjà commence?* in December 1951 or the first presentation of Gil J Wolman's *L'anticoncept* in February 1952. Nevertheless, he would have known about their work. See also my discussion of Klein's *Le vide* in relation to the performative in Cabañas, "Yves Klein's Performative Realism," *Grey Room*, no. 31 (Spring 2008), 6–31, as well as chapter 5, "Let This Be Said and Done," in Cabañas, *The Myth of Nouveau Réalisme: Art and the Performative in Postwar France* (New Haven, CT: Yale University

Press, 2013), 30–61, 131–34 (in relation to Lettrism). Indeed, my work on Lettrist cinema is something of a prequel to these earlier studies.

13 In the summer of 1972 at the Kunsthalle in Düsseldorf, Broodthaers presented the museum's "Section des Figures" under the title "The Eagle from the Oligocene to the Present." The exhibition comprised 266 objects representing eagles, with loans from forty-three "real" museums and private collections, including Broodthaers's own. Displayed in glass cases or hung on the wall, each eagle object (from banal objects such as postage stamps to appearances in military iconography and advertising) was accompanied by a small plastic plaque with the statement "This is not a work of art" printed in English, French, or German. As remarked by Broodthaers, the statement derives from "a formula obtained by the contraction of a concept by Duchamp and an antithetical concept by Magritte." See Marcel Broodthaers, "Ten Thousand Francs Reward," trans. Paul Schmidt, *October*, no. 42 (Fall 1987), 47. In submitting an upside-down porcelain urinal to an open entry exhibition with the assertion that "this is a work of art," Duchamp had contested the principles underlying the notions of both autonomous art objects and expressive artists. See Benjamin Buchloh's entry "1972a," in *Art since 1900: Modernism, Antimodernism, Postmodernism*, ed. Hal Foster, Rosalind E. Krauss, Yve-Alain Bois, and Benjamin H. D. Buchloch (London: Thames and Hudson, 2004), 549–53.

14 See, for example, Benjamin Buchloh, "The Museum Fictions of Marcel Broodthaers," in *Museums by Artists*, ed. A. A. Bronson and Peggy Gale (Toronto: Art Metropole, 1983), 45–56; the chapter "This Is Not a Museum of Art," in Douglas Crimp, *On the Museum's Ruins* (Cambridge, MA: MIT Press, 1993), 200–34; and Rachel Haidu's detailed study *The Absence of Work: Marcel Broodthaers, 1964–1976* (Cambridge, MA: MIT Press, 2010), esp. 107–18.

15 Program for a screening of Isidore Isou, *Traité de bave et d'éternité* (1951–1952), Palais des Beaux-Arts in Brussels, October 31, 1952, Bismuth-Lemaître Papers, Beinecke Rare Book and Manuscript Library, Yale University.

16 Program for a screening of *Le film est déjà commencé?* (1951), Palais des Beaux-Arts, Brussels, February 10, 1954, Bismuth-Lemaître Papers, Beinecke Rare Book and Manuscript Library, Yale University.

17 Marcel Broodthaers, "Le D est plus grand que le T," in *Marcel Broodthaers: Cinéma* (Barcelona: Funadació Antoni Tàpies, 1997), 58 (my translation).

18 Marcel Broodthaers, as cited in *Marcel Broodthears: Cinéma*, 52.

19 For a discussion of Broodthaers's turn to the devices of early cinema, see Eric de Bruyn, "The Museum of Attractions: Marcel Broodthaers and the Section Cinéma," in *Art and the Moving Image: A Critical Reader*, ed. Tanya Leighton (London: Tate Publishing/Afterall, 2008), 112–21.

20 See Devaux, *Le cinéma lettriste*, 143–57.

21 In his account of experimental film practice in the 1960s and 1970s, Peter Wollen describes the differences between avant-garde and formalist branches of film. I take Lettrist cinema to offer a third way, between these two alternatives, given that it both engages in formalist experimentation (and thus a politics of the signifier) and seeks to transform cinema as an institution. See Wollen, "The Two Avant-Gardes," in *Readings and Writings: Semiotic Counter-Strategies* (London: Verso, 1982), 92–104. Eric de Bruyn skillfully expands on Wollen's work in order to consider the specificity of what he calls "post-minimal" film, which develops alongside (or between) the formalist and political avant-gardes discussed in Wollen's text. See de Bruyn, "The Expanded Field of Cinema, or Exercise on the Perimeter of a Square," in *X-Screen: Film Installations and Actions in the 1960s and 1970s* (Vienna: Mumok, 2004), 152–76. De Bruyn claims, "In other words, what we need is a *history of avant-garde practices of film*, rather than a history of the discipline of avant-garde film" (154; my italics). Broodthaers's work is exemplary for de Bruyn.

SELECTED BIBLIOGRAPHY

I list here the interviews and primary sources that have been key to the research for this book. Secondary sources are listed in the notes.

ARCHIVES

Archiv Acquaviva, Berlin.
Bibliothèque Kandinsky, Centre Pompidou, Paris.
Bismuth-Lemaître Papers, Beinecke Rare Book and Manuscript Library, Yale University.
Fonds Guy Debord, Département des Manuscrits, Bibliothèque Nationale de France, Paris.
Gaumont-Pathé Archives, Paris.
Institute of Contemporary Arts archive, Research Centre for the Tate Library and Archive, London.
Archives Isou-Goldstein, Paris.
Gil J Wolman Papers, Beinecke Rare Book and Manuscript Library, Yale University. (Originally consulted at the home of the late Charlotte Wolman.)

INTERVIEWS

Frédéric Acquaviva, interview by author, November 3, 2009, and e-mail correspondence with author, August 11, 2013.
Michèle Bernstein, conversation with author, June 18, 2010.

Gérard Berréby, conversation with author, June 29, 2009.
Jean-Michel Bouhours, e-mail correspondence with author, November 16, 2009.
Richard Foreman, interview by author, June 20, 2013.
Catherine Goldstein, conversation with author, June 22, 2010; January 12 and 14, 2011, and e-mail correspondence with author, August 11, 2013.
Maurice Lemaître, conversation with author, January 16, 2011.
Marc'O, interview by author, June 15, 2010.
Maurice Rajsfus, interview by author, June 14, 2010.
Charlotte Wolman, conversation with author, June 17, 2009, and November 11, 2011.

FILMS

Debord, Guy. *Oeuvres cinématographiques complètes*. 1952–1973. DVDs. Paris: Gaumont Vidéo, 2005.
Dufrêne, François. *Tambours du jugement premier*. 1952. Sound film, 60 minutes. The copy consulted includes the 1973 recording at France Culture and the 1981 recording of the "Prodrome." Centre Pompidou Collection, Paris.
Dulac, Germaine. *La coquille et le clergyman*. 1928. Black and white, 88 minutes. DVD. Paris: Light One, 2009.
"Indochine: L'arrivée du Général de Lattre." *Journal Actualité (Journal Gaumont)*. 1950. Sound film, black and white, 13 seconds. Gaumont-Pathé Archives, Paris. REF 5051GJ 00004.
Isou, Isidore. *Traité de bave et d'éternité*. 1951. Sound film, black and white, 123 minutes. DVD. Paris: Re:Voir Video, 2008.
Lemaître, Maurice. "Annonce" (1979). *Le film est déjà commencé?* DVD. Paris: Fondation Bismuth-Lemaître.
———. *Le film est déjà commencé?* 1951. Sound film, color, 65 minutes. DVD. Paris: Fondation Bismuth-Lemaître.
Marc'O. *Closed Vision*. 1954. Sound film, black and white, 62 minutes.
Pomerand, Gabriel. *La légende cruelle*. 1951. Sound film, black and white, 22 minutes.
Védrès, Nicole. *Paris 1900*. 1947. Sound film, black and white, 75 minutes. DVD. Phoenix: Grapevine Video, 2012.
Wolman, Gil J. *L'anticoncept*. 1952. Sound film, black and white, 60 minutes. VHS. Paris: Éditions Allia, 1994.
———. *L'anticoncept à New York*. 1990. VHS. Sound film, color, approx. 65 minutes.

ADDITIONAL SOURCES

A.P. "A propos 'd'Anticoncept.'" *Le Figaro*, February 18, 1952.

———. "Quand l'avant garde abolit l'écran." *Le Figaro*, February 13, 1952.

"Applaudissements, injures et sifflets accueillent le film d'Isidore Isou." *Le Figaro*, January 26–27, 1952.

Artaud, Antonin. *Oeuvres complètes*, vol. 4. Ed. Paule Thévenin. Paris: Gallimard, 1970.

———. *Pour en finir avec le jugement de Dieu*. Paris: Éditions K, 1948.

———. *The Theater and Its Double*, trans. M. C. Richards. New York: Grove, 1958.

"Avec et contre le cinéma." *Internationale situationniste*, no. 1 (1958), 8–9.

Bazin, André. "Comment présenter et discuter un film!" *Ciné-club*, April 1954, 10.

———. "Nicole Védrès." *L'écran français*, September 30, 1947.

Berna, Serge, Jean-L. Brau, Guy-Ernst Debord, and Gil J Wolman. "Les lettristes désavouent les insulteurs de Chaplin." *Combat*, November 1, 1952.

———. "Position de l'International Lettriste." *International lettriste*, no. 1 (1952).

Chopin, Henri, ed. *Revue OU*, 1963–1974.

Cocteau, Jean. "Affaire Isou (avril 1951, en marge du festival de Cannes)." In *Entretiens sur le cinématographe*. Paris: Éditions Belfond, 1973.

"Contemporary Arts: Anti-Art." *Spectator*, July 12, 1957.

Debord, Guy. *Considérations sur l'assassinat de Gérard Lebovici*. Paris: Éditions Gérard Lebovici, 1985. Trans. Robert Greene, as *Considerations on the Assassination of Gérard Lebovici* (Los Angeles: Tam Tam Books, 2001).

———. *Contre le cinéma*. Aarhus, Denmark: Scandinavian Institute of Comparative Vandalism, 1964.

———. "Le détournement comme négation et comme prélude." *Internationale situationniste*, no. 3 (December 1959), 10–11.

———. "Encore un effort si vous voulez être situationnistes." *Potlatch*, no. 29 (November 1957), n.p.

———. "Grande fête de nuit" (preface) and "Hurlements en faveur de Sade" (script). *Les lèvres nues*, no. 7 (December 1955), 18–23.

———. "Hurlements en faveur de Sade." *Ion*, April 1952, 219–30.

———. *Oeuvres cinématographiques complètes (1952–1978)*. Paris: Champ Libre, 1985.

———. *Panégyrique tome premier*. Paris: Éditions Gérard Lebovici, 1989.

———. "Prolégomènes à tout cinéma futur." *Ion*, April 1952, 217–18.

———. *La société du spectacle*. Paris: Buchet-Chastel, 1967. Trans. Donald Nicholson-Smith, as *The Society of the Spectacle* (New York: Zone Books, 1995).

———. "Théorie de la dérive." *Internationale situationniste*, no. 2 (December 1958), 19–23.

———. "Totem and Taboo." *Internationale lettriste*, no. 3 (August 1953).

Debord, Guy, and Gil J Wolman. "Mode d'emploi du détournement." *Les lèvres nues*, no. 8 (May 1956), 2–9.

Desternes, Jean. "Dernière visite à Antonin Artaud." *Le Figaro littéraire*, March 13, 1948.

Dufrêne, François. "Une action en marge du Festival de Cannes 1952." In *Archi-made*, ed. Marie-Anne Sichère and Didier Semin. Paris: École Nationale Supérieure des Beaux-Arts, 2005.

———. "J'interroge et j'invective: poème a hurler / À la mémoire d'Antonin Artaud." *Ur: Cahiers pour un dictat culturel*, no. 1 (1950), 29–30.

———. "Marche." *Ur: Cahiers pour un dictat culturel*, no. 1 (1950), 27–28.

———. "Pragmatique du crirythme." *OU*, nos. 28–29 (1965), n.p.

———. "Prodrome." *Ion*, April 1952, 195–96.

———. "Tambours du jugement premier." *Ion*, April 1952, 197–214.

First International Symposium on Letterism, Lewis and Clark College, Portland, Oregon, May 24–29, 1976. Proceedings ed. Pietro Ferrua. Portland, OR: Avant-Garde Publishers, 1978.

Gautier, Jean-Jacques. "Au Studio de l'Etoile: 'Traité de bave et d'éternité." *Le Figaro*, January 28, 1952.

Hulse, Jerry. "Miniature World Unfolds at the Fair." *Los Angeles Times*, April 23, 1958.

Ion (April 1952). Paris: Centre de Création, 1952. Reprint, Paris: Jean-Paul Rocher, 1999.

Isou, Isidore. *Amos ou Introduction à la métagraphologie*. Paris: Éditions Arcanes, 1953. Reprint, Marseille: La Termitière, 2000.

———. *Contre l'internationale situationniste*. Cergy, France: D'ARTS, 2000.

———. *Essai sur la définition, l'évolution et le bouleversement de la prose et du roman* and *Les journaux des dieux*. Paris: Escaliers de Lausanne, 1950.

———. "Esthétique du cinéma." *Ion*, April 1952, 7–153.

———. *Fondements pour la transformation intégrale du théâtre*. Paris: Éditions Bordas, 1953.

———. "Introduction à l'esthétique imaginaire." *Front de la jeunesse*, no. 7 (May 1956).

———. *Introduction à une nouvelle poésie et à une nouvelle musique*. Paris: Gallimard, 1947.

———. *Isou, ou La mécanique des femmes*. Paris: Escaliers de Lausanne, 1949.

———. *Je vous apprendrai l'amour* and *Erotologie mathématique et infinitésimale*. Paris: Le Terrain Vague, 1957.

———. *Oeuvres de spectacle*. Paris: Gallimard, 1964.
———. "Préambule à un film." *Le film français (Cinémonde)*, nos. 9–11 (April 1951).
———. "Préface." In Maurice Lemaître, *Le film est déjà commencé?*, 2–36. Paris: Éditions André Bonne, 1952.
———. "Rectification à propos d'un film." *Combat*, April 26, 1951.
———. "Traité de bave et d'éternité." In *Oeuvres de spectacle*, 7–86. Paris: Gallimard, 1964. Reprint, Paris: D'ARTS, 2000.
———. *Traité d'économie nucléaire*. Paris: Escaliers de Lausanne, 1949.
J.N. "Traité de bave et d'éternité." *Franc-tireur*, January 29, 1952.
Klein, Yves. *Le dépassement de la problématique de l'art*. La Louvière, Belgium: Éditions Montbliart, 1959.
Lemaître, Maurice. "Base d'une éducation cinématographique du public par la critique permanente." *Ur: La dictature lettriste*, no. 2 (1952), 19–20.
———. *Cinéma, cinéma*. Paris: Centre de Créativité/Éditions Lettristes, 1979.
———. "Du lettrisme à la mégapneumie." In Gil J Wolman, *Résumé des chapitres précédents*, 14. Paris: Spiess, 1981.
———. *Le film est déjà commencé?* Paris: Éditions André Bonne, 1952.
———. *Marguerite Duras: Pour en finir avec cet escroc et plagiaire généralisée*. Paris: Centre de Créativité, 1979.
———. *Mes films (1951–1977)*. Paris: Centre de Créativité, 1977.
———. *Oeuvres de cinéma (1951–1981)*. Paris: Centre de Créativité, 1981.
———. *Oeuvres de cinéma, 1951–2007*. Paris: Éditions Paris Expérimental, 2007.
———. *Qu'est-ce que le lettrisme?* Paris: Éditions Fischbacher, 1954.
———. *Sistème de notasion pour les lètries*. Paris: Éditions Richard-Masse, 1952.
———. *Sur quelques erreurs commises à propos du film d'Isidore Isou, Traité de bave et d'éternité*. Paris: Centre de Créativité/Maurice Lemaître, 1995.
———. "Les vrais et les faux pionniers du cinéma." *Cahiers du cinéma*, no. 40 (1954), 54–55.
"Panorama intelligent de l'avant-garde à la fin de 1955." *Potlatch*, no. 24 (November 1955), n.p.
Pinel, Vincent. *Introduction au ciné-club: Histoire, théorie, pratique du ciné-club en France*. Paris: Éditions Ouvrières, 1964.
Philm, Dr. "Films expérimentaux." *Cinéma 52*, no. 4 (April 1952), n.p.
Pomerand, Gabriel. *Le cri et son archange*. Paris: Fontaine, 1948.
———. *Saint-Ghetto-des-Prêts ou Paris ton décor fout le camp (grimoire)*. Paris: O. L. B., 1950.
———. *Le testament d'un acquitté* and *Ses aveux publics*. Paris: La Porte Ouverte, 1951.

"La première du 'cinéma tridimensionnel' aura lieu sous la protection de la police." *France-soir*, December 8, 1951.
"La retraite." *Potlatch*, no. 28 (May 1957), n.p.
Schérer, Maurice. "Isou ou les choses telles qu'elles sont." *Cahiers du cinéma*, no. 10 (March 1952), 27–32.
"TRAITE de fleur de nave et d'hilarité." *Canard enchaîné*, no. 1597 (May 30, 1951).
Viénet, René. "Les situationnistes et les nouvelles formes d'action contre la politique et l'art." *Internationale situationniste*, no. 11 (October 1967), 32–36.
Waggoner, Walther H. "U.S. to Be Candid at Brussels Fair." *New York Times*, March 5, 1958.
Wolman, Gil J. *L'anticoncept*. Paris: Éditions Allia, 1994.
———. "Autour de la mégapneumie" (n.d.). In *Défense de mourir*, 22–23 (Paris: Éditions Allia, 2001).
———. "Le Cinématochrone—Nouvelle amplitude." *Ur: La dictature lettriste*, no. 2 (1952), 10.
———. *Défense de mourir*. Paris: Éditions Allia, 2001.
———. "Introduction à Wolman." *Ur: Cahiers pour un dictat culturel*, no. 1 (1950), 19–22.
———. "La mégapneumie." *OU*, no. 32 (1967), n.p.
———. "Pourquoi les spectateurs hurleront pendant la projection de *L'anticoncept*." *Cinéma 52*, no. 5 (May 1952), n.p.
———. *Résumé des chapitres précédents*. Paris: Spiess, 1981.
———. *Le sens perdu de l'interruption*. Paris: Éditions inconnues, 1987.

{~?~ST: begin chapter}

ILLUSTRATION CREDITS

All reasonable efforts have been made to identify and contact copyright holders for the works and photographs reproduced in these pages. The author apologizes for any inadvertent errors or omissions. Copyright holders not acknowledged here or in the image captions should contact the author to be acknowledged in future editions.

Illustrations appear courtesy of the following institutions and individuals: Archiv Acquaviva, Berlin (figs. 3, 5, 7, 10, 17, 24, 43, 55, 60, 63); Archives Isou-Goldstein, Paris (figs. 2, 9, 20); Beinecke Rare Book and Manuscript Library, Yale University (figs. 13, 18, 33, 35, 48, 57, 58, 75); Département des Manuscrits, Bibliothèque Nationale de France, Paris (figs. 61, 62, 64, 65); Rodrigo Garcia Dutra (fig. 1); Bradley Eros (fig. 71); Fondazione Torino Musei (fig. 69); Gaumont-Pathé Archives (fig. 30); National Reconnaissance Office, Declassified Records (fig. 53); Naval Historical Center (fig. 52); Prelinger Library (Internet Archive) (fig. 68); private collection, New York (figs. 8, 34, 41, 54, 56, 59); Museo Nacional Centro de Arte Reina Sofia (fig. 72); MACBA—Museu d'Art Contemporani de Barcelona (figs. 76, 77); Jorge Ribalta (fig. 47); Wikipedia Commons (fig. 51); Yves Klein Archives (figs. 73, 74).

PHOTOGRAPHY CREDITS

©2014 ADAGP, Paris/Avec l'aimable autorisation de M. Pierre Bergé, président du Comité Jean Cocteau, for all works by Jean Cocteau (fig. 23); ©Archives Isou-Goldstein, Paris (figs. 2, 8, 9, 10, 61, 62); ©2014 Artists Rights Society (ARS), New York/ADAGP, Paris, for all works by Paul Coline

and Yves Klein (figs. 4, 73, 74); ©Alice Debord (figs. 58, 59, 61, 62, 64, 65); ©Rodrigo Garcia Dutra (fig. 1); ©Gaumont-Pathé Archives, Paris (fig. 30); ©Gil J Wolman Estate, Paris (figs. 48, 57); ©2013 The Estate of Marcel Broodthaers/Artists Rights Society (ARS), New York/SABAM, Brussels, for all works by Marcel Broodthaers (figs. 76, 77); ©Fondazione Torino Musei (fig. 69); ©Maurice Lemaître (figs. 13, 33); ©Jorge Ribalta (fig. 47).
{~?~ST: end chapter}

INDEX

Page numbers in italic type refer to illustrations.